PRAY WITH PURPOSE

HOW PRAISING GOD A *to* Z WILL TRANSFORM YOUR LIFE

DEBBIE
WILLIAMS

PRAY WITH PURPOSE

LIVE *with* PASSION

HOWARD
PUBLISHING CO.

OUR PURPOSE AT HOWARD PUBLISHING IS TO:
- *Increase* faith in the hearts of growing Christians
- *Inspire* holiness in the lives of believers
- *Instill* hope in the hearts of struggling people everywhere

BECAUSE HE'S COMING AGAIN!

Published by Howard Publishing Co., Inc.
3117 North Seventh Street, West Monroe, Louisiana 71291-2227
www.howardpublishing.com

06 07 08 09 10 11 12 13 14 15   10 9 8 7 6 5 4 3 2 1

Edited by Laura Barker
Interior design by John Mark Luke Designs
Cover design by David Carlson
Cover photo by Getty Images

Library of Congress Cataloging-in-Publication Data

Williams, Debbie Taylor.
    Pray with purpose, live with passion : how praising god A to Z will transform your life
    / Debbie Williams.
        p. cm.
    Includes bibliographical references (p.).
    ISBN 1-58229-482-8
        1. Prayer—Christianity. 2. Praise of God. I. Title.

BV215.W48 2006
248.3'2—dc22

2005045636

All Scripture quotations, unless otherwise indicated, are taken from the *New American Standard Bible*® (NASB), © Copyright The Lockman Foundation 1960, 1962, 1963, 1968, 1971, 1972, 1973, 1975, 1977, 1995. Used by permission. (www.Lockman.org). Scripture quotations marked (NIV) are taken from the *Holy Bible, New International Version*®. NIV®. Copyright © 1973, 1978, 1984 by International Bible Society. Used by permission of Zondervan Publishing House. All rights reserved. Scripture quotations marked (KJV) are taken from the *King James Version*. Italics in Scripture quotations indicate author's added emphasis.

To KEITH, TAYLOR, *and* LAUREN, *with love*

In praise of

THE ALMIGHTY, BELOVED SON, COMFORTER, DOOR,
ETERNAL, FAITHFUL, GUARDIAN OF MY SOUL, HOLY,
IMMANUEL, JUST, KING OF KINGS, LIGHT, MAJESTIC,
GOD OF NEW LIFE, OVERCOMER, POTTER,
QUICKENING SPIRIT, RIGHTEOUS, SHIELD, TOWER,
UPHOLDER, VINEDRESSER, WONDERFUL, EXALTED,
YAHWEH, ZEALOUS GOD!

Contents

Contents

ADDITIONAL RESOURCES

Acknowledgments

A heartfelt thanks to the Howard Publishing family, to John and Chrys Howard and Denny and Philis Boultinghouse for allowing me the opportunity to serve the Lord with them through this book, and to Laura Barker whose editing expertise has been of invaluable help.

My family is my greatest blessing apart from the Lord. Keith, thank you for your love, prayers, and encouragement; for not minding when I slip out of bed in the wee hours of the morning to write; and for being the love of my life for thirty years! To Taylor and Lauren, our children, whose calls and prayers are a constant source of encouragement. I love you, thank you, and praise the Lord for you! My sisters, Linda McConnico and Vicki Tate, are my biggest spiritual encouragers apart from Keith, Taylor, and Lauren. I love you and thank God for you and your prayers! Though my parents, Q. B. and Bernice Taylor, are in heaven, their lives and prayers live in my heart. I am ever grateful for their walk with their Lord.

The Hill Country Ministries Board of Directors and volunteers are faithful friends and prayer supporters. In addition, I give my heartfelt thanks to Sandra Chapman, Janice Kubica, Kathleen Reeves, Barbara Duke, Jean St. Claire, Linda Schmidt, and countless others! A special thank you to Cynthia Itschner, a co-laborer, friend, and sister-in-Christ.

I've often laughed that writing a book on prayer has accomplished the objective of encouraging people to pray, for I've asked everyone I know to pray for me as I have written! To each who prayed, thank you—Women's Bible study, the CrossRoads Bible class, and my dear out-of-town sisters in Christ, Pam Couch, Jo Ann Dealey, Pam Kanaly, and Kellie Kendrick. What a blessing each of you is!

Special thanks go to a group of people who met weekly over a period of months and served as a critique group. My warmest thanks go to my friends

Cynthia Itschner, Crystal McGinnis, Kim Richards, Dorothy Schmidt, and Kathy Vinyard. Your wisdom, input, prayers, and encouragement were invaluable to me. This book is a better work because of you!

To you, the reader. May the glory of God's divine nature draw you to His throne. May you discover the joy of a transformed life as you look into the face of our Savior and praise Him.

Are You Ready *for a* Passionate Encounter *with* God?

Behold, the LORD *our God has shown us His glory and His greatness,*
and we have heard His voice from the midst of the fire;
we have seen today that God speaks with man, yet he lives.
Deuteronomy 5:24

Do you ever feel that your prayer life is in a rut? Are there times you don't feel like praying? When you do pray, do you find that you often repeat the same words to God? Do you consider your relationship with God to be important but not what you would call dynamic? Is prayer a one-way conversation, with *you* doing all the talking? Have you ever longed to hear God speak to you? Do you wonder at people whose prayers are infused with power and whose lives are characterized by passion for God?

If any of these things are true for you, let me assure you, you're not alone. However, God does not want us to stay on the outskirts of intimacy with Him! He has removed the veil that once separated men and women from His holy presence. He invites us to enter His glorious throne room, feast our eyes on His holiness, hear His voice, and be impassioned with His power.

Rather than settle for a less-than-vibrant prayer life, you truly can *pray with purpose and live with passion!*

Passion Comes from an Encounter with God

If you desire more fervency in your prayers and more passion in your relationship with God, He waits to receive you with open arms. Just as

Abraham, Moses, and others encountered the living God and were changed into men and women of purpose and prayer, you, too, can experience a life-transforming encounter with God.

Abraham's life was transformed through encounters with God. Abraham chose to walk with God. His relationship with God deepened and became more purposeful as Abraham grew to know the Lord more intimately. By picking up this book, you are responding to God's call to know Him more intimately and to pray to Him more purposefully. In the following pages you'll have the opportunity to know God increasingly on the basis of twenty-six aspects of His divine nature. As you purposefully have prayer encounters with God and learn to pray with His divine attributes in mind, your relationship will deepen and your passion will grow as you see His hand at work in your life.

Moses's life was transformed through encounters with God. Moses had no idea when he stopped to look at a burning bush that his life would forever be changed, that he would one day be parting waters and passionately leading others to know God. In the same way, you do not yet know all that God has in mind for you. However, your life will be filled with new purpose and passion if you'll make time to be in His presence, if you look into God's divine face and ponder the wonder of His glory. If you, like Moses, will follow the sound of God's voice, He will lead you to experience His passion and power in ways you never imagined!

Are You Ready for God to Rekindle Your Prayers and Life with Passion and Purpose?

The Bible says God is a consuming fire.[1] He is aflame with passion, and His appearance in Scripture is often marked by fire:

- With a flaming torch, God sealed His covenant relationship with Abraham.[2]

- God appeared to Moses in a blazing fire from the midst of a bush.[3]

- God led the nation of Israel to the Promised Land in a pillar of fire by night.[4]

- God consumed Elijah's offering with a fire from heaven when he stood against the false prophets of Baal and called the people to return to God.[5]

- Jesus's presence and words to the disciples on the road to Emmaus caused their hearts to burn within.[6]

- When God sent His Holy Spirit to believers at Pentecost, in accordance with His promise, the Spirit appeared in the form of tongues of fire resting on them.[7]

Acts 2 highlights the coming of the Holy Spirit, that moment of which Jesus had spoken to the disciples. Although the Spirit's coming was a fulfillment of Jesus's promise that they would receive spiritual power, the disciples participated in the encounter with God by obediently waiting in faith as Jesus had instructed, by continually devoting themselves to prayer, and by reading and acting on His Word.[8] Because of the disciples' willing participation and obedience, the Holy Spirit, symbolized by tongues of fire, inflamed and impassioned their hearts.

As we'll discuss in the following pages, since Pentecost the Holy Spirit has been given to Christians at the moment of salvation. He both impassions and empowers us to fulfill His purposes. However, the Holy Spirit can be grieved and quenched. Just as a joyful, vibrant woman can become grieved and subdued if she's continually ignored or quieted by her husband, so we can quench and grieve the Holy Spirit by ignoring Him and discounting His presence in our lives.

The apostle Paul understood the dangers of allowing spiritual passion to grow cold. He urged Timothy to "kindle afresh the gift of the God which is in you" (2 Timothy 1:6). In other words, we are responsible to tend the flame of the Spirit in our hearts.

When my children, Taylor and Lauren, were young, I wanted to illustrate for them the principle of not quenching the Spirit. I brought logs in from outside and placed them on the kitchen floor. With a lighted votive in the center of our "campfire," I explained that we put out a fire by quenching it with dirt. Just as dirt smothers a campfire, so sin quenches the Holy Spirit. However, a campfire can be rekindled, and so can the Holy Spirit, who glows as an eternal ember in our spirits. We can rekindle the flame of the Holy Spirit by throwing the wood of God's Word on the fire. Then our prayers, like the wind on a campfire, can ignite the flames and passion of the Holy Spirit.

Yes, my friend, you can initiate and ignite encounters with the living Lord. Why not begin right now? Kneel in God's presence. Tell Him you want the fresh wind of His Spirit to blow over the embers in your heart. Ask Him to fuel your mind and heart with His Word.

You will have the opportunity on the following pages to renew your vows to the Lord, to engage and invite Him to speak up in your life. As you do so, His purposes will propel you to serve Him in new ways, and His passion will ignite your prayer life!

WAYS TO USE THIS BOOK

Pray with Purpose, Live with Passion is designed to be used in a variety of ways. You can use it to deepen your personal prayer life, dig deeper in group study, and expand your intercessory prayers. It also can serve as an A to Z reference list of God's attributes and a tool for memorizing those attributes.

DEEPEN YOUR PRAYER LIFE

God's ultimate objective for us is to be transformed into His likeness as we live in His presence. One way to experience that transformation is by praying according to God's A to Z divine attributes. *Pray with Purpose, Live with Passion* will deepen your prayer life as you become acquainted with God's attributes and how He can meet your every need. Here are some ways to use this book as a devotional to help guide you into a deeper experience of prayer:

Read one chapter a day, beginning with the prayer. Rather than simply reading each chapter's opening prayer, pray the words to God, either aloud or in your heart. Ask Him to open your eyes to who He is and to the greatness of His divine nature. Ask the Lord to make the Scriptures come alive in your heart and transform you into His likeness.

Look up and meditate on the verses referenced in each chapter. Paul revealed his passion to know Christ when he stated in Philippians 3:8, "I count all things to be loss in view of the surpassing value of *knowing* Christ Jesus my Lord." Meditate on and highlight verses and statements that reveal God's divine nature. Looking up the referenced verses will deepen your understanding and personal application.

Take time to contemplate the Meditation Moments. At the end of each A to Z chapter, a Meditation Moment summarizes some of the ways that particular attribute of God affects you personally. Thoughtfully consider what you've read and spend time thinking about what those truths mean to you. Why? Meditating and "chewing" on God's Word helps you digest and absorb what you've read.

Kneel and PRAY. It is one thing to read about prayer. It is quite another to pray. After you read each chapter, humbly bow your heart, the innermost part of your being, before God. If you are able, kneel. Look up into the face of God. *Praise* and worship Him. *Repent* of any sin you have in relation to God's divine attribute. *Ask* God to forgive you and to bring His character to bear in your life. *Yield* to God's influence on your life as you give Him your hand and ask Him to lead you.

Delve Deeper in Group Study

In addition to your personal reading, you may choose to meet with others to delve deeper into what you are reading. Why meet with others? First, Jesus modeled meeting in a group with His disciples. He shared with them. He prayed with and for them. Second, we are able to learn from one another and stimulate one another in a group. Third, a group encourages us to practice what we are reading. "Delving-Deeper Study Questions" are provided in the additional resources section, along with a guide for group leaders.

Broaden Your Prayers for Others

Sometimes we find ourselves in a rut in the way we pray for family, friends, church, and others. *Pray with Purpose, Live with Passion* will help you break free of routine prayer and enlarge the way you pray for others as you learn to pray according to God's divine nature. For example, after reading, "Lord, You are Almighty," we might pray, "Lord, You are the Almighty God. Work in John's life in a powerful way today. Help him turn to You for strength." When we read, "Lord, You Are the Door," we may pray, "Lord, You are the Door. Prompt Sue to walk through the open door of prayer into Your presence and find help in her time of need."

If you are recording your prayers in the *Prayers of My Heart* prayer journal,[9] you may want to write "Lord, You Are" in the first column of *Week at a Glance*. Then you can record and praise God for a different A to Z attribute each day. In addition, you can use God's attribute as a springboard to pray for yourself and others that day. (See Additional Resources for a sample.) At the end of the month, you will have prayed through God's A to Z attributes!

Refer to God's A to Z Divine Attributes When You Have a Need

Pray with Purpose, Live with Passion is an easy-to-use reference when you have a particular need and want to pray according to God's divine nature. When you are discouraged or when temptation threatens your walk with God, look up an attribute of God that will help you pray. For example, if you are lonely, you can turn to "Immanuel" and be reminded that God is with you and will never leave you. If you are struggling, you can turn to the chapter that leads you to praise God who is Faithful.

Memorize God's A to Z Divine Attributes

Knowing God's divine attributes prompts us to pray with purpose and to live with passion. In the mornings when we rise to pray, praising God for His A to Z attributes awakens our hearts and minds to His glory and power. During the day, having God's divine attributes memorized arouses our minds to turn to Him when needs arise. As we become increasingly mindful of God, our hearts and spirits become tuned to the gentle touch of His guiding Spirit. Yielding to God's divine nature, A to Z, redirects our prayers and passions from being self-centered and worldly driven to being spiritually driven.

May you be blessed as you draw near the throne of God and praise Him, A to Z!

Part One

PRAY

But we all, with unveiled face, beholding as in a mirror the glory
of the Lord, are being transformed into the same image from glory
to glory, just as from the Lord, the Spirit.

2 Corinthians 3:18

CHAPTER 1

STOP, DROP, and PRAY

HOW TO BE TRANSFORMED AND LIVE WITH PASSION

Oh give thanks to the LORD, call upon His name.
PSALM 105:1

Lord, You are a great and awesome God, holy in word and deed. You have saved me by Your grace and reconciled me in Your mercy. Yet too often I don't live by Your divine nature. Help me repent of all that is not of You. Transform me to be a reflection of Your divine nature as I gaze upon Your glory and live for Your purposes. In Jesus's name, amen.

Many of us deal with an ongoing problem of sin, defeat, or spiritual apathy. Like the Israelites who looped in the wilderness instead of entering into the Promised Land, even after we become Christians and desire to change, we may find ourselves dealing with the same attitudes, worries, and temptations day after day instead of being transformed and living the abundant life promised by Christ. Some of us "settle in" with our fleshly dispositions. We may even call our unbecoming behavior a "pet sin" or believe it's "our little secret." Perhaps we excuse our thoughts and actions as being part of our personality—"That's just the way I am"—rather than move forward and live passionately for Christ.

However, our spiritual apathy, our sins of omission (not living passionately for Christ), and our sins of commission (doing those things He tells us not to do) are dangerous. Sin, by its nature, hurts others, the cause of Christ, and us. In addition, sins that we may consider to be "secret" are, in fact, not. The Bible says that God knows the secrets of our hearts, that nothing is hidden from His eyes.[1] Therefore we wear our sin and spiritual apathy as a billboard before our heavenly Father.

Perhaps we lack passion for the things of God because we haven't yet captured the vision that Christ's abundant life is a promised reality. Rather than petting our sin or excusing spiritual apathy, we can discover the joy of living a transformed life when we stop, look up, and pray in relation to God's divine attributes.

Wandering on a Wilderness Loop or Soaring Passionately for God?

Have you ever looked at people who live passionately for Christ and wondered how they do it or what makes them successful? People who live for Christ are distinct reflections of Him. Whether a Christian is a church usher with a contagious smile, a passionate youth worker, or a wife and mother who models Christ's passion in her home, people who live for Christ glorify God.

The question: How do we become like those who are passionate for Christ? If we are apathetic toward the things of God, how do we become enthused? If we are negative, how do we become positive? If lust has ensnared us, how do we break free? If we are sorrowful, how do we enter into Christ's joy?

Is there a way out of our wilderness loop, a way to move beyond where we are and live a passionate abundant life?

Yes! God would not give us the promise of a transformed life if it weren't possible. How do we break free? How do we live passionately? Taking Christ as our model—along with a firefighting illustration—let's begin!

Stop

If we want to break free of our wilderness loop of spiritual apathy or sin and become passionate for God, we must first learn to recognize when we are in danger. Firemen warn us that if we smell smoke, the first thing to do is stop! Don't walk through a closed door, where fire could be raging.

Likewise, the first key to escaping the sin of spiritual apathy is to stop. The moment we smell a defeated attitude or sin overtaking us, we can stop and turn to God's Word or stop and pray. Each of us has the opportunity to stop and think about what we are doing or about to do. We can stop and think about where our minds are going. We can stop and think about where our emotions are headed. We can choose to not put our hand on a door, on a keyboard, on a telephone, or to dwell on a past incident that keeps us looping in sin rather than living passionately for Christ. *read romance novels*

We can stop and, as Colossians 3:2 encourages, set our minds on the things above. We can stop and look into the divine face of God. We can stop and purposefully take "every thought captive to the obedience of Christ" (2 Corinthians 10:5). We can lasso sinful or apathetic thoughts, pull them in, and take them as prisoners to the throne of Christ. We can purposefully, prayerfully ask Him about them. Does the act or thought fit Christ's divine character? If not, don't do it or think it. Take the exit God provides.[2]

How did Jesus handle situations that would have prevented Him from soaring and doing the will of God? Perhaps there is no better place to look than the Garden of Gethsemane, where Jesus "stopped" prior to His arrest and crucifixion. "Then Jesus came with them to a place called Gethsemane, and said to His disciples, 'Sit here while I go over there and pray.' And He took with Him Peter and the two sons of Zebedee, and began to be grieved and distressed. Then He said to them, 'My soul is deeply grieved, to the point of death; remain here and keep watch with Me'" (Matthew 26:36–38).

The first point we learn from Jesus about living passionately for God is to recognize that there will be times of testing, grief, and distress in each person's life. They are not necessarily synonymous with sin or being out of God's will, but rather can be natural worldly trials and sufferings. However, in order to not become "grounded" in them, or stuck in their continual loop, we must stop in God's presence, as Jesus did.

Second, we learn that if we want to live passionately for God, we must, as Jesus did, keep watch. Jesus recognized that the fires of hell were being stoked. The enemy was plotting to incite the Jews to crucify Him. With the certainty of the cross at hand, Jesus stopped in His Father's presence. Though He strained against His flesh and grieved to the point of sweating drops of blood, He did not throw His hands in the air and say, "I can't go through with this!" Jesus stopped and told the disciples to keep watch with Him.

Jesus stopped. He recognized evil's presence and the weakness of the flesh. He knew He had a watch to keep that night in the Garden of Gethsemane. You and I need to ask ourselves if we know when we have a watch, when a certain behavior or sin threatens our walk with God, when Satan is stoking the embers of temptation to divert us from praying with purpose and living with passion. *clinging onto China as if it was where I found my passion, not God himself.*

? What experience or sin keeps you grounded rather than soaring passionately? Is it a time-consuming habit? Is it a certain place? Is it when you are under pressure or tired? Is it when you get home from work or the children challenge you or you're paying the bills? Is it when you check your e-mail and enticing pop-up ads appear? Is it when you'd rather sleep than go to church or rather watch television than pray?

Do we recognize, as Jesus did, how important it is to stop and keep watch if we want to pray with purpose and live with passion for Christ?

Drop

After we've stopped, our next step in being transformed into people who live passionately for Christ is to drop. Those who know the danger of fire warn us to stop and drop to the floor if we are caught in fire or smoke with no immediate escape. Why? Smoke rises. Continuing to walk upright in a smoke-filled room can be deadly.

In like manner, when we see or smell the smoke of spiritual apathy or of sin filling our hearts—in the form of laziness, a flashback of a wrong done to us, an enticing food or drink to which we are addicted, a hole of self-pity,

snappy

→ Pray for other likeminded people - other Kaylei + Elizabeth

14

an unhealthy relationship, a pornographic picture, or a swell of anger—we have an opportunity to drop to the floor. Rather than walk in mediocrity or sin, we can drop to our knees in prayer.

Consider how Jesus responded with passion rather than apathy after He asked the disciples to keep watch with Him: "And He went a little beyond them, and *fell on His face*" (Matthew 26:39). Pressed by temptation to avoid the cross and aware of the excruciating pain soon to be inflicted on His body, Jesus stopped and dropped to the ground in prayer.

Like our beloved Savior, when we are pressed by temptation or trials, we can look up, through the smokescreen, into the glorious face of God, who is clothed in radiance. He will carry us safely through the fires of temptation and give us wings to soar as eagles when we drop to our knees in prayer.

PRAY

The third word of instruction firemen give is to roll if our clothes catch on fire. Why? To smother the fire. To put it out as quickly as possible.

So what do we do when temptation, sin, or spiritual apathy burn within our hearts? The answer is to PRAY! Listen to the words of Jesus: "My Father, if it is possible, let this cup pass from Me, yet not as I will, but as You will" (Matthew 26:39). Jesus prayed this three times.[3] In Jesus's passionate prayer we find that He did four things that transformed Him and gave Him strength:

First, He praised *God*. He acknowledged God's sovereign will over His. This is the highest form of praise, to look into the divine face of our heavenly Father and acknowledge Him and His will.

Second, although Jesus had no sin to confess, He repented. He confessed that He wanted to go in a different direction than the cross. However, He expressed His willingness to submit to His Father's will.

Third, He asked *God*, "Let this cup pass from Me." Perhaps this is the most moving prayer Jesus ever prayed. It is the only time I recall Jesus's asking His Father for something and being told no. Should we ask? Yes! Consider how many hundreds and thousands of prayers Jesus prayed and His Father answered yes. "Yes, the blind can see. Yes, the lame can walk. Yes, raise Lazarus from the dead." Then, "No, You cannot avoid the cross." The penetrating question is, will we accept God's no as well as His yes?

Fourth, Jesus yielded *His will to His Father.* Jesus not only said, "Your will be done," He *did* God's will at great sacrifice and cost. Jesus took our scourging. He was nailed to the cross to pay for our sins. Can we do any less than live passionately for Him?

When, like Jesus, we stop, drop to our knees, and PRAY—Praise, Repent, Ask, and Yield—we'll break free of the wilderness loop that keeps us tethered in sin and spiritual apathy. We'll discover the joy of a transformed life!

Soar with Christ

Pray with Purpose, Live with Passion is designed to help you break free from the wilderness loop and live with passion as you PRAY according to God's divine attributes. In the next four chapters, we're going to further explore what it means to PRAY. Then we're going to look at twenty-six attributes of God and how they can help guide your prayers.

Why PRAY on the basis of God's divine attributes? Because we are freed from looping in our sin or spiritual apathy as we look at the divine face of God. Praying according to God's divinity helps us "not be conformed to this world, but be transformed" as our minds focus on who He is (Romans 12:1–2). Beholding God's divinity gives us a visual of all that is "true . . . honorable . . . right . . . pure . . . and lovely" (Philippians 4:8).

As we consider the needs of others and ourselves and then stop, drop, and PRAY, we discover that God is gloriously sufficient for every situation. Whether we're at home, driving a car, or sitting in a doctor's office, we can PRAY according to God's A to Z divine nature.

Will the divine Lord, the God of the Universe, hear us when we *praise*, *repent*, *ask*, and *yield* to Him in prayer? Indeed He will! Psalm 145:18 encourages us, "The Lord is near to all who call upon Him, to all who call upon Him in truth."

I invite you to join me as we *praise* our glorious Lord, *repent* of our sin, *ask* God for His divine help, and *yield* our hearts to His divine will.

Chapter 2

Praise God

Look Up!

*Praise the LORD! Oh give thanks to the LORD, for
He is good; for His lovingkindness is everlasting.*
Psalm 106:1

*Lord, You are the Almighty, Beloved Son, Comforter, Door, Eternal, Faithful,
Guardian of my soul, Holy, Immanuel, Just, King of kings, Light, Majestic, God
of New Life, Overcomer, Potter, Quickening Spirit, Righteous, Shield, Tower,
One Who Upholds me, Vinedresser, Wonderful, eXalted, Yahweh, Zealous God.
I love You and praise Your Holy Name!*

The voice on the telephone was barely audible, "Can you help me?" Time
and silence passed as we shared her moment of suffering. With a quivering
voice she confided, "I don't know what to do. Everything in my life is falling
apart."

Have you, like my suffering friend, ever felt the pain of utter desperation? At one time or another, nearly all of us will. The pressures of life,
the overwhelming power of sin, and the sorrow of sickness and death are
inescapable realities of a fallen world. What is the antidote to the pain?
What can we do when we find ourselves in the pit of despair or when sorrow overwhelms our hearts? Among the many words of counsel, one stands
proven: praise.

Perhaps you think, as I once did, that praising God and thanking Him
in all things is unrealistic. However, I've learned that praise does not mean
pretending to be happy about an awful situation. Rather, it means looking

19

Brother Yen—
Heavenly Man

up at God in the midst of every situation and worshiping Him who sits enthroned on high, above the world, sovereign. In praise, we lift up our eyes from the pit of sorrow and see the light of His countenance. In praise, we fix our hope on Him who was faithful to us in the past and who will be faithful in the future. Rather than wallow in despair, rather than be held in the bonds of Satan, we fix our eyes on the One who overcame sin, death, and the grave. We rejoice that our Lord is enthroned above all kingdoms.

Amen!

The diadem is on His kingly head. The royal scepter is in His hand. When the storms of life are blowing us off course, when we are losing our bearings, we can look up at God, our guiding Star. He is a fixed hope. We can swim to Him in our pool of tears.

I grew to understand the power of praise several years ago when my teaching, writing, and home responsibilities were overwhelming and my dear sick mother had moved to Kerrville to be near to us. When I found myself sinking in responsibilities, God taught me to look to His presence, to His light, and to the hope found in Him. I came to understand the counsel I offered to my friend on the telephone: "Look up and praise."

WHAT IS PRAISE?

The word "praise," or a form of it, appears 327 times in the Bible. While several Hebrew words describe praise, the one most frequently used is the verb *halal*, from which we get the word "hallelujah." This primitive root word means to "shine, to flash forth light, boast."[1] When life is good, we can sing "hallelujah" to our Lord. However, when darkness surrounds us and nothing good is happening in our lives, we can also look heavenward and focus the eyes of our hearts on Him. Like a huge beam shining through the night that draws attention to a fair, the praise we send heavenward shines on God. We are drawn into His presence and transformed by His glory when we praise.

The Greek word for praise is *aineo* and means to "extol, to sing praises in honor to God."[2] Praise focuses our minds and hearts on the exalted Lord

20

who was, who is, and who is to come. Praise is the spirit dancing in delight with the Lord. Praise is the soul choosing to boast in the Lord. Praise is a choice. Praise is a command. "Give praise to our God, all you His bond-servants, you who fear Him, the small and the great" (Revelation 19:5). As biblical scholar Dr. Gleason Archer points out, "give" in this verse is "a present imperative verb, a command to keep on doing an action as one's general habit or lifestyle. It is a commitment to a long-term way of doing something."[3] We are commanded to have a lifestyle of praising God. ★ *Key.*

WHAT DIFFERENCE DOES PRAISE MAKE?

Those who obey the command to praise God receive the reward of being transformed into His image. Second Corinthians 3:18 states, "We all, with unveiled face, beholding as in a mirror the glory of the Lord, are being transformed into the same image from glory to glory." As we look into God's glorious face and praise Him, we become increasingly intimate with and knowledgeable of the God whom we praise.

God doesn't tell us to praise Him because He craves flattery. God tells us to praise Him in order to direct our hearts to His throne. Praise realigns our souls like a chiropractor realigns a spine. When we praise the Lord, we discover that He is our comforter in times of sorrow. He is with us when our souls rejoice. He is with us when our babies are born and when we bury our mothers. We can walk purposefully and passionately through life's ups and downs when we fix our eyes on God and praise Him. *for our good — ultimately why we are for his glory too? we couldn't handle the spotlight*

Through the examples of those who've gone before us, we see that praise makes a difference in our lives and relationship with God. Let's first consider a person who did not praise God and how his countenance and actions were affected:

So it came about in the course of time that Cain brought an offering to the LORD of the fruit of the ground. Abel, on his part also brought of the firstlings of his flock and of their fat portions. And the LORD had regard

21

for Abel and for his offering; but for Cain and for his offering He had no
regard. So Cain became very angry and his countenance fell. Then the LORD
said to Cain, "Why are you angry? And why has your countenance fallen?
If you do well, will not your countenance be lifted up? And if you do not
do well, sin is crouching at the door; and its desire is for you, but you must
master it." Cain told Abel his brother. And it came about when they were in
the field, that Cain rose up against Abel his brother and killed him.

GENESIS 4:3–8

There are several points for us to notice in this passage regarding praise. First, God personally knows each of us. He knows our names. Second, He sees if we praise and worship Him from a sincere heart. Third, God notices our emotions and countenance. Fourth, He counsels us in order to transform us. He sees sin that crouches close by and warns us to master it.

How should we respond to a God who takes note of even our countenance and emotions? Our response should be to praise Him, to honor Him with our lives as well as our lips. Cain, however, did not praise God. Rather, he killed his brother.

In direct contrast to Cain's example is David, who purposefully chose to praise God and live passionately for Him, even when he faced enemies, discouragement, times of spiritual failure, family and marital disappointments, and challenges leading Israel. Often David entered prayer with a troubled or downcast spirit, but through the process of praising and worshiping God, he was transformed.

For instance, consider David's words in Psalm 3:1–3: "O LORD, how my adversaries have increased! Many are rising up against me. Many are saying of my soul, 'There is no deliverance for him in God.'" Now notice his next words carefully: "But you, O LORD, are a shield about me, My glory, and the One who lifts my head."

How differently David and Cain handled their troubling situations, their downcast countenances, and their relationships to God. Cain ignored

God and with a fallen, angry countenance killed his brother. David took his sorrows, fears, and problems to the Lord. He purposefully focused on God in prayer, praised Him for being his shield, glory, and the One who lifted his head and was therefore transformed and used mightily of God.

— drive to prayer bc need him — ? Craig

May I ask, how do you respond to God in the midst of sorrows, temptations, or troubles? Do you purposefully enter into prayer, look up into the face of God, and praise Him who reigns on high? Or do you go through your day with a fallen countenance, allowing sin to master you?

stress does master me — even w/o sorrow. Stress i create myself.

Paul and Silas provide additional examples of those whose countenances were lifted as they praised the Lord. After being beaten with rods, they sat in a dungeon with their feet in stocks. Yet they didn't give way to discouragement and defeat. Acts 16:25 tells us that "about midnight Paul and Silas were praying and singing hymns of praise to God, and the prisoners were listening to them." In the darkest pit of night, with pain searing through their bodies and the stench of the dungeon rising about them, Paul and Silas looked up. They set their minds on God. They set the eyes of their hearts on Him who held the keys to their emotions. Though their bodies were bound, their spirits were free to sing! What did they sing? The Greek word for "praise" in this verse is the word *humneo* and means to "sing the praise of, sing hymns to." The hymns they most likely sang were what the Jews call the "great Hallel," Psalms 113–18 and 136.[4] *— cool!*

I encourage you to read these psalms. As you read them, envision Paul and Silas, beaten and chained in a filthy dungeon yet choosing to sing praises to God. Listen as their coarse, thirsty voices ascend in praise to the Lord. Imagine what Christ felt as He looked upon His two faithful servants.

When many of us would have despaired, God made a way for these men not only to keep their sanity but also to greatly rejoice and thereby be witnesses to those in prison with them. In fact, the witness of their praising God in the midst of their trouble no doubt contributed to the jailor's conversion that night.

We, too, have the opportunity to be witnesses in the midst of hard times and difficult days. As the prisoners listened to Paul and Silas, so our family members, coworkers, and friends notice how we respond to trying circumstances. Are we pouting or praising, whining or worshiping, complaining or choosing to purposefully lift our eyes to the Lord?

When you find yourself beaten, in a dungeon of despair, in stocks you cannot escape, you can look up and, like Paul and Silas, praise God. Others will see and hear and be encouraged to look to the Lord whom you praise.

God Hears Our Praise

Some people distinguish worship from praise, saying that worship is based on who God is and praise is based on what He does. However, often praise and worship intermingle. In the following psalm, the psalmist praises God for His great and awesome name, while at the same time he exhorts us to worship at God's footstool.

> *The LORD reigns, let the peoples tremble;*
> *He is enthroned above the cherubim, let the earth shake!*
> *The LORD is great in Zion,*
> *And He is exalted above all the peoples.*
> *Let them praise Your great and awesome name;*
> *Holy is He. . . .*
> *Exalt the LORD our God*
> *And worship at His footstool;*
> *Holy is He.*

PSALM 99:1–3, 5

Just as praise and worship go hand in hand, so do praise and thanksgiving. Psalm 106:1 states, "*Praise* the LORD! Oh *give thanks* to the LORD, for He is good; for His lovingkindness is everlasting." Praise brings to mind that for which we are thankful, such as God's provisions of joy, salvation, and wisdom. A natural heartfelt response is to give glory and praise to God in a flash flood of thanks. In other words, often praise and thanks mingle in one harmonious sonnet to the Lord. "Lord, You are worthy of our praise. You hear from heaven and answer prayer. You show forth Your lovingkindness every day in the rising of the sun and the air we breathe. You give peace in storms, light in darkness, and hope in despair. *Thank You!* I praise Your holy name."

The more we give our needs to God, the more opportunity we have to raise our voices in praise and thanksgiving, glorifying Him for acting on our behalf. The more despair we experience and grief we encounter, the more opportunity we have to find our boast in the Lord and thank Him for His provisions.

Does Jesus notice our praise or lack of it? Does our "Thank You" reach God's ears? Absolutely! Remember the story of Jesus's healing the ten lepers? Luke 17:15–18 records the scene that followed: "Now one of them, when he saw that he had been healed, turned back, glorifying God with a loud voice, and he fell on his face at His feet, giving thanks to Him. And he was a Samaritan. Then Jesus answered and said, 'Were there not ten cleansed? But the nine—where are they? Was no one found who returned to give glory to God, except this foreigner?'"

Jesus noticed who turned back to give Him glory and who did not. The word "glory" is translated from the Greek word *doxazo*, which means to "praise, extol, magnify, celebrate."[5] Only one who cried for mercy returned to praise and thank Jesus. Only one returned to magnify what Christ had done and celebrate that he had been healed.

How easy it is to ask for God's blessings and then, when they come, hurry on with our lives, forgetting to praise and thank Him. For years I sang the words of the doxology in church, "Praise God from whom all blessings flow." However, as I repeated those words, week after week, I wasn't thoughtfully praising God for how He had answered specific prayers. Often I mindlessly sang the words by rote, thinking of where we might eat lunch or who I wanted to visit with after the service.

What about you? Do you sing and say words of liturgy without truly praising God from your heart? During the week do you daily, throughout the day, return to Jesus, fall on your knees and celebrate what He is doing in response to your prayers? I want to be like the leper who turned back! What about you?

JESUS MODELED PRAISE

When Jesus taught the disciples to pray, the first words out of His mouth— "Our Father"—direct us to look up.[6] Jesus modeled an attitude of thanksgiving and praise when He thanked God for the fish and bread provided by the little boy.[7] Jesus modeled praise when He stood outside the tomb and raised His eyes before He raised Lazarus.[8] Jesus modeled praise when, after the Last Supper, He led the disciples from the Upper Room to the Garden of Gethsemane, singing a hymn.[9]

Think of a situation that causes you despair, frustration, stress, or worry. Would you be willing to follow Jesus's example? Would you be willing to practice praising God?

- Praise directs our hearts to focus on God.

- Praise interrupts sorrow. It literally turns a frown upside down.

- Praise redirects our minds' focus from ourselves and what we can't do, to God, who can and will accomplish all that is right, good, and pure in accordance with His divine will and nature.

- Praise interrupts temptation. We cannot at the same time embrace sin and praise God.

- Praise transfers problems from our weak backs to God's strong right hand.

Praise brings the light of God's direction to our darkest hour as we sit quietly in His presence and look into His holy face. In every despair, mood swing, or ailment, we can practice the discipline of praising God A to Z. Instead of spotlighting our inability or another's faults, we can shine the spotlight of praise on God, who sits enthroned above. We can experience the blessing of a transformed countenance, as we look full into His wonderful face!

He did immeasurably more w/ a job — he can do it with a spouse too.

↑
won't be all its cracked up to be

↑
wasn't all the answer — still lingering stress, new ones

Chapter 3

Repent *and* Confess Sins

I'm Forgiven!

*If we confess our sins, He is faithful and righteous to forgive
us our sins and to cleanse us from all unrighteousness.*
1 John 1:9

*Lord, You are a holy God, powerful, exalted above the heavens! How is it that
You are mindful of me? How is it that You are so loving and good and kind that
You sent Jesus to die for my unrighteousness? Lord, I love You and praise You. I
thank You for the incredible gift of forgiving my sins. Cleanse me, Lord, and fill
me so that I might be useful in Your kingdom! In Jesus's name, amen.*

My daughter Lauren's coal black miniature dachshund, cute beyond words,
is so much fun to play with. However, as a puppy Bailey had a distinct
odor that lingered on Lauren, even after she put her down. Although
Lauren bathed Bailey regularly, her puppy odor would quickly return as
Bailey played and got into places she wasn't supposed to be. I once "puppy
sat" while Lauren went out of town. Before long, I was attached to Bailey,
cuddled her close to me, and even did what I never thought I would do . . .
let her sleep with Keith and me. One morning I woke up and realized that
I smelled like Bailey!

Whether we're talking about pets or something else, it's a fact that we
begin to smell like whatever we hold close to us. When we hold sin close
to our hearts, we begin to carry its odor in our lives. Pride, prejudice, unforgiveness, self-pity, anger, lust, selfishness, jealousy, lying, and lukewarm

fear worry

spirituality are all odious. Are we holding anything close to our hearts that is not of God? Are we sleeping with unconfessed sin? If so, the good news is, we can be washed! We can go to God in repentance and confession and be bathed in His righteousness. The aroma of the Lord—not sin's unpleasant odor—can be the fragrance of our lives.[1] *I want this.*

① The Bible teaches us that confession of sins and answered prayers go hand in hand. For instance, unconfessed sin can affect our prayer requests for health. If we refuse to repent of gluttony or drunkenness, our health may be affected, regardless of how much we pray. If we harbor unconfessed resentment or covetousness, our nerves and health can be affected. If we refuse to confess that money is our god, *what is the cause of* stress-related illnesses may affect our bod- *mine?* ies. James 5:16 offers the encouraging solution: "Confess your sins to one another, and pray for one another so that you may be healed." Confession of sin is often the first step toward our prayers for healing being answered.

lack of trust
high exp. of self
pride

② Our prayer life can also be affected by how we treat others. God says in Isaiah 1:15, "When you spread out your hands in prayer, I will hide My eyes from you; yes, even though you multiply prayers, I will not listen. Your hands are covered with blood." We may give a sigh of relief and say, "Thank goodness, I don't have blood on my hands." However, let us remember that God looks at our hearts. He goes on to say, "Wash yourselves, make yourselves clean; remove the evil of your deeds from My sight. Cease to do evil, learn to do good; seek justice, reprove the ruthless, defend the orphan, plead for the widow" (Isaiah 1:15–17).

Clearly, God cares about how we treat others. In the Sermon on the Mount, Jesus made it clear that when we harbor anger toward someone, we are as guilty before God as if we had committed murder. When we commit adultery in our hearts, we have sinned.[2] What is God teaching us? Our relationships with others affect our relationship with Him. Peter affirmed that our relations with others can affect whether or not our prayers are answered: "You husbands in the same way, live with your wives in an understanding way, . . . and show her honor as a fellow heir of the grace of life, *so that your prayers will not be hindered*" (1 Peter 3:7). Our prayers are hindered when we do not honor God and others.[3]

If we want to move forward in our relationship with God, we must become serious about repenting and confessing. The Greek word for "confess" is *homologeo* and means "say the same thing, i.e., agree with."[4] When we agree with God that we have sinned, when we admit our guilt before Him, we no longer bear the stench of sin but the pleasing fragrance of a life submitted to God.

WHY WE MAY NEGLECT TO CONFESS OUR SINS

Why do we so often ignore our sin rather than repent? How is it we go day after day without confessing our sin?

One reason may be that *we don't have regular prayer time each day.* Although "arrow prayers"—brief sentence prayers throughout the day—can be a valuable way of communing with God, there is something to be said for a set time to meet with God each day. The Gospel of Mark tells us that Jesus purposefully woke early and went to a secluded place to pray before His day began: "In the early morning, while it was still dark, Jesus got up, left the house, and went away to a secluded place, and was praying there" (Mark 1:35). If Christ needed early-morning solace with God, how much more do you and I? The Bible teaches us to meditate both in prayer and on the Word of God. Yet many of us fail to center our minds, emotions, and will on God. Perhaps our first confession should be that we've ignored God's counsel and Christ's example. I wonder how much heartache, how many mistakes, how much depression, anxiety, and indulgent behavior might be avoided if at the beginning of each day we "centered" on God, meditated on His Word, and confessed our sin.

A second reason we may fail to confess our sin is that *we don't praise our heavenly Father.* Too often we rush into prayer, giving God our latest to-do list rather than first entering with praise. As we saw in the previous chapter, when we humble ourselves before God and worship Him, we become mindful of who He is and who we are not! When we praise God, we become aware of our unholiness. The stench of our sin rises in our nostrils. Thus, praise quickens our hearts and leads us to repentance.

A third reason we may not confess our sin is because *we are stiff-necked.* Although we get a whiff of our sin, we don't want to give it up. However, Deuteronomy 10:16 warns us, "Circumcise your heart, and stiffen your neck no longer." What is God saying? He is telling us to cut off any passion, thought, inclination, appetite, speech, or action that is an affront to Him. In other words, "Stop the offensive sin!" When we don't repent and cut off sin, we become even more stiff-necked. Second Chronicles 30:8 also warns us against becoming hardened by sin or indifferent to God's conviction: "Now do not stiffen your neck like your father, but yield to the LORD and enter His sanctuary which He has consecrated forever, and serve the LORD your God, that His burning anger may turn away from you." As long as we carry our stinky sins close to us, we are walking as stiff-necked persons. No wonder so many of us have neck aches!

THE CONSEQUENCES OF UNCONFESSED SIN

Unconfessed sin results in numerous consequences, including anxiety, loss of joy, defeat, and missing out on God's blessings.

Unconfessed sin brings anxiety. In Psalm 38:18 David said, "For I confess my iniquity; I am full of anxiety because of my sin." David recognized that sin creates tension between God and us, as well as between others and us. We become anxious because of the tension between what we know is right and the wrong we've done or are doing. Like a rubber band pulled tightly, we may feel like we're about to break! In Psalm 32:3–6 David wrote more about the tension and anxiety sin can cause and encourages us to confess our sin:

When I kept silent about my sin, my body wasted away
Through my groaning all day long.
For day and night Your hand was heavy upon me;
My vitality was drained away as with the fever heat of summer. Selah.

Lord, I need accountability over my anxiety.

32

I acknowledged my sin to You,
And my iniquity I did not hide;
I said, "I will confess my transgressions to the LORD";
And You forgave the guilt of my sin. Selah.
Therefore, let everyone who is godly pray to You in a time when You may
be found.

Is there anxiousness in your life due to your refusal to confess your sin? If so, why not purposefully kneel and confess your sin right now? Why not humble yourself in the presence of the One who loves you so much He died so that you might be forgiven?

Unconfessed sin is a joy breaker. Sinning is like pulling the plug on the One who is our source of joy. When we refuse to admit that we have sinned, we remain an empty basin, unfilled with the Lord's flowing supply of Living Water, His Holy Spirit. We aren't filled with His love, joy, peace, patience, kindness, goodness, gentleness, faithfulness, and self-control flowing through us. Many ailments, such as depression and anger, can be linked to unconfessed sin. For example, Christ explains that we are tormented when we don't forgive others. Our sin of not forgiving others keeps us emotionally imprisoned. However, forgiving others opens the door to restored joy!

Unconfessed sin brings defeat. When we sin, and especially if we willfully continue in sin, we become aware that we are living a defeated Christian life rather than the victorious life to which Christ calls us. If only we could say that we cannot help but sin, we might find comfort. However, we cannot say that, "for nothing will be impossible with God" (Luke 1:37). Through the Holy Spirit we are empowered to walk in the ways of Christ.[5] Therefore, let us heed the warning in 1 Kings 8:33 that Israel was "defeated before an enemy, because they . . . sinned." Let us refuse to be defeated by sin and, instead, boldly approach the throne of grace, "so that we may receive mercy and find grace to help in time of need" (Hebrews 4:16).

Unconfessed sin causes us to miss God's blessings. Adding to our sense of defeat is the fact that we miss God's blessings when we refuse to recognize

and confess our sin. First Kings 8:35 describes Israel's loss of God's blessings: "The heavens are shut up and there is *no rain, because they have sinned
against You.*" The passage continues by describing the hope that comes with
confession: "[When] they pray toward this place and confess Your name and
turn from their sin when You afflict them, then hear in heaven and forgive
the sin of Your servants . . . and teach them the good way in which they
should walk. And send rain on Your land, which You have given Your people
for an inheritance" (1 Kings 8:35–36).

God wants us to know the spiritual blessings of His presence. What sin
is holding you back from receiving them? Why not repent and confess that
sin? God will not withhold His forgiveness from the repentant.

The Blessings of Confessing Our Sin

We've seen that unconfessed sin brings serious consequences. However, repentance and confession bring hope and reconciliation.

Confessing our sin brings forgiveness and cleansing. Romans 3:23 declares
that "all have sinned and fall short of the glory of God." However, the wonderful news is that when we confess our sins, God is faithful to "forgive us
our sins and to cleanse us from all unrighteousness" (1 John 1:9). As a matter of fact, Psalm 103:12–14 says, "As far as the east is from the west, so far
has He removed our transgressions from us. Just as a father has compassion
on his children, so the LORD has compassion on those who fear Him. For
He Himself knows our frame; He is mindful that we are but dust." God
yearns to bathe us in His righteousness. That's why Jesus came. He put
on our filthy rags and clothed us in His righteousness so that we might be
cleansed and reconciled to God.[6]

Confessing our sin brings freedom from guilt. In addition to the blessing
of being forgiven, when we repent and confess, God removes the guilt of
our sin. If you are carrying the weighty guilt of past sins, read carefully the
wonderful words of comfort found in David's prayer in Psalm 32:5–6: "I
acknowledged my sin to You, and my iniquity I did not hide; I said, 'I will

confess my transgressions to the LORD'; and You *forgave the guilt* of my sin."
David's advice in the next verse? "Let everyone who is godly pray to You in a
time when You may be found." Why not acknowledge your sin and guilt to
God, as David did? Why not confess and experience the blessing of having
the guilt of your sin wiped away?

Confessing our sin results in restored fellowship with God. God, who in
Christ reconciled the world to Himself,[7] desires for us to live in daily fellowship with Him. Proverbs 28:13 blesses us with both the warning and encouragement that "he who conceals his transgressions will not prosper, but
he who confesses and forsakes them will find compassion." Knowing that
God wants to live in union and oneness with us,[8] let us confess and forsake
our sin and discover the blessing of restored fellowship with Him. Let us
daily, moment by moment, run into the arms of God our Father and, when
we stray, quickly return to the blessing of His loving arms!

Confessing our sin leads to meaningful service. Reconciled and walking
in fellowship with God, we are able to serve as "ambassadors for Christ"
(2 Corinthians 5:19–20). Rather than living for ourselves, we can purposefully repent of sin and choose to "no longer live for [our]selves, but for Him
[Christ] who died and rose again" on our behalf (2 Corinthians 5:15). Have
you 'fessed up? Are you cleansed, ready to be "a vessel for honor, sanctified,
useful to the Master, prepared for every good work" (2 Timothy 2:21)?

None of us is sinless. However, we can guard against sin taking root in our
lives by including repentance in our quiet time and keeping short accounts with
the Lord and others. We can be careful to not harbor sin in our hearts. We can
be cleansed vessels who open our lives for the Holy Spirit to fill our sails.

Therefore, as we look into the glorious face of Christ and are convicted
about our sin, let us agree with God that our sin stinks, and repent. Cleansed,
let us run into the loving arms of Christ. Then let us spread the good news,
"I'm forgiven!" and share with others how they can be forgiven.

[Handwritten margin notes: "why comp. linked to confessing sin?"; "where anxiety keeps me"]

[Handwritten notes at bottom of page:]
confess ignoring Josiah - not visiting CA this summer
anxiety over everything - having/ not having job, mentoring
Gleneden, Mom, Craig, SR, e-mail
(it is not fun - why do I let it linger? I want to cast it
away for today - + Tomorrow I'll cast it away for tomorrow

Little things	Medium things
texting Amy prayers	blogging
convo w/ Carly	Rosetta Stone
Prayer stuff @ church	
Liu Xing	
Kaylee	
Comp. kids	
outings w/ Mom	
" w/ Rachael	

CHAPTER 4

Ask

I'll Take a Crumb!

This is the confidence which we have before Him, that,
if we ask anything according to His will, He hears us.
1 John 5:14

Lord, You teach me to come to You and ask for my needs. Thank You for the
promise that whatever I ask in Your name, You will do. Thank You for Your
Spirit who helps me pray. Help me be faithful to make my heart a place of prayer.
In Jesus's holy name, amen.

"The Christian life is not a constant high," writes the great evangelist Billy
Graham. "I have my moments of deep discouragement. I have to go to
God in prayer, with tears in my eyes, and say, 'O God, forgive me,' or
'Help me.'"[1]

Everyone in this world has needs, from Billy Graham to the neighbor
next door. We, or those we love, may need healing from illness, comfort in
the midst of tragedy, money to buy groceries for a hungry family, wisdom
in addressing a conflict with a coworker, help in coping with a night of
sleeplessness, or patience to deal with a child. Often our needs change day-
by-day, sometimes even moment-by-moment. Whether we are praying for
our own concerns or for those of others, God invites us to lay our needs at
His feet.

What can we expect when we do so? Will God hear and answer our
prayers? Indeed He will, if we come to Him in faith. An example of coming

to Jesus and asking in faith is the woman who sought help for her demon-possessed daughter. Imagine the anguish she must have felt as she pleaded, "Have mercy on me, Lord, Son of David; my daughter is cruelly demon-possessed" (Matthew 15:22).

What happened when Jesus didn't immediately respond to her request? The woman continued to desperately shout and ask for His help, to the point that the disciples begged Him to send her away. Jesus responded by stating that He was sent to the lost sheep of the house of Israel. The woman, a Canaanite, came and bowed before Jesus, begging Him, "Lord, help me!" (v. 25). His reply seems strange: "It is not good to take the children's bread and throw it to the dogs" (v. 26). While His words may seem cruel to us, she understood in the language of the day that His reference was to her as a foreigner. He explained that His ministry was currently directed toward the Jews.

I can imagine the woman at Jesus's feet, tears streaming down her face. Jesus was her last hope. She persevered in faith: "Yes, Lord; but even the dogs feed on the crumbs which fall from their masters' table" (v. 27). So desperate was her daughter's need that she was willing to take whatever bit of help, whatever bit of glory and power Jesus had to give her, even if it was a crumb.

> *I'll take a crumb from Your table, Lord,*
> *I don't need riches or fame*
> *Only what falls from Your glorious hand*
> *From the power of Your name.*
> *I'll take a crumb from your table, Lord*
> *For even Your crumb's filled with might*
> *I wait on Your heavenly manna to fall*
> *Your crumb is my soul's delight!*
> *I'll take a crumb from Your table, Lord*
> *Your presence and face I crave*

Feed me and fill me with heaven's crumbs
As I wait on You day by day.[2]

Jesus's response is tender. "'O woman, your faith is great; it shall be done for you as you wish.' And her daughter was healed at once" (v. 28). No fanfare. Just healed. Jesus answered a woman's persevering plea for her daughter.

In the account of the Canaanite woman, we learn several points about asking God for our needs and those of others. First, when we have a need, we can boldly approach God. Second, we should ask in faith. Third, though we boldly approach God's throne to find help in time of need, our prayers should be offered in reverence and humility. Fourth, we must not give up if our prayers aren't immediately answered, but rather persevere in prayer.

Why Should We Ask God for Our Needs and the Needs of Others?

At times people tell me that they don't ask God for their needs, reasoning that God gave them a brain to use and they don't want to "bother" Him. Their logic, however noble it may be, is contrary to the counsel of God, who teaches us to come to Him and pray about everything.

Contemplate the following reasons for purposefully asking Him for your needs and those of others.

Ask because Jesus, by His words and actions, taught us to ask. Jesus stopped funerals and asked for lives to be restored. He prayed all night before He chose His disciples. He asked for sick people to be healed. Jesus prayed at meals when there wasn't enough food to feed the multitude. He prayed when He was tempted to avoid the cross. He asked for a way other than the cross, if it was God's will. In Matthew 7:7 Jesus says, "Ask, and it will be given to you; seek, and you will find; knock, and it will be opened to you. For everyone who asks receives, and he who seeks finds, and to him who knocks it will be opened." We ask God for our needs because Jesus taught us to ask, and keep on asking; to seek, and keep on seeking; and to knock at heaven's door, and keep on knocking. Why? Because Jesus wants us to enter His presence through prayer, find His answers, and receive His blessings.

Ask because God cares for you. Peter, the big fisherman, wrote, "Cast all your anxiety on him [God] because he cares for you" (1 Peter 5:7 NIV). Note that Peter said we are to "cast," or throw as a fishing net, *all* our worries on God. God cares if our spirits are downcast. He cares if our children are sick. He cares if our finances are running out, our temperament is out of sorts, or our marriage is suffering. He cares if we are stressed with work. He cares if we are lonely. Our greatest worries are not too great for God, and our smallest concerns are His. Do you have a boatload of problems? Tie them to the end of your fishing line and cast them heavenward. Why? Because God cares for you.

Ask to avoid losing heart. Have you ever felt discouraged or disheartened? Jesus knew there would be times we felt that way. Therefore He told the disciples a parable to "show that at *all* times they ought to pray and not to lose heart" (Luke 18:1). In the parable a widow kept going to a judge and asking for legal protection. Although the judge was unrighteous, he eventually answered her request. Jesus concluded that if an unrighteous judge responded, certainly God, who is righteous, would respond to those who cry out to Him. The next time a wave of despair floods your soul, run to Jesus with your needs. He will keep you from losing heart if you stay in His presence and, believing, ask for His help!

Ask in order to be transformed. Our face, or countenance, is an expression of our innermost being. If we are happy, our eyes smile. If we are down, it is reflected in our countenance. When we have a fallen countenance—when we are sad, angry, or worried—we can go to God and ask Him to help us with whatever is on our heart. I love the account of Jesus taking Peter, John, and James up the mountain to pray. Luke 9:29 states, "*And while He was praying*, the appearance of *His face became different*." When we pray, the appearance of our face can be transformed. We may enter prayer with a

Jesus/ HS/ all praying for you—he knows what to pray

sad or furrowed brow. However, by looking at Christ's glory and laying our requests at His feet, we are able to rise from our prayer time with a countenance of peace, confident that God has heard our prayers.

Ask in order to be filled with the knowledge of God's will and spiritual wisdom. Is the future a worry? Are you in a state of unrest because you don't know what to do about a family, business, or church situation? Ask God to reveal to you His will and fill you with His wisdom. Paul wrote in Colossians 1:9, "We have not ceased to pray for you and to ask that you may be filled with the knowledge of His will in all spiritual wisdom and understanding." James 1:5 reinforces Paul's prayer. "If any of you lacks wisdom, let him *ask* of God, who gives to all generously and without reproach, and it will be given to him."

Ask in order to resist temptation and walk in God's will. In the Lord's Prayer, Jesus purposefully asked God, "Do not lead us into temptation, but deliver us from evil." In the Garden of Gethsemane, Jesus told the disciples, "Keep watching and praying that you may not enter into temptation; the spirit is willing, but the flesh is weak" (Matthew 26:41). In addition, Jesus asked in Matthew 26:39, "My Father, if it is possible, let this cup pass from Me; yet not as I will, but as You will." Jesus asked God for a way out of what He faced. However, He also yielded to God's will, even if it led Him the way of the cross. If Jesus asked for help in resisting temptation and walking in God's will, should we not also do the same?

Ask in order to bear abundant spiritual fruit through the power of the Holy Spirit. Jesus told the disciples, "You did not choose Me but I chose you, and appointed you that you would go and bear fruit, and that your fruit would remain, so that whatever you *ask* of the Father in My name He may give to you" (John 15:16). Jesus chooses, appoints, and empowers us to go and bear spiritual fruit. Through Christ in us we are able to do "far more abundantly beyond all that we ask or think, according to the power that works within us" (Ephesians 3:20). The fruit that is born out of a Spirit-filled Christian's life is a by-product of Christ's Spirit filling us when we pray and walk in His will. Is your spiritual fruit basket empty? Is all that is born out of your life markedly "you" and not Christ? Why not ask God to fill you with His Spirit so that you might bear spiritual fruit?

How Should We Ask God?

Are there right ways and wrong ways to approach God's throne? The following scriptures offer helpful insights.

Ask believing you will receive. Jesus emphasized the importance of faith when we ask God for our needs: "And all things you *ask in prayer, believing,* you will receive" (Matthew 21:22). What was the context of Jesus's words? Jesus had just cursed a fig tree for its lack of figs, which symbolized the nation of Israel's not bearing fruit for God. However, Jesus wanted His followers to know that past or present spiritual barrenness doesn't dictate that there will never be spiritual fruit. Christianity was born from the vine of Israel, even though she appeared dead. In the same way, we may look at our lives and feel discouraged by the lack of spiritual fruit. Yet Christ's promise is for us. If we ask in faith, believing, we will receive.

Ask in Jesus's name. Years ago I would not have thought there would be a question regarding to whom we pray or in whose name we pray. However, in recent years I've heard people say that it doesn't matter to whom we pray. They say we can pray to a witch or a deceased person or that conversation between two people is prayer. Such words are contrary to Christ's teaching: "Pray, then, in this way: 'Our Father who is in heaven, hallowed be Your name'" (Matthew 6:9). In addition, Jesus teaches us to ask in His name: "Whatever you *ask in My name,* that will I do, so that the Father may be glorified in the Son. If you *ask Me anything in My name,* I will do it" (John 14:13–14). Access to God is through Christ.

Ask with the spirit and the mind. The apostle Paul wrote, "I will pray with the spirit and I will pray with the mind also" (1 Corinthians 14:15). The spirit is the means by which we commune with God, who is spirit. However, our communion with Him is to be based on the Word of God and "the mind of Christ" (1 Corinthians 2: 16). That's why it's so important for us to be continually in God's Word. The more we know God's mind and His words fill us, the more we will ask according to God's will. Asking God for our needs and interceding for others is an intelligent exercise of the mind expressed through the spirit to God.

Ask with the right motives. James minced no words when he wrote, "You do not have because you do not ask. You ask and do not receive, because *you ask with wrong motives,* so that you may spend it on your pleasures" (James 4:2–3). God looks not only at our words but also at our hearts. Is our request motivated by a desire to glorify God? If so, "this is the confidence which we have before Him, that, *if we ask anything according to His will,* He hears us" (1 John 5:14). How can we be sure that we're asking according to His will? Jesus told His disciples, "If you abide in Me, and My words abide in you, *ask whatever you wish,* and it will be done for you" (John 15:7). A practical way to abide in Christ and pray according to His will is to pray the Scriptures. For instance, Galatians 5:16 says, "Walk by the Spirit, and you will not carry out the desire of the flesh." Therefore, we can ask, "Lord, help my children walk by Your Spirit today and not carry out the desires of the flesh." When we abide in Christ and His Word abides in us, we can have confidence that our motives are right and God will hear our prayers.

Will God Give Us What We Ask For?

God answers prayers, but His answers may not always be what we expect. We may pray for peace, but the enemy still rages. We may ask for a certain job but, in praying God's will, discover that He has opened a door for us at a different place. We may ask for healing but not receive it in our lifetime. We may ask God to save someone, but the person may not come to salvation for years—perhaps not until we are already in heaven.

Let us be mindful that God wants to speak to our hearts and direct us even in how to pray. Romans 8:26 states, "In the same way the Spirit also helps our weakness; for we do not know how to pray as we should, but the

Spirit Himself intercedes for us with groanings too deep for words; and He who searches the hearts knows what the mind of the Spirit is, because He intercedes for the saints according to the will of God."

We may not always know God's will, but the Spirit does, and He prays for us as we pray. What a comforting thought! Knowing that, we should rush to our knees every morning and throughout the day and night. We must never shrink from prayer out of fear we will pray the wrong thing. We may not know exactly how to pray for our children, marriages, work, or others, but if we put our bodies, minds, and spirits in the position of prayer, the Holy Spirit will intercede and pray for us in accordance with God's will.

Someone once said, "God always answers in the deeps, never in the shallows of our soul."[3] Are we in deep intimacy with God when we pray? Or are we splashing in the shallow end before we rush off to our day? The Canaanite woman fell at Jesus's feet and asked for even a crumb of His power and glory. Jesus saw her faith and answered her prayer.

hmm...

Am I a failure b/c I need acupuncture for stress + tension? I have access to the greatest power source — + I choose to keep it on my own shoulders — "Do it myself." Like when I needed a anti-depressant for not having enough joy. Tension always is here — @ times stronger or more dormant — but it is always there. I'd rather have Jesus' peace.

44

Chapter 5

Yield

Give Him Your Hand!

Now do not stiffen your neck like your fathers, but yield to the LORD and enter His sanctuary which He has consecrated forever, and serve the LORD your God, that His burning anger may turn away from you.
2 Chronicles 30:8

Lord, You are a great and awesome God, powerful and holy in all Your ways. You have given me Your Spirit by which to live and walk. Yet too often I walk in my own strength. Forgive me, Lord. Take my life and fill my mind, emotions, and will with Your Holy Spirit. Teach me to increasingly listen and yield to You, to give You my heart and hand. In Jesus's name, amen.

Prayer involves praising God, repenting of our sins, and asking Him for our needs. But prayer involves more than just speaking to God; it also involves yielding to His voice. Consider how ineffective our prayers would be if God didn't listen to us. Likewise, those who live passionately for Christ not only speak to God but also listen to Him. They yield their hearts and wills to His voice.

Yielding Requires Waiting on God to Speak

Although we may not often think of listening as a part of prayer, it is, in fact, a vital organ of our prayer life. In order to hear God speak, we must wait on Him. Just as we cannot hear someone if we leave while they are talking, we cannot hear God if we rise from prayer without waiting for Him to speak to our hearts and minds.

Imagine how frustrating your relationships would be if the conversations were only one-way. If your spouse expected you to listen all the time but never lingered to hear your responses, how would you feel? If your children gave you requests from the time they woke up until they went to bed but never waited to hear your thoughts, what kind of relationship would you have? If your friend talked all the time but didn't answer the telephone when you called, what kind of friendship would that be? If your business partner shared his ideas but never wanted yours, how effectively could you manage a joint venture?

At salvation, we enter into a relationship with God through Jesus Christ. Our relationship is characterized in numerous ways: as Jesus being our Savior, Friend, Brother, Mediator; as God being our Lord, Father, King; as our being Christ's bride, ambassador, steward, and friend. What kind of friend, child, sister, subject, or steward would talk to God but never allow Him to speak, never listen and yield to His voice?

David knew the value of not rushing through prayer but rather waiting on God:

> *To You, O LORD, I lift up my soul.*
> *O my God, in You I trust. . . .*
>
> *Make me know Your ways, O LORD;*
> *Teach me Your paths.*
> *Lead me in Your truth and teach me,*
> *For You are the God of my salvation;*
> *For You I wait all the day.*
>
> PSALM 25:1, 4–5

Are we only to listen to God when we open our day in prayer? No. An intimate relationship with Him involves tuning our hearts in the morning to listen to His voice "all the day."

While out of town recently, I drove through a car wash, but before I did, the attendant took the antenna off my car and placed it on my dashboard. Later, on the road back to Kerrville, I became frustrated that I couldn't get a channel on my radio. Then I noticed the antenna on my dashboard and realized I was unable to hear any stations because my antenna was not up. I drove on in silence, wondering how often God had spoken to me but my spiritual antenna had not been up; I was not "tuned in" to God.

How can we keep our spiritual antennae up? The first way is by starting the day "tuning in" to God in prayer and Bible study. The second way is by staying within range of His voice through the day and listening closely.

Several years ago I began praying that God would teach me to be sensitive to His voice. I cannot tell you the joy I've experienced as a result. It is exciting to sense the Almighty's prompting and guiding voice even in the midst of an ordinary day, such as when my sisters and I recently returned to our hometown to attend a funeral. On the way to the church we had several stops to make, including a visit to our old high school. What fun it was to walk down the halls and reminisce. As we did, we visited with an administrator who was preparing for a meeting with the school's cheerleaders. When Linda shared she was in the school's first graduating class, was a cheerleader, and had helped write the school song, his eyes brightened. When he learned that I, too, had been a cheerleader and Vicki, our sister, had gone to state in drama, he invited us to come to the meeting and share the value of our high-school years. What a privilege it was to share how during my high school years I learned that God wants us to live not only on a physical level but also on a spiritual level with Him.

What does that have to do with listening to God? As we drove around that morning, determining which stops to make and in what order, I had been conscious of following the Lord's guiding Spirit. Had we gone to the school at any other time, the opportunity would not have presented itself.

Could it be that our prayers are often stagnant and our lives less than passionate because we don't take time to put up our spiritual antennae and listen to God's voice? I believe when we purposefully pray to be sensitive to His Spirit, we will be amazed at how He guides us and at the "coincidences" in which we find ourselves able to encourage others in their walk with God!

YIELDING IS GIVING OUR HANDS TO GOD

How do we listen and yield to God's voice? The word "yield" is a combination of two Hebrew words: *nathan*, which means "give"[1] and *yad*, which means "hand, power, or strength."[2] Thus, to yield means to give one's hand, power, or strength to the Lord. Biblical scholar Matthew Henry described what it means to "yield yourselves unto the Lord":

> Give him your hand, in token of giving him your heart. Lay your hand to his plough. Devote yourselves to his service, to work for him. . . . Be absolutely and universally at his command, at his disposal, to be, and do, and have, and suffer, whatever he pleases.[3]

In 2 Chronicles 30 and 2 Kings 19, we read how King Hezekiah yielded to God in a time of difficulty, when Israel was threatened by sin. First, King Hezekiah *implored the people to yield* to the Lord: "Now do not stiffen your neck like your fathers, but *yield* to the LORD and *enter His sanctuary* which He has consecrated forever, and *serve the LORD* your God, that His burning anger may turn away from you" (2 Chronicles 30:8).

Hezekiah's charge included the promise of God's blessings if they yielded: "For if you return to the LORD, your brothers and your sons will find compassion before those who led them captive and will return to this land. For the LORD your God is gracious and compassionate, and will not turn His face away from you if you return to Him" (2 Chronicles 30:9).

Later, Hezekiah modeled *yielding his hand* to the Lord when he received a threatening letter from Sennacherib, a powerful king and enemy who declared his intention to destroy Jerusalem. Rather than calling the nation to arms,

> [Hezekiah] *took the letter from the hand of the messengers and read it, and he went up to the house of the LORD and spread it out before the LORD. Hezekiah prayed before the LORD and said, "O LORD, the God of Israel, who are enthroned above the cherubim, You are the God, You alone, of all*

the kingdoms of the earth. You have made heaven and earth. Incline Your ear, O LORD, and hear; open Your eyes, O LORD, and see; and listen to the words of Sennacherib, which he has sent to reproach the living God. Now, O LORD our God, I pray, deliver us from his hand that all the kingdoms of the earth may know that You alone, O LORD, are God."

2 KINGS 19:14–16, 19

Notice God's response: "'Because you have prayed to Me about Sennacherib king of Assyria, I have heard you. . . .' Therefore thus says the LORD concerning the king of Assyria, 'He will not come to this city or shoot an arrow there; . . . By the way that he came, by the same he will return, . . . For *I will defend this city* to save it for My own sake and for My servant David's sake'" (2 Kings 19:20, 32–34).

What if Hezekiah had not gone to the Lord in prayer? What if he had not waited to hear the Lord's response and had not yielded to His voice? Oh, dear friend, so often God wants to speak to us, but we rise from our prayer time without waiting for God to speak. We leave without hearing His counsel, comfort, or warnings.

However, when we lay our needs and problems before the Lord, as Hezekiah did with the letter, and, listening, give God our hands, He is able to lead us through whatever maze of problems, challenges, hurts, or decisions we face. Yielding to God means giving Him our ears, hands, strength, and power and responding as He directs.

YIELDING IS ACTING ON WHAT GOD TELLS US TO DO

The Bible relates many accounts of those who listened to God and yielded to Him. Consider Noah, who built the ark in obedience to God's voice. Ponder anew the awesome relationship Abraham had with God, how he went out from his country not knowing where he was going but following the voice of the Lord. Consider the great model we have in Moses and the way God talked to him as a man talks to his friend. Study Samuel's life and how he learned to discern God's voice.

What might God want to speak to you about? Whatever you have prayed about! If you've taken your concerns to God about your organization structure at work, He may guide you in how to better organize. If you've prayed about your attitude, God may give you insight into what's going on in your heart, as He did with Cain. God may lead you to a new city, job, or ministry if you give Him your ear and hand. God may respond to your prayer about your relationship with your spouse by giving you ideas for strengthening your marriage. God may respond to your prayer concerning your children by directing you in how to discipline them.

When Lauren's strong will became evident during the toddler years, I went to the Lord with my concerns about how to best parent her. In the quiet of the early morning, God encouraged me that He could use her strong will! Jesus blessed me with the knowledge that if I guided her to love Him, He could make her a bold, uncompromising witness as a teen and throughout her life. How did God speak to me? Did I hear an audible voice? No. He spoke to my mind as I searched His heart for help. Was God right? Imagine the smile in my heart at Lauren's three-year-old birthday party when she announced, "Let's pray!" before her friends delved into the birthday cake. Imagine the joy I felt as she practiced her faith throughout her teen years, went on mission trips, served as a counselor at a Christian camp and as a college youth intern at church. Imagine the joy I now experience when she accompanies me to retreats and conferences to lead the "Prayers of My Heart" Breakout Session and teaches others how to journal their prayers.

God showed Himself faithful to hear my prayers when I gave Him my ear to listen for His answers and gave Him my hand to lead me.

If we want to pray with purpose and live with passion, let our prayer lives be characterized by looking up, into the face of our glorious Lord. Let our hearts be repentant when we sin. Let our needs flow before His throne and our ears be open to God's voice when He speaks. Let us give our hands to the Lord, yielding ourselves to be used as He wishes.

Part Two

LORD, YOU ARE . . .

*I will exalt you, my God, the King; I will
praise your name for ever and ever.*

PSALM 145:1 NIV

In the following chapters you'll have an opportunity to be transformed as you behold, as in a mirror, the glory of the Lord's divine attributes. At the end of each chapter is a section titled "Kneel and PRAY," in which you'll be guided to stop, drop to your knees, and PRAY. By the end of the book, you will have PRAYed for twenty-six of God's divine attributes to transform your life and the lives of those for whom you pray.

May God's blessings and joy fill you as you pray with purpose and live with passion!

2 Cor 4:7 But we have this treasure in jars of clay, to show that the surpassing power belongs to God & not to us.

Col 1:9—

Zech 4:6 Not by might, nor by power, but by my Spirit says the Lord of hosts.

Rom 4:20-21 No distrust made him waver concerning the promise of God, But he grew strong in his faith as he gave glory to God, fully convinced that God was able to do what he had promised.

Mark 1:35 And rising very early in the morning, while it was still dark, he departed & went out to a desolate place, and there he prayed.

John 15:4 Abide in me, & I in you. As the branch cannot bear fruit by itself, unless it abides in the vine, so neither can you, unless you abide in me.

CHAPTER 6

LORD, YOU ARE ALMIGHTY

WHEN I AM WEAK,
I FIND STRENGTH AND POWER IN YOU

He who dwells in the shelter of the Most High
will abide in the shadow of the Almighty.

PSALM 91:1

Lord, You are the Almighty God, the most powerful one. You produce fruit in my barrenness. You judge and rule in righteousness. You are a father who holds sway over all things. In You I find shelter for my soul. Help me remember the awesome privilege of coming to You in prayer! In Jesus's name, amen.

The scene must have been odd. Had we been there, we would have seen an old man falling to his knees, not due to a stumble but deliberately. Genesis 17:1–3 explains: "Now when Abram was ninety-nine years old, the LORD appeared to Abram and said to him, 'I am God *Almighty*; walk before Me, and be blameless. I will establish My covenant between Me and you, and I will multiply you exceedingly.' Abram fell on his face, and God talked with him."

Although we may have read or studied the account numerous times, we should never cease to be amazed that Almighty God talks to humans. We should never cease to be amazed that the Almighty invites us into His presence to share the joys, burdens, and concerns of our hearts!

The Old Testament word for "Almighty" is the Hebrew word *Shaddai*, which means "most powerful."[1] "Some scholars suggest that *šadday* is related to the word *šadû* that means breast or mountain or both. So *šadday*, when

53

used of God, refers either to His ability to supply abundantly ['the Abundant One'] or to His majestic strength ['the Almighty One'].["2] The Greek
word *pantokrator*, translated as "Almighty" in the New Testament, means
"he who holds sway over all things, the ruler of all."[3] Together, these words
reveal that the Almighty is the most powerful, majestic being who holds
sway over all things.

Abram had known the Lord as "God Most High, possessor of heaven
and earth" (Genesis 14:19). He had known God as his "shield" (Genesis
15:1). However, Abram had yet to experience God's majestic strength and
abundant ability to supply his needs. He had yet to experience the Almighty
holding sway to bring forth a son and nation through whom all people on
the earth would be blessed.

Perhaps today we are like Abraham in that we know God in certain
ways, but we haven't yet experienced His mighty power. We may know Him
as our Father but still succumb in weakness to sin. We may know Him as
Savior yet not experience "the power of His resurrection" (Philippians 3:10).
If so, let us kneel before the Almighty as Abraham did. Let us purposefully
pray to learn more fully how the Almighty desires to work in us by His all-
powerful Spirit.[4]

THE ALMIGHTY PRODUCES FRUIT IN OUR BARRENNESS

Have you ever felt defeated, unable to fulfill God's commands? We've probably
all felt that way at times. We read God's promises in the Bible, knowing they
are meant for us, yet find it impossible to lay hold of them. We try to be the
godly people God wants us to be—we try to produce love, joy, peace, patience, kindness, goodness, faithfulness, and self-control—and fail miserably.

Even Abram, the great man of faith who left behind everything he knew
in obedience to God, found himself barren, unable to fulfill God's promise
to make of him a great nation. God had told Abram that his descendants
would be numerous as the stars.[5] However, his wife, Sarai, wasn't able to
conceive. Abram tried every means he knew to produce the son God had

My devos in the AM are my anti-stress times - getting it
all out of my system. Replacing anxiety w/ the truth of God's
word.
ALMIGHTY ‣ CHAPTER 6

promised. He offered to adopt a servant and confer on him the rights and
privileges of a son. When God rejected that idea, Abram fathered a child
through Hagar, Sarai's maid, according to the custom of the day. However
the Almighty rejected Ishmael as the son through whom all the nations
would be blessed.

Abram finally learned a great truth about God: What the Almighty
promises, only the Almighty can produce.[6] Mighty promises require mighty
power, not fleshly, human power.[7]

2 Cor 4:7 - all supp. power belongs to God
Col 1:10-11 - his glorious might
Zech. 4:6

From Abraham we learn that our human efforts can never produce what
the Almighty requires in us. Only through His Spirit are we able to conceive
and produce spiritual gifts and works. Only when we, like Abraham, confess
to God, "I'm dead, barren. I can't be righteous apart from You. I can't do
what you are requiring of me," are we capable of God's promises being born
in our lives.[8] The Almighty's promises are for us, yet they are not produced
by us but in us, through the Holy Spirit, as we seek His power in prayer.[9]

key
I'm unable to not worry - unable to trust You - Praise you that that ability to trust comes from You.
2 Cor 12:9
Rom 4:21
Phil 4:19

When we despair of our inability to produce the goodness, patience,
and love that God demands, let us go to the Almighty and humbly pray,
"You are Almighty. I am weak. Please fill me with Your all-powerful Spirit so
that I may please you and bring glory to Your name."[10] — *Rom 4:19-20*

make you famous, I love those verses on God's might!

I want faith like this - to believe God & give him glory
"No distrust made him waver concerning the promise of God."

THE ALMIGHTY PROVIDES SHELTER
AND SHADE IN OUR TRIALS

How did Abraham eventually experience the power of the Almighty and
bear the son of God's promise? He stayed in God's presence. As stated earlier, *Shaddai* is a word picture of God as a mountain of strength and His
presence as a majestic shelter and shade.

Does it seem that trial after trial is beating down relentlessly upon your
family? Are you exposed to a constant barrage of temptation, discouragement, or doubt? If so, you, as Abraham, can experience the Almighty's shelter and shade. How? By dwelling in His presence. God's words in Psalm
91:1 are for you: "He who dwells in the shelter of the Most High will abide

in the shadow of the Almighty." The Hebrew word for "dwell" is *yashab* and means "to remain, sit, abide, stay."[11] The Almighty's invitation is not to occasionally visit His holy hill in prayer, but rather to stay in a constant state of His majestic, all-powerful presence. To walk before Him, as He instructed Abraham.[12] Or to abide in Him, as Jesus taught[13]

what does this look like lived out?

We dwell in the Almighty's presence through prayer. We live in His presence by purposefully going to Him with our hurts, bruised souls, wandering minds, lustful passions, and doubts. We are invited, in fact compelled, by the Almighty, to come and sit with Him, to drink richly from His breast, to "sup" or "dine" with Him (Revelation 3:20 KJV and NASB).

Psalm 121 reminds us that we, like the psalmist, can lift up our eyes to the mountains and find help in the Almighty Lord who made heaven and earth. We can experience the blessedness of the Almighty being the "shade" on our right hand.

Our Almighty God is standing on His holy hill. He is not shaken by the events that shake us. We can run to Him a thousand times a day and find shelter and shade. We can kneel in His presence each morning and return to Him throughout the day.

Hallelujah!

The Almighty Judges and Reigns in Righteousness

Almighty God not only produces fruit in our barrenness and provides shelter and shade, He also judges and reigns in righteousness. Abraham witnessed the Almighty's righteous judgment in the events recorded in Genesis 18:17–19:29. Following His announcement that Sarah would give birth to Isaac the following year, the Lord confided to Abraham that He was going to see the wickedness of Sodom and Gomorrah. Having seen it, He destroyed the two cities in righteous judgment. However, the Almighty spared Lot out of the judgment of the wicked.

Today many ignore the Bible's warning that the Almighty is coming again to judge the world and reign in righteousness. However, Revelation

wants to be in communi- decisions — ask for power Kaylee

Gen 17:1

Jn 15:4

8/14 – Be Almighty over Amy + her family situation.

19:15 provides a visual of His impending judgment and reign: "From His mouth comes a sharp sword, so that with it He may strike down the nations, and He will rule them with a rod of iron; and He treads the wine press of the fierce wrath of God, the Almighty."

What does this mean for us? First, it means that the Almighty to whom we pray will one day judge the living and the dead. Those who have called on Him for the forgiveness of their sins will experience the salvation of their souls and His glorious eternal presence. Those who refuse the Almighty's mercy will experience His almighty wrath. Therefore, let us purposefully pray for those who have not yet confessed Jesus as Lord, that they will turn to the Almighty. Let us passionately live for the Almighty in anticipation of His return.

using all resources—time, $, ... as a way to get friends in kingdom.

LiuXing   LMN peeps
MIK   extended
JIC   family
Nicky
Nichole
HCCS Teachers

The Almighty Is Our Father Who Holds Sway over All Things

result of knowing this

As we have seen in Abraham's life, the Almighty, *pantokrator*, "holds sway over all things." Is this "ruler of all"[14] a distant dictator who manipulates us to do His will? Hardly! In 2 Corinthians 6:18 the Almighty describes Himself in the most personal of ways—as our Father. "'I will be a father to you, and you shall be sons and daughters to Me,' says the Lord Almighty." Rather than being an impersonal God, the Almighty relates to us as a loving father who influences us for our good and who allows us to be tested so that we might discover His strength.

Abraham demonstrated what it means to allow Almighty God, our Father, to influence us, to hold sway over our actions. When God called on him to do the most difficult thing imaginable—to sacrifice Isaac—Abraham did not rebel. Instead, he bowed his will at the altar of sacrifice. He came under God's divine influence. He trusted his Almighty Father and said to those who accompanied him and Isaac, "We will worship and return to you" (Genesis 22:5).

Had Abraham not been willing to sacrifice Isaac, he would never have known the Almighty's provision of a ram substitute, which foreshadowed Christ's substitute for us. How often do we miss the Almighty's blessings and provisions because we refuse to come under His divine sway?

As the Almighty tested Abraham, He tests us to reveal if we are allowing Him to hold sway over our hearts and lives. What can we do when we are tested in our marriages, tested by a rebellious child, tested to remain morally pure in an impure society? What can we do when we have a decision to make but no clear direction? What can we do when the Almighty calls us to sacrifice our personal preferences to do His will? We, like Abraham, can listen and respond to the voice of the One who is speaking. Following the example of Jesus, we can fall on our faces in the Almighty's presence and yield to His influence.[15] We can meet with Him early in the morning, even while it is still dark, so He can influence our hearts and minds how to best serve Him.[16] We can pray for the Almighty to sway our hearts to accomplish His divine will when we face decisions.[17] We can stay in prayer under the Almighty's influence when our flesh is weak and our calling difficult.[18]

Isn't it amazing that He who holds sway over all things, He who is able to influence kingdoms, powers, and principalities invites us into His presence so we can make our hearts' desires known to Him and He can make His desires known to us?[19] Our Almighty Father invites us to tell Him "good morning" each day so that He might purposefully influence us for good. He invites us to intentionally pray for our needs and the needs of others.

Are we found at His footstool each morning, purposefully praying for the Almighty to influence our loved ones' hearts, to influence our nation for Christ? Do we return to the Almighty throughout the day to find rest in the shadow of His majestic presence? Are our ears passionately tuned to His voice throughout the day? Are we purposefully praying for His empowerment, through the Holy Spirit, to walk blamelessly before Him? Are we returning to the Almighty and thanking Him when we see how He has powerfully influenced and held sway over circumstances?

Raylee –
challenge –
use rest of
summer for God
devos when
school
begins
healthy
schedule

Meditation Moment

The Almighty God invites you into His majestic presence, produces fruit
in your barrenness, and provides shelter and shade for your soul. Your Almighty Father lovingly desires to influence you, so that you can know the
joy of His presence and the empowerment of His Spirit.

KNEEL *and* PRAY

A sample prayer can be found in Additional Resources.

WORSHIP THE ALMIGHTY GOD

P   *Praise* the Almighty, most powerful God, who produces fruit in
barrenness, provides shelter and shade, judges and reigns in righteousness,
and as a loving Father influences you for His divine purposes.

Fought for Israelites, Joshua 10 ; As Almighty now
as when I was in China – can still teach me here –
He's not limited to a location.

R   *Repent* of any ways in which you seek to live in your own strength rather
than relying on the Almighty. Confess if your heart is hardened and you
don't give your ear to the Almighty's voice and influence. *short memory of*
what you've done – who you
– forget you're Almighty – past faithful deeds → trust self.
– forget you're A over my family   instant reaction ... to
are –
worry
A   *Ask* the Almighty to fill you with His Spirit so that you might live *instead.*
by His divine power and influence. Pray for others to come under the
Almighty's divine influence and for the unsaved to turn to the Almighty for   *8/13/14*
PR in SP
the forgiveness of their sins. *Be A. over reflection today –*
looking forward (today + tomorrow + Fri) – using every   *8/23*
moment for you. Be almighty over my reli. with
Jenny – my stress level – my body –
Y   *Yield* to the Almighty who wants to influence your heart and life so *my sat*
vacation
that you might know His joy. Pray to be increasingly sensitive to His sway.
Purposefully listen to His voice and give Him your hand. *help me hear*
you & obey – in all convo. w/ teachers, parents, students

Husband dept - You've been Almighty to give me short friendships each that teach me something, not too long to distract or derail my emotions completely. You were Almighty to call me to singleness for a majority of my time overseas - I didn't need the extra distractor.

Job dept. - You were Almighty to provide a job I'm already in love with, a job load I can ease back into, an environment that will use my China experience + language - a position everyone says, " fits me like a glove"; + I agree! Something I'm skilled for, passionate about, enjoy, fills me up... + makes sense why I came home from China fa. You are Almighty over my career + future!

Family dept. - You will show yourself Almighty as you grant wisdom to how to still pour into family when they're not #1 priority. You will show yourself continually Almighty over mom's health + stroke + tests + energy + personality + memory - Almighty over the fear + concern which want to creep in, the holding tighter or pushing away I default to.

   You are Almighty over Carly's anxiety - her meds - her psychiatrist, her view of you + your word - her soul searching - her book - her daughter - her own family.

CHAPTER 7

Lord, You Are *the* Beloved Son

When I Feel Unloved,
I Remember That I Am Precious to You

After being baptized, Jesus came up immediately from the water;
and behold, the heavens were opened, and He saw the Spirit of God
descending as a dove and lighting on Him, and behold, a voice out of the
heavens said, "This is My beloved Son, in whom I am well-pleased."
MATTHEW 3:16–17

Heavenly Father, thank You for loving me so much that You gave Your Beloved
Son for me. Forgive me for taking Your love and Your Son for granted. Help me
to increasingly love others as You do. In Your Beloved Son's name I pray, amen.

When our children, Taylor and Lauren, were born, there were no words to describe our love for them. Keith and I loved, adored, and prayed for our son and daughter from the time they were conceived. We looked at photographs of their development in the womb and celebrated every movement of their wiggly bodies. We loved Taylor and Lauren before our eyes gazed on them or our hands laid hold of them. When they were born, our love exploded into deep affection.

How much more passionately must God the Father, whose very being is love, have felt when His precious Son was born?

The Beloved Son Holds a Special
Place in the Father's Heart

Picture the quiet village of Nazareth, where the culmination of an eternal promise is about to be put into motion. The Holy Spirit moves upon the

61

virgin Mary, and the heavenly Father begins weaving the Savior of the world within her womb. Imagine Him forming every fiber of Jesus's body, shaping His eyes that would one day penetrate the masses, His hands that would touch disease-ridden bodies and bring healing, His lips that would teach us to pray. Consider the care with which the Father formed His Beloved Son's tiny back, knowing it would one day carry the weight of our sins at Golgotha.

Imagine how the Father must have hovered in anticipation when Mary went into labor, how He must have proudly watched the birth of His Beloved Son. What rejoicing must have echoed through heaven when Jesus let out His first cry and the heavenly host looked on the innocence of Jesus, Savior of the world.

Never before and never since has a father celebrated his baby's birth in such a spectacular manner. Our heavenly Father placed a glorious star in the sky to herald His Son's birth. He sent musical birth announcements by way of angels. He invited shepherds to come and see His Beloved Son. The Father sent birthday gifts fit for a king by way of wise men.

As great as the Father's love was that first Christmas, consider God's love and pleasure as He watched His Beloved Son grow in stature and favor with mankind. Imagine the heavenly excitement on the day of Jesus's baptism when the Holy Spirit descended as a dove and the Father spoke from heaven, "This is My beloved Son, in whom I am well-pleased" (Matthew 3:17). The Greek word translated "beloved" is *agapetos*, which means "esteemed, dear, favorite, worthy of love."[1] The Father loved and esteemed His only begotten Son.

How could it be, then, that the Father was silent when His Beloved Son was tied to a whipping post? Where was His Father when Jesus endured scourging almost to the point of death? Where was His Father when Jesus stumbled and fell under the weight of the cross? Where had He turned His gaze when His Beloved Son cried to Him, "Why have You forsaken Me?" (Matthew 27:46).

The Father's love-filled eyes were looking at you and at me.

We Hold a Special Place in the Father's Heart

As hard as it is for us to imagine, the Father allowed His Beloved Son to suffer the punishment that we deserve, to carry the weight of our sins to the cross, and to die in our place. Why? Because the Father loves you and me too.

The Bible is replete with scriptures that point to the fact that we are God's children and that He loves us. Paul, in Acts 17:24–31, states that our Father made the world and all the things in it and that we are to seek Him, even grope for Him, though He is not far from us. Paul passionately explains, "For in Him we live and move and exist . . . 'For we also are His children'" (Acts 17:28). Paul concludes that because we are God's children we should live in relation to Him. We should grope for Him.

When trouble comes upon us, we should go to our heavenly Father who loves us. When we become aware of sin, we should repent and run into our Father's arms. We should be mindful that our Father does not take lightly the sacrifice of His Beloved Son on our behalf. Therefore, let us not merely quote John 3:16, the familiar verse that tells us God so loved us that He gave His only begotten Son for us; let us also purposefully pray and passionately live in light of its truth, in light of our Father's love.

We Hold a Special Place in the Beloved Son's Heart

Not only does the Father love His Son and us, the Beloved Son loves us too. Jesus could not have been more specific in defining His love for us than when He explained in John 15:13, "Greater love has no one than this, that one lay down his life for his friends."

How did we rank becoming the Beloved Son's friends? We didn't. The Beloved Son's love for us is not based on our goodness. Jesus loved us before we were born. His love is active, not passive. The account of God's interacting with mankind is the story of His pursuing love, of God's saving us from sin and evil. Why? Because "God is love" (1 John 4:16). Love is His nature, the essence of who He is.

Jesus demonstrated His love not only in the sacrifice of His life on the cross but also in touching the sick and healing them, tirelessly teaching the good news of heaven, welcoming little children into His arms, forgiving sinners, and calling all to follow Him.

It is easy in our world to feel unloved. Whether you are single, married, divorced, widowed, have children, live alone, are busy or bored, working or retired, just beginning your life, "over the hill," in the sandwich generation, golden years, or final hours of your life, pain and disappointment are inevitable. We make mistakes that cause us to feel unlovable or undeserving of love. However, let us never question the Beloved Son's love for us.

Why? Because He carried out the ultimate act of love. He laid down His life for us while we were sinners. He took our scourging. He carried our cross. He literally lay down and allowed His hands and feet to be cruelly hammered into heavy crossbeams. The Beloved Son not only gave up His glory when He left His Father's side, He humbled Himself to the point of hanging on the cross for our sins. Why? Because we hold a special place in His love-filled heart.

LET US PRAYERFULLY LOVE
AS THE FATHER AND BELOVED SON LOVE US

Knowing that the Father and Beloved Son love us should cause us to pray and live differently than if we didn't have such assurance. We should confidently approach the throne of grace to pray not only for ourselves but also for others.[2] We should purposefully pray to love others as God loves us.[3] Are you having a hard time loving a child, a spouse, a relative, or perhaps someone with whom you work? If so, the Beloved God's arms are open wide. Run into them and ask Him to give you His love for others, to give you eyes to see others as He does, to give you His heart with which to love them. The Bible says that no one has seen God, but that "if we love one another, God abides in us, and His love is perfected in us" (1 John 4:12). It is through God's indwelling Holy Spirit that we experience and express His love toward

64

others.[4] Therefore, let us purposefully approach the throne of God and ask Him to fill the reservoirs of our hearts with His love.

Let us also purposefully pray to have God's heart of love for those who don't yet know the Beloved Son as their Savior. Luke 19:10 tells us that the Beloved Son came to earth "to seek and to save" those who are lost, as sheep wandering aimlessly in sin. The Beloved Son's heart is that no one die in sin but that all "come to repentance" (2 Peter 3:9). The Father's heart of love desires that every man, woman, and child experience the joy and fullness of what it means to be His adopted children and heirs, filled with His Spirit.[5]

The Beloved Son is worthy of our praise, for He willingly laid down His life for us. Shouldn't we therefore daily profess our love for Father and Son? Shouldn't we honor them by living passionately for them? Shouldn't we tell others of their love? Let us confidently pray to the Lord who loves us so much that He gave His only begotten Son for us. Let us never feel unloved, but rather recognize the Father and Son's love for us and purposefully pray to love others as They have loved us.

Meditation Moment

God the Father and Jesus, His Beloved Son, love you not only in word but in deed. The expression of their love culminates in the cross. Their love can fill you today through the Holy Spirit and empower you to love the Father, the Beloved Son, and others.

KNEEL and PRAY

WORSHIP THE BELOVED SON

P   *Praise* the heavenly Father and Beloved Son for Jesus's giving His life so that you might be saved, becoming His adopted heir, receiving His love, the Holy Spirit, and an eternity in heaven. _____

_____

_____

R   *Repent* and confess aspects of your life that do not reflect the Beloved

65

no. @ my school my goal is to stake my claim.

Son's love. Consider how you treat others and whether you are motivated by Christ's love and the desire to see all persons come to God through the forgiveness of their sins. annoyance @ not sleeping 100% — @ still having to do a simple diet — irritability — selfishness

God is source of all love — even to love him

A *Ask* the Lord to make you an instrument of His love. Purposefully pray for others to see God's love in you and be drawn to the Savior.

so embarrassed I call myself a Christian Marcella — Jeannine — for help to love others like God does

Y *Yield* your heart and mind to the Beloved Son. Ask Him to fill you with His Spirit of love and to give you an abounding love for Him and others. Give Him your hand so He can lead you and show you how to love others.

Towards mom + her SR email — I'm being stubborn, selfish, petty — I want my own space + I only have it in my car.

1 Cor 13

Love is patient
        kind
doesn't envy
        boast
is not rude
is not self-seeking
keeps no record of wrongs
doesn't delight in evil but
        rejoices with the truth
Always protects, hopes,
trusts, perseveres.
Love never fails.

But when the fullness of time had come, God sent forth his son, born of woman, born under the law, to redeem those who were under the law, so that we might receive adoption as sons. God has sent the Spirit of his Son into our ♡'s, crying, Abba! Father! So you are no longer a slave, but a son, + if a son, then an heir through God. Gal. 4:4-7

Let us therefore draw near with confidence to the throne of grace, that we may receive mercy + find grace to help in time of need. Heb 4:16

66

CHAPTER 8

LORD, YOU ARE *the* COMFORTER

WHEN I AM DISCOURAGED,
I FIND ENCOURAGEMENT IN YOU

Blessed be the God and Father of our Lord Jesus Christ,
the Father of mercies and God of all comfort.
2 CORINTHIANS 1:3

Lord, You are the God of all comfort. Thank You for the comfort You give me.
Forgive me for the times I don't experience Your comfort because I don't pray.
Help me be a source of Your comfort to others. In Jesus's name I pray, amen.

On a cold winter evening, nothing feels quite as cozy as snuggling in bed
under the warmth of a soft comforter. However, no blanket can compare to
the God of all comfort when life blows us off course, when a person's sharp
tongue chills us to the bone, or when the howling wind of despair beats
upon our hearts.

The Bible tells us that God is "the Father of mercies and God of all
comfort" (2 Corinthians 1:3). The Greek word for "comfort" is *parakaleo*,
which means "to call to one's side, speak to, in the way of exhortation, console, teach."[1] How awesome it is that God gives every believer the gift of His
presence through the Holy Spirit, whom the Bible calls our Comforter. This
Comforter is an abiding presence who will never wear out, become thread-
bare, or leave us. He calls us to His side, warms our hearts, encourages and
consoles us, and teaches us God's ways so we can walk in His will. The closer
we stay to God in prayer and Bible study, the more fully we experience the
warmth of His abiding presence. Where we go, our Comforter goes. The

good news is, we don't have to be like Linus, carrying around a blanket. Our Comforter blankets us on the inside with His love, warmth, and encouragement as we come to Him in prayer.

GOD'S COMFORT TAKES MANY FORMS

When we're caught in a raging blizzard of chaos, pain, or disappointment, what a joy it is to realize that God doesn't leave us as orphans in the cold. Rather, He pulls us close to Him and bundles us in His everlasting arms, offering comfort in a number of ways.

First, He comforts us through the Holy Spirit. Prior to His death, Jesus comforted, taught, and encouraged the disciples as He walked alongside them in person. Before He went to the cross, Jesus prepared His followers for a new way in which they would experience His comforting presence. He explained that, although He was leaving, He would send the Holy Spirit in His place: "I will ask the Father, and He will give you another Helper, that He may be with you forever; that is the Spirit of truth, whom the world cannot receive, because it does not see Him or know Him, but you know Him because He abides with you and will be in you. I will not leave you as orphans, I will come to you" (John 14:16–18). Just as Jesus was present with the disciples, He is present with believers today through the Holy Spirit, who lives in us to teach us, comfort us, and encourage us.

Second, God comforts us through the Bible. The psalmist wrote, "This is my comfort in my affliction, that Your word has revived me" (Psalm 119:50). How did God's Word revive the psalmist? The next few verses explain that, when arrogant people derided him, he continued to follow God's instructions, finding comfort in remembering God's words. Perhaps, like the psalmist, you find comfort in bringing to mind certain verses. For many, Jeremiah 29:11 brings comfort, "'For I know the plans that I have for you,' declares the LORD, 'plans for welfare and not for calamity to give you a future and a hope.'" Just as curling up under a comforter and taking a nap revives us, resting in the comfort of God's Word revives us. Make a daily habit of reading God's Word. Highlight favorite passages and rest in them. Memorize God's Word, and you'll have a ready supply of His comforting words close to your heart. Pray God's Word when you don't know what to pray. He will blanket you with His love and warm your heart and mind.

Third, God comforts us through godly people. Although God's internal comfort cannot be replaced, He often comforts us through the words or presence of another person. The apostle Paul wrote about such an experience: "God, who comforts the depressed, comforted us by the coming of Titus" (2 Corinthians 7:6). Lasting comfort doesn't come through those who speak off the top of their heads or by reason of their own counsel, as did Job's friends. However, other people can bring genuine comfort when the source of their words and wisdom is God's Word, communicated through the Holy Spirit. Comforters come in all sizes and shapes. Don't miss the godly people God sends you. Rather, thank God for them and pray to be a source of God's comfort to others.

Fourth, God comforts us in prayer. Suffering and weakness are parts of life, as Paul noted in Romans 8:18 and 8:26. However, God, our Comforter, doesn't leave us alone in our weaknesses. Rather, He invites us to His throne room, where He comforts us with His presence, where the Holy Spirit helps us and even intercedes for us, according to the will of God. He comforts us with the knowledge that "God causes all things to work together for good to those who love God, to those who are called according to His purpose" (Romans 8:28).

Often I light a candle when I pray, as the priests of the Bible did upon entering God's presence in the temple. As the fragrance of the candle fills the room, I am comforted, knowing that my prayers are ascending as a fragrant aroma to God.[2] Experience the comfort of God as you draw near to Him in prayer.[3]

GOD'S COMFORT IS ALWAYS AVAILABLE

Have you ever known someone who refused to be comforted? Have you, perhaps, fallen unknowingly into this trap? Do you choose to dwell on the

[handwritten at top: "maybe... all my comparing to self?"]

past rather than live in the present? Do you punish yourself for past sins rather than accept God's forgiveness? Do you choose to think sad, worrisome thoughts rather than focus on that which is true, honorable, right, pure, lovely, of good report, excellent, and worthy of praise, as Paul advises in Philippians 4:8?

[handwritten left margin: "9/13 yes — all the time!"]

God wants us to be comforted. He encourages us in 2 Corinthians 13:11 to "rejoice, be made complete, be comforted." Are you purposefully praying to experience God's comfort in the midst of your affliction, depression, or suffering? Or do you push the Comforter aside and then wonder why your heart is cold and you feel emotionally beaten? Let us find renewed joy and comfort by purposefully looking up, into the face of our glorious Comforter!

[handwritten left margin, running vertically: "In some ways the best 4 weeks have been the hardest of my year, home. The first few mo. were tough — grief, transition, health, adjusting. Now I'm struggling to balance — gov, work, life, health. huge —"]

God Comforts Us in Our Affliction

[handwritten above heading: "on the stress + mvg people; I'm not crazy for struggling... to be crazy to not struggle"]

Sometimes we may think of God's comfort as something that *follows* tragedy or pain or crisis. However, 2 Corinthians 1:4 says that God "comforts us *in* all our affliction." In other words, in the midst of being troubled or afflicted, we can experience God's comfort by going to Him in prayer.

I have found that in the quiet of morning, when I kneel before the Lord with a troubled heart, He is there to comfort me. I have found that when my children call with burdens, I can kneel and pray for God to comfort them in the midst of whatever they face. I have learned that when a loved one is hospitalized, I can look up into the heavens as I drive to the hospital and receive comfort as I praise God, who is seated on the throne and who I know will comfort my loved one through the illness. We can pray with our eyes open during a stressful meeting, a highly charged discussion, or when children are quarreling. God's Comforter is wherever we are, ready to comfort us *in* our affliction!

God Comforts Us When We Are Depressed

The Comforter also stands ready to console us when trials are ongoing, threatening to drain our reserves of strength and hope. Have you lost a loved one? Does a load of troubles weigh you down? Are financial problems an ever-present source of worry? Is your heart heavy? You'll find no place more comforting than God's presence. Second Corinthians 7:6 says that God comforts the depressed. Purposefully go to Him in prayer. Look up and praise God. Repent of any anger or unforgiveness that drains you of His joy and peace. Ask the God of all comfort to encourage you with the knowledge that, even though you cannot see Him, He is present with you and in you, and He will never leave you. You are His. Yield yourself to His comforting arms of love.

I don't want it to drain away— I need all I can get.

God Comforts Us When We Suffer for Him

Recently I led a retreat with Pam Moore, Corrie ten Boom's former traveling companion. Listening to her account of Corrie ten Boom experiencing God's comfort in the midst of a concentration camp brought to mind the reality of Paul's words, "Just as the sufferings of Christ are ours in abundance, so also our comfort is abundant through Christ" (2 Corinthians 1:5).

Although few of us will endure such persecution, we may suffer for our faith in other ways. Spouses may suffer the grief of living with a partner who doesn't know the Lord. Parents may suffer over children who refuse to follow Christ. Employees may suffer for refusing to compromise their Christian values at work. Those who yield their ministries and work fully to the Lord will face times of suffering and discouragement.

What can we expect in the midst of our suffering? We can expect the Comforter to walk alongside us. We can expect the Comforter to give us assurance, as only He can, as we draw close to Him in prayer. When trials and suffering come our way, rather than pull the bed covers over our heads, let us pull the Comforter over our hearts! *ahh, yes...*

Meditation Moment

God is the God of all comfort who comforts you through the Holy Spirit, His Word, godly people, and prayer. He is worthy of your praise!

KNEEL *and* PRAY

WORSHIP THE GOD OF ALL COMFORT

P *Praise* the God of all comfort who comes alongside you and encourages you through the Holy Spirit, the Bible, godly people, and prayer._____

_____

_____

_____

R *Repent* and confess ways you resist the Holy Spirit's comfort. If you haven't been seeking God's comfort, change your mind about to whom or what you turn for comfort. don't show your comfort — stubborn to not recieve yours

[left margin: no time to repent → worry, stress, anxiety]

A *Ask* the Comforter to fill your heart with His Spirit. Ask Him to comfort and encourage you through His Word and in prayer. Pray for others to find their comfort in God. Ask Him to use you to be a source of His comfort to others. Remind me — comfort me when I think the insurmountable tasks are by myself. I'm never alone, Hallelujah!! By your strength abiding in you, bearing

[left margin: yes 9/13]

Y *Yield* to the Comforter as you go through your day, returning to Him in prayer and Bible study as He prompts you and draws you to His side. for eternity. yield to instead of anxiety — it's one or the other. Help me let you give me comfort. @ a

[left margin: no time to yield...do on own + mess up + take time or take sleep or lose out on others]

[right margin: fruit eternity. I day @ a time]

This is my comfort in my affliction, that your word has revived me. Ps 119:50

If God is for us, who can be against us? He gave me a great idea for Sent. Composing. Why would I think He's deserted me or that I'm on my own now? 9/6/14 After 1st wk of school.

9/13

I don't know how to boast in my weakness. I see ---
- not enough energy. "insurmountable tasks". feeling sick (stomach/cold)
+ think defeat, discouragement, impossible. Help me see your equation ... weak + big task + no energy = God's strength made perfect

CHAPTER 9

LORD, YOU ARE *the* DOOR

WHEN MY HEART LONGS FOR HEAVEN, I ENTER THROUGH YOU

I am the door; if anyone enters through Me, he will be saved.
JOHN 10:9

Lord Jesus, You are the Door. You are not just any door but rather a heavenly Door that ushers me into the Father's presence. Thank You for opening the door to heaven, a door by which my family, friends, neighbors, and the world can be saved. Forgive me for not coming into Your presence more often. In Your name, amen.

Have you ever been locked out of a place you desperately needed to be?

One night several years ago, I was awakened by a phone call from my mother, who at the time was living in an independent retirement apartment. My heart lurched when I heard her say, "Deb, I think you'd better get over here." Assuring Mama I was on my way, I literally jumped out of bed and tossed the phone to my husband, Keith, asking him to call 911.

On the desperate drive to her apartment, I prayed that I would get to Mama in time, that I could be with her in her suffering until an ambulance arrived. I knew that the outer doors to her building were locked at night for security, but an attendant would be available to open the doors to those who arrived after hours.

Arriving at the building, I ran to the door and yanked, but it was locked. The attendant was nowhere in sight. In desperation I rang the night buzzer, beat the door, ran to another door, grabbed my cell phone, and called the front desk. No response.

Panicked, I continued to pound the door and buzz the doorbell, knowing my mother was suffering alone while I stood outside the door, unable to get to her. Eventually, the attendant, who had been caring for another patient, arrived and flung open the door. I rushed up the stairs, along with the medical technicians who had arrived, and found my mother gasping for breath. Days later I was able to bring her home from the hospital, but not without looking differently at the door that had finally let us into her presence so that her life could be saved.

Thankfully, none of us has to face such a situation when we try to reach our heavenly Father. God doesn't lock us out of His presence. He loves us and opens the door to His presence through Jesus Christ.

If you're not a Christian and feel as if you're on the outside looking in, that there must be more to life than you're experiencing, it may be that you're on the threshold of heaven. Or perhaps you have entered the door of salvation but have yet to fling open the doors to God's throne room each day and walk in His grace. Whatever the case, I encourage you to take Jesus and His offer seriously: "Ask, and it will be given to you; seek, and you will find; *knock*, and it will be opened to you. For everyone who asks receives, and he who seeks finds, and *to him who knocks it will be opened*" (Matthew 7:7–8).

Jesus Is the Door to Salvation

Jesus stated in John 10:9, "I am the door; if anyone enters through Me, he will be saved." The Greek word for "door" is *thura*, which means "a vestibule, entrance, way or passage into."[1] Jesus is the passageway by which we enter into God's presence and abundant life.

The image of Jesus being the door of salvation dates back to the Exodus of the Israelites from Egypt. The Israelites were enslaved to the Egyptians when God called Moses to lead them to freedom. Pharaoh repeatedly ignored God's command through Moses, "Let My people go." Through devastating plagues, God revealed His power and authority, providing Pharaoh an opportunity to change his mind and release Israel. Still he refused, and the final plague was announced: the death of every firstborn son across the land. To protect Israel from this plague of death, the Lord provided a door of opportunity by which death would not touch them. God told Moses to instruct each family to take a lamb for their evening meal and apply its blood to the doorposts of their homes.[2] "When I see the blood I will pass over you, and no plague will befall you to destroy you when I strike the land of Egypt" (Exodus 12:13). The lamb's death served as a substitute sacrifice for the firstborn child in the home. The blood-smeared doorway was their means of being saved.

Fast-forward to first-century Jerusalem and stand at the foot of the cross. Look up at Jesus, hung on two wooden beams, bleeding, taking our judgment, being our means of salvation. Jesus hangs between heaven and earth, Son of Man, Son of God, a blood-smeared door through which we enter into God's presence. When we look to Christ for forgiveness, God, who once would have seen only our sin, now sees the substitute blood of His Son, the Lamb sacrificed in our place, the Door by whom we are saved.

Have you entered through Him? If not, He is a prayer away. Experience the joy of being forgiven and entering God's presence through Christ!

JESUS IS THE ONLY DOOR TO HEAVEN

When I was growing up, my family often watched *Let's Make A Deal*, a television game show in which contestants guessed whether the prize was behind door number 1, door number 2, or door number 3. If they guessed correctly, they received the prize behind the door. If they guessed wrong, they went home empty-handed.

Sometimes people approach eternity by supposing that there are lots of doors to heaven. They believe they can enter through good works or church attendance or whatever form of religious faith appeals to them. However, those who think God has provided numerous doors of salvation are mistaken.

Jesus warned, "I am the way, and the truth, and the life; no one comes to the Father but through Me" (John 14:6).

All nationalities and people are welcomed in heaven, but all must enter through the same door: Jesus. He is a sure door—the only Door—that opens to the prize of God Himself!

JESUS IS THE DOOR TO ABUNDANT LIFE

Recently I visited a friend who had moved into a new home. As I stepped through the door into her entry, I stopped in amazement. It was absolutely beautiful. I gazed at the winding staircase, the ornate decorations, the gorgeous furniture, and beautiful paintings. I stood in the vestibule of her home trying to take in everything. "Come on!" she finally urged, eager to show me the rest of her home.

In the same way, as believers we may pause at the entrance to our salvation, take a deep breath at the beauty of being saved, and stop right there, so enthralled that we don't hear God calling us, "Come on!" We may neglect to realize that God is urging us to move beyond the doorway and enter into the riches that are ours in Jesus. Christ's promise, "I came that they may have life, and have it abundantly" (John 10:10) is not only for after we die but for today.

What are these riches that are ours through Jesus? Take a peek:

Jesus is the door to love. Although we know we are supposed to love, we may not find love in our hearts toward others. When we wake up feeling cranky or we're harboring resentment toward someone, we can purposefully pray, *Lord, You are love. Forgive me for being so unloving, for being so selfish and only looking out for my interests. Please fill me with Your love today. Help me overflow with love toward_____. I yield my heart to You.*

Jesus is the door to joy. Many live day-in, day-out with no joy. Even holidays and vacations can be times of tension and sadness. What is the key to having joy? Matthew 25 offers a powerful parable that reveals that joy isn't something we acquire by living for ourselves. Rather, joy is something

9/29 - my need for this week - to walk w/ me daily.

76

use talents – invest what we've been given *look like?*

we enter into when we do God's bidding. Only when we lose our lives for Christ's sake do we discover the door to joy.

Jesus is the door to peace. Turmoil can rise unexpectedly in our hearts like a tsunami. We can be having a smooth day when a gust of bad news blows us off course. Instead of blowing up at someone or pretending things are fine when they are not, we can go to our all-knowing Father. We can bow on our knees and praise Him for being the Prince of Peace. We can repent of our anger. We can let off steam with Him. We can ask God to give us His perspective and fill us with His peace.

Jesus is the door to patience. Had I been Jesus, enduring the belittling of the Pharisees or putting up with the disciples' quarrels over who among them was the greatest would have certainly tested my patience. However, Jesus met each friend and foe with patience. If we want patience, then let us recognize that it doesn't come by counting to ten. It is a fruit of God's Spirit, a result of entering into Christ's presence and opening the doors of our hearts to His patience.

Jesus is the door to kindness. How do we respond to people who interrupt us? Are we equally kind to both the rich and poor, to those who can help us and those who call on us for help? Jesus dealt gracefully with many interruptions and was kind to both rich and poor, sinner and saint. Let us kneel and purposefully pray for Christ to fill our hearts with kindness. Let us repent when we are unkind to family, friends, business associates, or strangers.

Jesus is the door to goodness. We cannot attain goodness by trying hard. Goodness, like other spiritual fruit, is a result of the overflow of Christ's goodness within us. When we confess our inability to generate goodness and look to the Lord, we discover Christ's goodness filling us.

Jesus is the door to gentleness. As with kindness, there is a gentleness that is recognizably that of Jesus. When we ask, seek, and knock, Christ opens the door to a gentleness that is not synonymous with weakness but that demonstrates His power under control.

Jesus is the door to faithfulness. When we are "tied up" in the hectic pace of life, absorbed in our favorite television shows, or caught up in the throes of meetings, appointments, and activities, prayer and Bible study may be shoved aside. Rather than serving Christ as His ambassadors, we may be unfaithful to Him. However, when we stop, drop to our knees, and knock on the door of heaven, God faithfully flings open the door to His presence. He rejoices when we repent. He is ever ready to forgive. As we ask for His help, we discover His faithfulness compelling us to be more faithful to Him.

Jesus is the door to self-control. Christ, who could have called legions of angels to His rescue when Roman soldiers arrested Him in the Garden of Gethsemane, is the highest example of self-control. Through the Holy Spirit living within us, we can access this same form of strength. When we confess our self-indulgent behavior and repent of our lack of self-control, God's ears are open to our honesty. Let Him hear our plea to be filled with His self-control and respond to His guiding Spirit in relation to how we think, speak, act, eat, and drink.

Jesus is the Door to both eternal life in heaven and abundant life here and now. Let us determine to pray purposefully and live passionately through Christ, the open Door. He invites us, "Come!"

I'll race you to the Door!

Meditation Moment

Jesus is the Door to God, eternity, salvation, and abundant life. Through Christ you have access to the Lord of lords, to pray for not only your needs but also the needs of others. Pause in awe of God's amazing invitation to enter into His presence and to receive His gifts.

Kneel *and* PRAY

Worship the Lord Jesus Christ, the Door

P   *Praise* God for Christ, the door of salvation, the door to heaven, and the door to abundant life._____

_____

R *Repent* if you've failed to enter the door of salvation. Confess Jesus as Lord and ask Him to forgive your sins and save you. If you are a Christian, confess if you fail to daily enter into intimacy with God and do not walk in the abundant life He's opened to you. _____

_____

_____

A *Ask*, seek, and knock in prayer as Jesus, the Door, has invited you to do. Ask Him to fill you and clothe you with His Spirit. Pray for those who _9/20_ _~ as I do school - rest - friends_ have not yet entered salvation, that they will seek and enter into eternal life through Jesus._____

_____

_____

Y *Yield* to the Holy Spirit's leading. If He calls you to His throne room during the day, rush into His presence. If He prompts you to speak to someone about Jesus's being the door to heaven, do so. Keep the door of your heart open to God, as He keeps the door of His presence open to you. _____

_____

_____

CHAPTER 10

LORD, YOU ARE ETERNAL

WHEN LIFE SEEMS FUTILE, I FIND PURPOSE IN YOUR EVERLASTING ARMS

*The eternal God is a dwelling place,
and underneath are the everlasting arms.*
DEUTERONOMY 33:27

Lord, You are the Eternal God. You have existed forever. Forgive me for being shortsighted and preoccupied with things that are passing away. Help me to live in the awareness of Your eternal presence and serve Your eternal purposes. In Jesus's name, amen.

Most of us can relate to how a car trip with small children can seem like an eternity. Such was the case as Samantha headed down the road with her three little ones. "Mommy, how much longer?" Martha whined, as she swung her legs, kicking the front seat where eight-year-old Chad grew increasingly irritated. Before Samantha could catch his hand, Chad turned and hit his little sister. "Quit kicking me!" he yelled. Martha burst into tears, which woke up Jason. "How much longer, Mommy?" the children echoed as Samantha pulled out of the city limits to begin the twelve-hour drive to Grandma's.

How Samantha wished this were a fun trip instead of a desperate attempt to find a job and place to live. She had hoped to be able to make it on her own, but everything her mother said about her had come true. She had no job and no money—nothing to show for herself except three children born into two disastrous marriages. She finally gave in to the tapes playing in her head, "You're nothing. You never will be. You're a good-for-nothing daughter. You're a good-for-nothing wife."

Where are you, God? Samantha pleaded as she searched the sky through her bug-splattered windshield.

Unlike Samantha, who felt her life was a failure, Saul strode through the streets of Jerusalem with an air of confidence. A leading persecutor of Christians, his preparations were well under way to imprison any Jew who had become a follower of Jesus. Unlike Samantha, Saul wasn't looking for God. He believed himself to be God's right-hand man. Then one day the Eternal God stopped Saul dead in his tracks. Saul, who prided himself in his religious beliefs, fell to the ground in the presence of the Lord Jesus Christ.[1] Saul was forever changed when he realized that he did not exist for his religious beliefs but for the Eternal God. He later wrote to his young friend Timothy:

> *I thank Christ Jesus our Lord, who has strengthened me . . . even though I was formerly a blasphemer and a persecutor and a violent aggressor. Yet I was shown mercy because I acted ignorantly in unbelief; and the grace of our Lord was more than abundant. . . . It is a trustworthy statement, deserving full acceptance, that Christ Jesus came into the world to save sinners, among whom I am foremost of all. . . . Now to the King eternal, immortal, invisible, the only God, be honor and glory forever and ever.*
>
> 1 Timothy 1:12–15, 17

Whether we feel defeated like Samantha or successful and proud like Saul, the fact is, the Eternal God loves each of us and has a plan for our lives. Yet often—amid the car problems, broken washing machines, office politics, family feuds, and other minor crises—we lose sight of what's truly important. What does the Eternal God want us to remember? That He is a dwelling place for us.[2] His everlasting arms are outstretched. He invites us to join His eternal purposes.

Eternal God Invites Us to Dwell in Him

The Hebrew word translated as "eternal" is *ad* and means "forever, of continuous existence."[3] The Greek word translated as "eternal" in the New Testament is *aionios*, which means "without beginning and end, everlasting."[4]

As difficult as it is for our finite minds to grasp, the Lord to whom we pray is a self-existent God. He has always existed and always will exist. What difference does it make that God is "self-existent"? God, who has eternal power and glory,[5] is a dwelling place.[6] He invites us to dwell in Him. What an awesome description God gives of Himself! He doesn't give us limited visiting privileges; He says we can live in Him.

Dear friend, if we think of Christianity as church attendance and prayer, as something we do occasionally, we're missing out on what it means to live with passion. The Eternal Lord does not explain Himself or our relationship to Him as a water spigot to be turned on and off, but as a wellspring of life, of living water flowing in and through us.[7]

What difference does it make to us that Eternal God is a dwelling place? First, we have boldness and confident access to God through our faith in Jesus. This is God's eternal purpose.[8] The next time you have a need, rather than fret and fuss, go directly into the presence of the Eternal God. You can boldly approach His throne with confidence, knowing that He gives eternal comfort.[9] You may not always like the events of your life. You may be unhappy about choices you've made. You may have lost your job or be discouraged by someone's thoughtless words. However, no one can take from you the comfort found in Christ's presence.

Second, rather than living for that which will pass away, we are to passionately live by His power and Spirit for that which will last for eternity. We can live and bear fruit that will result in eternal rewards and joy.[10] This fruit is different from results we get by working in our own power. Therefore, we should purposefully, daily enter into God's presence and ask Him what work He has for us to do. Rather than our days passing and counting for nothing, our lives can have eternal value when we dwell in the Eternal God and live for Him.[11]

Eternal God Invites Us to Ceaseless Prayer

As we increasingly recognize Eternal God as our dwelling place, we increasingly accept His invitation to pray about everything and ask Him for our needs.[12] When our days are long and our fuses short, we ask God to give us His eternal perspective. When we see those who do not know Christ, we ask Him to use us in their lives to point the way to Him. When we have a financial decision to make, we go to Him over whose money we are stewards.

Eternal God invites us not only to bring Him our requests but also to remain in constant conversation with Him. First Thessalonians 5:17–18 says, "Pray without ceasing; in everything give thanks; for this is God's will for you in Christ Jesus."

Brother Lawrence in *The Practice of the Presence of God* impacted me with his description of what it means to live in a state of ceaseless prayer:

> During our work and other actions—let us stop a few minutes, as often as we can, to adore God in the depths of our hearts, to enjoy Him—in passing and in secret. He is in the depth and center of your heart, why should you not cease your exterior occupations—at least from time to time—to adore Him interiorly, to praise, petition Him, to offer Him your heart, and to thank Him?[13]

Eternal God invites you to ceaseless prayer. Leave the faucet of prayer open. Praise and thank Him for the little things. Repent immediately when you sin. Ask Him for your needs as you go through your day. Talk to Him as you would a friend. Yield to His Holy Spirit by giving Him your hand and following His promptings.

Eternal God Gives Eternal Life and Warns of Eternal Judgment

Eternal God, in His foreknowledge of sin and because of His all-consuming love, established a plan by which all who call on Him can be saved. Only the unrepentant, those who refuse to acknowledge their need for forgiveness and a Savior, will experience eternal separation from God.

While many today try to explain away hell as a myth, it is all too real. Jesus spoke of eternal fire and eternal punishment,[14] making it clear that we need to decide where we want to spend eternity. Just as God speaks of eternal punishment for those who do not repent of sin and confess Jesus as Lord,[15] He speaks of eternal life for those who receive the forgiveness of sins.[16]

Jesus defined eternal life in His prayer to His Father, "This is eternal life, that they may know You, the only true God, and Jesus Christ whom You have sent" (John 17:3). *The Bible Knowledge Commentary* explains:

> Eternal life, as defined here by Jesus, involves the experience of knowing the only true God through His Son. It is a personal relationship of intimacy which is continuous and dynamic. The word *know* . . . is often used in the Septuagint and sometimes in the Greek New Testament to describe the intimacy of a sexual relationship. Thus a person who knows God has an intimate personal relationship with Him. And that relationship is eternal, not temporal. Eternal life is not simply endless existence. Everyone will exist somewhere forever (cf. Matt. 25:46), but the question is, In what condition or in what relationship will they spend eternity?[17]

Knowing that all people will spend eternity in heaven or hell, should we not be concerned for those who have not confessed Jesus as Lord? Should we not purposefully pray that God would use us to speak the truth in love about eternity as He gives the opportunity?

ETERNAL GOD GIVES ETERNAL REWARDS

God's eternal purpose for our lives is that we live in His presence, bear the fruit of His Spirit, and be a light for unbelievers—and He promises eternal rewards to those who do so: "Behold, I am coming quickly, and My reward is with Me, to render to every man according to what he has done. I am the Alpha and the Omega, the first and the last, the beginning and the end" (Revelation 22:12–13).

What eternal rewards does God promise? Colossians 3:24 speaks of "the reward of the inheritance." Although we don't know the extent of our inheritance, 1 Peter 1:4 describes it as "an inheritance which is imperishable and undefiled and will not fade away, reserved in heaven for you." The Eternal God could have simply spared us from going to hell, yet He also promises us the reward of His presence and heaven. What an awesome reason to fall on our knees and praise Him!

If you're discouraged, look up. Take a glimpse of your eternity! Look into the heavens and know that this life is not all there is. Each day we live is but a moment in time, a snapshot in the photo album of eternity. God, with whom all things are possible, is working out all things in accordance with His will. Pray to be a part of His eternal purposes!

Let us also remember, when it is hard to stand by our Christian convictions, God "is a rewarder of those who seek Him" (Hebrews 11:6). He promises rewards for those who build on the foundation Christ laid.[18] When you make decisions about how you spend your time and energy, purposefully prioritize in light of eternity. When your work for the Lord seems to be in vain or unappreciated, remember that your Father "who sees what is done in secret will reward you" (Matthew 6:6).

Prayerfully live before Eternal God, offering your days and moments to Him.

Meditation Moment

God is eternal, self-existent. Meditate on the fact that He who gives eternal life, in whose hands are eternal rewards and judgments, invites you to dwell in Him and to ceaseless prayer. Worship the Eternal God who makes your life of eternal value through Christ Jesus your Lord.

KNEEL *and* PRAY

WORSHIP ETERNAL GOD

P *Praise* God, who is self-existent, a dwelling place for you, who invites you into His presence, who gives eternal rewards, and makes your life of eternal value. _____

eternal plan –
fix our eyes on
Jesus

We just can come – w/o our act together – weary +
laden – w/ a cold – in need of wisdom

R *Repent* and confess ways you do not dwell in God's presence or live
passionately in light of eternity. – *not w/ Jenny, not w/ the*
pride or fleshly desires w/ Luke, not w/ the
fear + apprehension about making a wrong move

A *Ask* God to open your eyes to His eternal purposes for you and to help
you live passionately for Him. Pray for others to turn to God for eternal life *– + Luke*
and to live for His eternal purposes. ' _– faith proved genuine_
2 _– clothe self in humility_
nations may know + see

Y *Yield* your heart, will, and day to God Eternal. Ask Him to fill you with
His Spirit so that you walk by His power and do works that will last for
eternity. _school – LP – Jenny partnership –_
Luke – how to take support from family

God, I'm struggling w/ this in light of Luke - how you
led me to trust him but he ended up being a jerk - or
creep - unhealthy. Will that be the case w/ Emanuel too?
Can I trust your hand to walk into unknown waters -
to be vulnerable + transparent + be open to being
hurt by him - he's also a sinner, a man w/ a sex
drive.

He who fears is not made perfect in love.
Perfect love drives out fear.
Can I follow a broken person? who will
make mistakes?

4/4/15

Chapter 11

Lord, You Are Faithful

When I Am Unfaithful,
You Remain Steadfast and True

*And I saw heaven opened, and behold, a white horse, and He who sat on it
is called Faithful and True, and in righteousness He judges and wages war.*
Revelation 19:11

*Lord, You are faithful. Your words are faithful. Your works are faithful. You are
trustworthy, steadfast, and sure. Forgive my unfaithfulness and help me to be
more faithful to You in my words and actions. In Jesus's name, amen.*

Compelled by God's love and compassion, Carrie McDonnall traveled with
David, her husband of less than one year, to join other Christians in carrying humanitarian relief to war-shattered Iraq. On March 15, 2004, as they
were scouting for water purification sites, shots rang through the air. David
McDonnall and three other Christians were killed. Carrie, though seriously
injured, was the lone survivor.

When she later spoke about the tragedy, Carrie warned her listeners not
to be surprised when everything goes wrong and life gets hard. "There are
times when you will need to focus on the Lord's faithfulness," she said. "He
is the one who is faithful and true. In those times when nothing seems to
go right and all you can cling to is the call you have obeyed, remember this:
God is faithful. That is His name."[1]

Carrie's statement calls to mind the words of the apostle John: "I saw heaven
opened, and behold, a white horse, and He who sat on it is called Faithful and
True, and in righteousness He judges and wages war" (Revelation 19:11).

God is Faithful and True. That is His name. God's Word also is faithful and true. If God speaks it, it will come to pass. Since the beginning of time, He has been faithful to keep His covenant, answer our prayers, work wonders, call us into fellowship with Jesus, protect us from the evil one, and forgive our sins.

God's Faithfulness Exceeds All Human Measure

What does it mean to look up into the heavens and glory in God's faithfulness? The Hebrew word for "faithfulness" is *emuwnah* and means "firmness, fidelity, steadfastness."[2] The Greek word for "faithfulness" is *pistos* and means "trustworthy, sure."[3] When you're going through a difficult time, when the road of life is bumpy or you can't see through the fog, you can look heavenward at God who is with you and praise Him for the following ways in which He is steadfast.

God Is Faithful to Keep His Covenant and Lovingkindness

Faithfulness is hard to find these days. Approximately 40 percent of marriages in America end in divorce. Corporate executives break their promises to employees and stockholders. Employees often fail to live up to job responsibilities. Politicians fail to keep their campaign promises.

Only One is faithful to fully keep His covenant and lovingkindness, and that is the Lord God.

Deuteronomy 7:9 describes Him as "the faithful God, who keeps His covenant and His lovingkindness to a thousandth generation with those who love Him and keep His commandments." Although people may break promises to us and we may fail to live up to our words, God is faithful to keep His covenant of salvation.

God Is Faithful to Answer Our Prayers

Have you experienced the frustration of needing to talk to someone but not being able to reach the person? You phoned your husband's office looking for him, but your call went into voice mail. You called your child who was supposed to be playing nearby, but no one answered the phone. You dialed the number of your parents for the umpteenth time, but no one picked up.

What would happen if we had a God who didn't answer when we called? We read in 1 Kings 18 of such a god. The prophets of Baal tried repeatedly to obtain a response from their false god. Although they cried with loud voices and cut themselves with swords and lances, still their god did not answer.[4] The righteous prophet Elijah suggested that perhaps the god to whom they prayed was occupied, asleep, or on a journey.

Consider the very different response Elijah received to his prayer:

> At the time of the offering of the evening sacrifice, Elijah the prophet came near and said, "O LORD, the God of Abraham, Isaac and Israel, today let it be known that You are God in Israel and that I am Your servant and I have done all these things at Your word. Answer me, O LORD, answer me, that this people may know that You, O LORD, are God, and that You have turned their heart back again." Then the fire of the Lord fell and consumed the burnt offering and the wood and the stones and the dust, and licked up the water that was in the trench. When all the people saw it, they fell on their faces; and they said, "The LORD, He is God; the LORD, He is God."
>
> 1 KINGS 18:36–39

Elijah knew that the God to whom He prayed—the same God who invites us to make our requests known to Him—is faithful! He is never away, asleep, or on a journey.

God Is Faithful to Work Wonders

On rare occasions we have the opportunity to witness human wonders. Twins joined at birth are separated and live. A new space venture is successful. However, no man or woman can create a universe. No person can set the stars in the sky. Only One is faithful to work wonders, and it is to Him, our Faithful God, we look.

Isaiah, who was given a vision of God high and lifted up, exalted and praised God for His faithful working of wonders: "O LORD, You are my God; I will exalt You, I will give thanks to Your name; for You have worked wonders, plans formed long ago, with perfect faithfulness" (Isaiah 25:1).

Isaiah stopped what he was doing and looked up. When he did, he saw God's faithful working of wonders. Prayer is a time to stop what we're doing and purposefully place our trust in the Faithful God who wants to work wonders in our homes, families, and relationships. It is a time to praise God for the faithful wonders He has done.

God Is Faithful to Reach Out to Us

Have you ever dropped the ball on a friendship? Have you promised to write to a friend who moved away, but months passed before you got around to it? Have you promised to stay in touch with someone you met at a conference but then lost the person's e-mail address? Have you promised to phone and check up on a friend in need but the time got away from you? Even precious friendships can diminish through lack of contact or fellowship.

Usually one person in a relationship is better at keeping in touch. In the case of our relationship with God, Paul makes it clear who is faithful: "God is faithful, through whom you were called into fellowship with His Son, Jesus Christ our Lord" (1 Corinthians 1:9).

Praise God for His faithfulness and for calling you into fellowship with His Son. Repent if you have not been faithful to "keep in touch" with Jesus through prayer and Bible study. Ask God to help you be more faithful. Yield when He prompts you to spend time with Him.

God Is Faithful to Forgive Us

You've probably heard of Old Faithful, the geyser in Yellowstone National Park that was so named for its faithful performance. People travel great distances to see Old Faithful erupt into a spectacular display of water!

Even more predictable and spectacular than Old Faithful is the One whose name is Faithful and True. When we do something that hurts another or brings shame to God or ourselves, we may feel that we can't forgive ourselves. However, even if we have ignored God's path of escaping temptation and have given in to sin, that doesn't change God's faithful love for us. Although we may suffer the consequence of our sin, 1 John 1:9 assures us, "If we confess our sins, [God] is faithful and righteous to forgive us our sins and to cleanse us from all unrighteousness." God *is faithful* to forgive our sins. God *is faithful* to cleanse us.

As a fountain of living waters, God erupts not in anger but in mercy every time we ask for forgiveness, without fail. The question is, are we faithfully seeking His forgiveness?

GOD IS FAITHFUL AND COMPASSIONATE EVERY MORNING

I recently saw a napkin that was imprinted, "Some mornings I wake up grouchy. Other mornings I let him sleep." Although humorous, the fact is, some mornings we, or those we live with, may wake up in a grouchy mood. A poor night's rest, feeling sick, discord among family members, pressure at work, and the strain of life can provoke a negative attitude. However, there is One who is faithful and compassionate. Far from being grouchy, our Faithful God lovingly awaits us each morning.

Jeremiah, known as the weeping prophet because his writings are filled with such anguish, stated in Lamentations 3:21–23: "This I recall to my mind, therefore I have hope. The LORD's lovingkindnesses indeed never cease, for His compassions never fail. They are new every morning; great is Your faithfulness."

You may want to reread that verse. It is full of glorious promises! First, Jeremiah points to the source of his hope: God, who is Faithful. Rather than placing our hope and expectations in others to make us happy, let us practice placing our hope each morning in God. He alone can satisfy the desires of our hearts. In Him alone we can rest.

Second, Jeremiah pointed out that the Lord is faithful to be loving,

93

kind, and compassionate every morning. I don't know about you, but I cling to God's faithful love, kindness, and compassion. He knows that I am but flesh. I fail Him. I sin. I fail others. I do wrong things that I don't want to do. If God were a divine tyrant who belittled me, who held my sin over my head, who berated me, I could not daily go into His presence. My heart could not bear the constant shame. However, we do not worship a tyrant. Rather, we worship and pray to One who is faithful in His compassion every morning!

If you are a weeping saint, if you battle depression or moodiness, follow Jeremiah's example: Recall to your mind the Lord's love and kindness. Think on His compassion that is new every morning. Sing the hymn "Great Is Thy Faithfulness" or another song that reminds you of God's faithfulness.

God's Faithfulness Protects Us from the Evil One

My husband's claim to fame in his high-school physics class was building a balsa-wood bridge that could bear more weight than anyone else's. The average bridge could only bear 35 pounds. Keith's bridge was able to bear 725 pounds!

Like that bridge, specially equipped to stand strong, Christians are unique from those who do not know Christ. We have an internal support system: our Faithful Lord. Although Satan is on the prowl and we are tempted in many ways, 2 Thessalonians 3:3 promises, "The Lord is faithful, and He will strengthen and protect you from the evil one." If you ever feel that you cannot bear the circumstances of your life, remember who is faithfully supporting you!

In addition, 1 Corinthians 10:13 says that our Faithful God never allows us to face more temptation than we can bear. Just as a fire escape provides a route to safety, so God provides an escape from temptation. Are you using His escape? If not, ask Him to show you how to escape your temptation. God may direct you to hide a particular scripture in your heart. A favorite

8·18·19
Praise you for being the true faithful just God.

Repent of trusting my own faithfulness, of puffing myself up, of trusting my own righteousness, of looking down on others.

Ask Help me remember my imperfection + rely on your ability to save + keep covenant. Help me obey

Yield to your faithful plan in my marriage + life - to fix my eyes on you.

verse I learned as a child is, "Thy Word have I hid in mine heart, that I might not sin against thee" (Psalm 119:11 KJV). Or He may lead you to call a friend to pray with you. James 5:16 says, "Confess your sins to one another, and pray for one another so that you may be healed." Or your escape route may be Christian music.

Whatever your situation, our Faithful God will provide a way out. Our job is to be watchful and to pray, to praise God for His faithfulness and to take the escape route He provides. Let us remember that God is Faithful and True. He will be there for us and for our loved ones. Are we faithful to Him?

Meditation Moment

God is Faithful and True. That is His name. Pause to consider His amazing faithfulness, which exceeds all human standards, promises unconditional love and compassion, protects you from the evil one, and brings cleansing from your sins.

KNEEL and PRAY

WORSHIP GOD, WHO IS FAITHFUL IN ALL THINGS AND IN ALL WAYS

P *Praise* God for His faithfulness, for keeping His covenant of salvation, for answering your prayers, calling you into fellowship with Jesus, providing an escape in temptation, and forgiving your sins.

[handwritten: 4/5/15 Eileen - the word - BCC - Micah convo.]

R *Repent* and confess any unfaithfulness to God on your part.

[handwritten: acting in the moment instead of in the Spirit trusting self to solve problem instead of God]

A *Ask* God to help you be increasingly faithful in your prayer time, study of His Word, and serving Him. Pray for others to be faithful to God.

[handwritten: don't want to do w/ E - surrender to you. Keep my eyes on His faithfulness, not man or my kayday — I felt I had to pray Luke to become the man to God he needed to become — too much responsibility. He needed to seek you apart from me. small : outweigh the glory revealed - glass dimly]

[right margin handwritten: He is the only foundation - = my foundation for, source of wisdom, future + salvation, from anxiety, of how to step forward, make godly plans, ul work n relationships. Quick to fear unknown - to distrust human affirmations of love - to bottle myself up]

[left margin handwritten: I'm not faithful to obey or trust the word or circumstances, I'm not obeying your word, look k to cross that I can't forget, as proof that you...]

_____

_____

Y *Yield* to the Holy Spirit when He prompts you to be faithful in prayer, faithful in service, faithful in speaking of Him to others, and faithful to Him when tempted. _____

_____

_____

❧ CHAPTER 12 ❧

LORD, YOU ARE *the* GUARDIAN *of* MY SOUL

WHEN I AM FEARFUL, I TRUST IN YOUR PROTECTION

*For you were continually straying like sheep, but now you
have returned to the Shepherd and Guardian of your souls.*
1 PETER 2:25

*Lord, You are the Guardian of my soul. You encircle me with Your love. You
guard me as the apple of Your eye. You are my rear guard, protecting me from
the Enemy. You go before me. Forgive me when I am fearful. Help me rest in the
comfort of Your presence. In Jesus's name, amen.*

Thunder, the one-year-old black Lab, paced around Daisy, alert to every
nighttime sound, every crackle of brush. He had protectively followed the
blonde two-year-old when she wandered from her backyard into a wooded
area behind her home.

Her mother, brothers, and sisters had stepped into the kitchen for just
a few moments when they realized Daisy was not with them. The following
hours brought only increasing worry for Daisy's family and friends, who
realized how dangerously close she must be to the Ohio River. The search
team worked through the long night without success, clinging to the hope
that the dog might protect the precious little girl.

Finally, the next morning the search team found fresh dog tracks in the
sand. They followed the Lab's prints to the wet, barefoot toddler, who rested
just six inches from the water's edge. The search team joyfully returned Daisy

safely to her home—but not without first noticing Thunder's prints, which encircled the spot where they found Daisy. Thunder had paced around Daisy all night, protectively guarding her as well as keeping her from wandering further into danger.[1]

Whether we realize it or not, you and I have a protector who is even more vigilant than Thunder. God, as our faithful Guardian, offers protection from our sins, encircles and protects us, goes behind and before us, and guards our hearts and minds.

The Guardian of Our Souls Bore Our Sins on His Body

First Peter 2:25 describes God as the Guardian of our souls. The word "guardian" is translated from the Greek word *episkopos* and means an "overseer, a man charged with the duty of seeing that things done by others are done rightly."[2]

The Secret Service agents who guard the president of the United States are charged with the duty of "taking a bullet" for the president. They will bear the marks on their bodies that are intended for the one they guard. Christ loves us so much that, as our Guardian, He took the hit, the lash, the sting of judgment intended for us. First Peter 2:24 says that Jesus "bore our sins in His body on the cross, so that we might die to sin and live to righteousness." As the manager, the overseer, and Guardian of our souls, Jesus protectively, lovingly put His arms around us and used His body as the buffer for our lashes. What an overseer! Praise the Lord Jesus, Guardian of your soul!

The Guardian of Our Souls Encircles and Protects Us as the Pupil of His Eye

Deuteronomy 32:10 states that God found Israel "in the howling waste of a wilderness." Then, "He encircled him, He cared for him, He guarded him as the pupil of His eye." What an awesome visual! Have you ever had sand or something else in your eye? If so, you remember how much it hurts! We instinctively guard our eyes. If a ball is thrown in our direction, we protect our eyes. If a bug is swarming our face, we swat it away from our eyes. We shield our eyes from the sun's harmful rays. We guard the pupils of our eyes—and so does God guard His chosen people.

The Hebrew word for "guard" in Deuteronomy is *ca'an*, a primitive root word translated by the *King James Version* of the Bible as "warrior."[3] God guarded Israel, the pupil of His eye, as a warrior. God protected Israel from annihilation in Egypt. God guarded Israel as the pupil of His eye during the plagues on Egypt. God fought as a warrior on Israel's behalf all the way to the Promised Land.

In the same way, God is a mighty warrior on our behalf, guarding and protecting us as the pupil of His eye. If you ever feel unprotected or uncared for, remember God loves you and is guarding your soul in ways you are not even aware of! When you're in bed and afraid at night, pray to the Lord, who encircles you in His love. When fear for your children or spouse grips you, realize that no matter what happens, God, the Guardian of our souls, encircles the one you love.

THE GUARDIAN OF OUR SOULS GOES
BEFORE AND BEHIND US

I learned most of what I know about western life and scouts by watching the television show *Wagon Train* as a child. In case you're of the *Friends* generation, let me explain that scouts played a vital role when Americans moved west in covered wagons. The scout rode ahead of a train of wagons and checked the route to see if it was safe. He also used his knowledge to guide the wagons in the best way to go.

In the same way, when God led the Israelites out of Egyptian bondage, He went before them. And when the Egyptians pursued them, the Lord went behind them. Exodus 14:19–20 says, "The angel of God, who had been going *before* the camp of Israel, moved and went *behind* them; and the pillar of cloud moved from before them and stood behind them. So it came between the camp of Egypt and the camp of Israel." God not only led Israel, He was also their rear guard.

In addition, as the Israelites continued on their way, God assured Moses that they would not be on their own: "I am going to send an angel before you to guard you along the way and to bring you into the place which I have prepared" (Exodus 23:20). Imagine the relief Moses felt!

We have an awesome Guardian of our souls! He both leads us and protects our backs! We don't know what tomorrow holds, and the past may be a source of concern. How awesome it is to know that the Guardian of our souls goes before and behind us to make certain we arrive safely to the place He is leading us.

We must keep in mind, however, that God's protection comes with conditions. Prayerfully meditate on the following words from Isaiah, noting particularly the nonitalicized words, to see if perhaps you've let your rear guard down.

Then your light will break out like the dawn,
And your recovery will speedily spring forth;
And your righteousness will go before you;
The glory of the LORD will be your rear guard.
Then you will call, and the LORD will answer;
You will cry, and He will say, "Here I am."
If *you remove the yoke from your midst,*
The pointing of the finger and speaking wickedness,
And if *you give yourself to the hungry*
And satisfy the desire of the afflicted.

ISAIAH 58:8–10

God is a rear guard, but guess whose rear He's guarding? God is guarding the rear of the one who is following Him!

100

The Guardian of Our Souls Guards Our Hearts and Minds

Often we're not fighting a flesh-and-blood enemy but rather an enemy within: our thoughts, the battle in our minds. Even here, Philippians 4:4–9 declares, the Guardian of our souls protects us. The Greek word for "guard" used in this passage is *phroureo* and means "to protect by a military guard, to prevent hostile invasion."[4] God's Word gives the following instructions by which our Lord guards our hearts and minds:

1. "Rejoice in the Lord always" (v. 4). We may not have anything to be joyful about except the Lord, but we can always rejoice in Him. This is when praising God A to Z is a powerful prayer tool. If we set our minds on God's glory and power when we are discouraged, He is able to guard us from hopelessness.

2. "Let your gentle spirit be known to all men. The Lord is near" (v. 5). We may at times feel destitute spiritually or physically. At other times we may feel that we must stand up for our convictions. Whichever the case, we are to remember that God is near. He guards us by telling us to have a gentle spirit—even in the midst of adversity.

3. "Be anxious for nothing" (v. 6). How is it possible, in a world filled with pain, uncertainty, sickness, and trouble, to avoid being anxious? The Guardian of our souls protects us by telling us: "In everything by prayer and supplication, with thanksgiving, let your requests be made known to God" (v. 6). Prayer is an alternative to worry. Instead of preoccupying your mind with worry, preoccupy your mind with prayer. Tell Him your needs. Thank Him for what He has done and is doing. If you do, "the peace of God, which surpasses all comprehension" will guard your heart and mind in Christ Jesus (v. 7).

4. Finally, whatever is true, honorable, right, pure, lovely, of good repute, "if there is any excellence and if anything worthy of praise,

dwell on these things" (v. 8). God guards us by counseling us to set our minds on the things above.[5]

Encouraging us that God guards us not only today but for eternity, the apostle Paul wrote, "For I know whom I have believed and I am convinced that He is able to guard what I have entrusted to Him until that day" (2 Timothy 1:12). We can trust God with every circumstance of our lives, now and for eternity! Praise be to Him!

on apartment decision

Meditation Moment

God, the Guardian of your soul, guards you against the lash on your back and against eternal punishment for your sins. He encircles and protects you. He both goes before you and is your rear guard. He protects you from the Enemy. He guards your heart and mind in Christ Jesus. Rejoice in Him!

KNEEL *and* PRAY

WORSHIP THE LORD, THE GUARDIAN OF YOUR SOUL

P *Praise* God for being the Guardian of your soul, for encircling you in His love, for guarding you as the pupil of His eye, for going before you and being your rear guard, for guarding your heart and mind in Christ Jesus.

when I worry, do I not let him guard my Ⓞ mind? Where do I turn? Ⓗ around

_____

_____

(losing 1st love) pretend I don't need guarding

R *Repent* and confess ways you have failed to follow the Guardian of your soul, ways that you have perhaps strayed from His protective guidance and instruction. apartment search, age when having kids, Emanuel integrating, rel. w/ Joe + Carly, Stomach, Sleep, jet lag. worry over weddings + babies of next summer

storing up "flaws" in Emanuel.

A *Ask* the Guardian of your soul to lead you and guide you, to help you follow Him and practice His ways, to guard your heart and mind in Christ Jesus. Pray this for others too. _____

esp. to not take up others' worries or any "shoulds"

guard Corley + from worries I induced

Y *Yield* your life to God, allowing Him to guard your heart, mind, and actions in Christ Jesus. our apartment — Ting Tings visit

Begin each AM - you go ahead + behind me - can step forward with confidence.

I am so faulty + cracked - how will anyone love me when they see it? When I don't have my full devo time + have kids hanging on me? In marriage where my deepest sins become seen?

(1st love)

I'm missing the passion oo I used to live life with - the urgency - the focus - financially frugal // focused on the lost - mission-minded. I'm settling down + my eyes are not on the priorities these days, God. It's when I sit back + listen that I see the slight change - the growing apathy - the enjoyment of comfort.

You hem me in behind + before - you've laid you hand upon me.

While I was w/ them, I kept them in your name, which you have given me. I have guarded them, + not one of them has been lost except the son of d. that the S. might be

fulfilled.

103

CHAPTER 13

LORD, YOU ARE HOLY

WHEN I SIN,
I FIND CLEANSING AND HOLINESS IN YOU

Exalt the LORD our God and worship at His footstool; Holy is He.
PSALM 99:5

Lord, You are Holy. There is none like You. You are exalted in holiness and purity. I bow down and worship You. I confess my sins and seek Your forgiveness and cleansing. Fill me with Your Holy Spirit so that I might please and honor You. In Jesus's name, amen.

It had been another frustrating day. I had *hoped* to "be good," a catch-all phrase for pleasing God. I had *hoped* to be loving and kind, to not say or even think unkind thoughts. Kneeling at God's throne in the quiet of prayer, I apologized once again, "Lord, You are holy. I am not."

There are several Hebrew words for "holy," but the primitive root word for "holy" is *qadash*, which means to "consecrate, sanctify, dedicate, be set apart, treat as sacred."[1] The Greek word for holy is *hagiazo* and means to "separate from profane things and dedicate to God, consecrate things to God, dedicate people to God, free from the guilt of sin, to purify internally by renewing of the soul."[2]

At the moment of salvation, believers are given the Holy Spirit, who positionally sets them apart as God's. But our habits, practices, and thought patterns are not always instantly transformed. We want to please God, but it often takes time to transform patterns of sinful behavior and thinking.

What is to be our response to our unholy actions and thoughts? Are we to give up or give in? Hardly! Christ's seed, His Holy Spirit, is a dynamic, powerful force implanted in our hearts to transform us into the holy people God has called us to be.

By setting ourselves apart from the world each day and entering into His presence through the Word, we absorb God's holy mind. By choosing to pray according to His divine nature, we boldly demonstrate that we want to be transformed into His likeness.

HOLY GOD IS WHOLLY RIGHTEOUS AND PURE

If you were to take a snapshot of God, what would He look like? Would the photo album of your mind show God as a white-bearded grandfather sitting in the clouds? Or perhaps as a rugged carpenter with a gentle smile? Is your mental picture of God that of Jesus on the Mount of Transfiguration or a bludgeoned Messiah hanging on a cross? What does Holy God look like to you?

To even begin to grasp a concept of Holy God to whom we pray, we have to read the Bible, which is exactly why it is important to do so. He who holds the stars in place and holds our hearts in His hands, who is invisible yet visibly came to earth, is a divine, incomprehensible God.

Although thinking on God may rouse images of a teacher, Savior, and healer, perhaps the most awesome images of God are those of Him in His throne room. Isaiah gives us a glimpse:

> *I saw the Lord sitting on a throne, lofty and exalted, with the train of His robe filling the temple. Seraphim stood above Him. . . . And one called out to another and said,*
> > *"Holy, Holy, Holy, is the LORD of hosts,*
> > *The whole earth is full of His glory."*
> > *And the foundations of the thresholds trembled at the voice of him who called out, while the temple was filling with smoke.*
> > *Then I said,*

"Woe is me, for I am ruined!
Because I am a man of unclean lips,
And I live among a people of unclean lips;
For my eyes have seen the King, the Lord of hosts."

Isaiah 6:1–5

Isaiah wasn't the only one who saw Holy God in heaven. John recorded in Revelation 1:13–17 the following portrait:

In the middle of the lampstands I saw one like a son of man, clothed in a robe reaching to the feet, and girded across His chest with a golden sash. His head and His hair were white like white wool, like snow; and His eyes were like a flame of fire. His feet were like burnished bronze, when it has been made to glow in a furnace, and His voice was like the sound of many waters. In His right hand He held seven stars, and out of His mouth came a sharp two-edged sword; and His face was like the sun shining in its strength.
When I saw Him, I fell at His feet like a dead man.

Notice that both Isaiah and John were overwhelmed by Holy God's presence—and these men were righteous prophets!

God alone is holy. He is set apart from us, yet by His grace and through Christ's shed blood, all who call on Him are saved and declared holy, set apart for Him. With that in mind, let us humbly fall on our knees every day and, looking up, worship Holy God.

Holy God Makes Us Holy by His Presence in Our Lives

The word "holy" first appears in the Bible in Exodus 3:5 when God told Moses to remove his sandals because the place on which he was standing was holy ground. In this first use of the word, we get a glimpse of what makes an object or person holy: it is God's presence. The ground on which Moses stood was not made of heavenly dust. The bush was not made of angel hair.

The ground and bush, though common, became holy because Holy God inhabited them.

This gives us hope. My home is made of wood and stone, unholy materials in and of themselves. But if I dedicate my home to God, it can be used for His holy purposes. I am composed of fat, muscles, blood, water, and bones. There's absolutely nothing holy about me. But God, by His indwelling presence, makes me holy. That which is common—you, me, our thoughts, words, deeds, ministries, businesses, leisure, and relationships—is transformed from common to holy by the presence of Holy God.

Recently Keith and I decided to clear some trees off the property on which we live. In preparing to do so, I walked among the trees and marked which ones were to be cut down and thrown onto the wood pile to be burned and which ones were to be saved. As I used orange tape to mark the trees to be cut down, I was humbled as I thought about how Holy God walked among mankind and marked as His own those who repented of their sins. He marked them then, and He marks now all who call on Him to be saved.

How do we invite Holy God into our lives? If you're not saved, the first step is to recognize that Holy God does not want anyone to perish, but for all to come to salvation.[3] Unlike trees that cannot express their desires, God gives us a voice by which we can call on Him to be saved.[4] If you aren't yet marked for salvation, now is the time to repent of your sin. Confess Jesus as Lord. Ask Him to take up residence in your heart and seal you with His Holy Spirit.

Holy God Wants to Use You for His Holy Purposes

When we are saved, God marks us with His Holy Spirit. We are set apart for God and enabled to live holy lives by His indwelling and empowering Holy Spirit. We have the privilege of being used by God for His holy purposes. Indeed, we're shortsighted if we think our salvation is simply for a future time. Receiving God's Holy Spirit alters everything now. Our hands are no longer simply extensions of our arms; they are extensions of Christ's holy arms of love and can be used to touch people in His name. Our mouths are no longer ours to speak whatever we wish; as the mouthpieces of Holy God, we can speak His words to others and encourage them in their walk. Our ears are no longer limited to hearing people; we're able to hear Holy God speak in our inner being. Our minds are no longer limited by our acquired knowledge; we're given holy wisdom from above. Our emotions are no longer prisoners of our genetic makeup; we're given a spiritual infusion of holiness that affects even our emotions. We are recipients of the Holy Spirit's love, joy, peace, patience, kindness, goodness, faithfulness, gentleness, and self-control.[5]

How does Holy God perfect His work within us? Although God does not visibly walk on earth today, He lives among us through His Spirit, infusing our thoughts, emotions, and will with His holiness. We feel Holy God flagging our sin as with orange tape when we do not walk in His ways. Anything that is not of Him, anything that is not holy, anything that is sin, He wants cut out and taken to the wood pile.

HOLY GOD WILL TRANSFORM OUR LIVES AS WE YIELD TO HIM

As the workmen cut down one tree and then another, an amazing change took place on our property. Our small pond became more visible as the trees blocking the view were removed. I began watching in anticipation as each marked tree fell, literally transforming the appearance of our land. I was excited about each new reflection of water I could see!

How Holy God must rejoice as each sin we repent of falls and more of His holiness becomes visible in our lives! If sin, like unwanted underbrush, is covering the radiance of the Holy Lord who is in you, you can do something about it. You don't have to stand by and let sin consume you. Instead, you can follow Paul's advice in Romans 12:1–2 and purposefully present yourself to God as a living sacrifice. Kneel before His holy throne and say, "Take the chain saw to my life. Remove anything that is unbecoming, anything that covers the radiance of Your holiness." Submit your body to God, moment-by-moment, and ask Him to transform you through His Word and His Holy Spirit.

Several years ago I was convicted that, although I attempted to daily yield my life to God, I had failed to understand the importance of yielding my physical body to Him. Although I quoted 1 Corinthians 6:19–20, which says that our bodies are not our own, I didn't grasp how critical it was that I care for my body, the Lord's temple. With a busy schedule and the constant demands of family, ministry, and church, I realized one day that too little sleep, too much caffeine, and not enough exercise were taking a toll on me. God brought to my attention that my physical condition was important to Him and my body needed to be set apart for Him. In other words, I needed to take care of my body so that I could "run the race" He has set before me. I became convicted that I needed to eat healthy foods, get adequate rest, and say no to those things that are not good for my body. The fact that my body is not my own became clearer when I wrote *If God Is in Control, Why Do I Have a Headache?*—a study of six women of the Bible and how God cared for them physically, emotionally, and spiritually.

I learned that when God says our bodies are not our own, He literally means it. My body belongs to God. He bought it with a price: the blood of Jesus Christ. Therefore, as a steward of my body, I am to keep it fit and healthy so that my Lord can use it for His holy purposes.

What does Holy God want you to realize is not yours but His? Your tongue? Your mind? Your home? Perhaps your children? Might it be your finances or time? Whatever it is, begin to purposefully pray and dedicate all that you are and have to Holy God. He will transform you, and you will increasingly discover the joy of His holy presence.

Meditation Moment

Holy God desires to make you holy, use you for His holy purposes, and transform your life to more clearly reflect His holy presence. Spend some time considering what these truths mean in your life.

KNEEL *and* PRAY

WORSHIP HOLY GOD

P *Praise* Holy God for the gift of salvation through Jesus Christ and for the Holy Spirit who seals you for the day of redemption and by whom you are empowered to lead a holy life. _____

_____

_____

R *Repent* and confess any underbrush of sin and guilt that keeps the radiance of God's holiness from being reflected in your life. *avoiding sin*
for the sake of pride. prolonged hugs. thinking of sex or touching E.
w/o clothes.

A *Ask* God to give you a hate for any sin in your life and to fill you with His holy presence so that you can be an extension of His holy arms, feet, mind, and mouth. _____

_____

_____

Y *Yield* all that you are and have to the Holy Lord: your day, home, time, money, body, and relationships. Pray to be increasingly sensitive to the Holy Spirit's promptings. Say no to anything that is not holy.

_____

_____

have lost their grip on me. Praise you—
Hallelujah!

CHAPTER 14

LORD, YOU ARE IMMANUEL

WHEN I FEEL ALONE,
I REMEMBER YOU ARE WITH ME

*Therefore the Lord Himself will give you a sign: Behold, a virgin will be
with child and bear a son, and she will call His name Immanuel.*
ISAIAH 7:14

*Lord, You are Immanuel, ever present with me and in me. I praise Your holy
name. Forgive me when I take You for granted and ignore Your holy presence.
Cleanse me and fill me with Your Spirit so that I might hear Your voice, follow
Your ways, and bear much fruit that glorifies You. In Jesus's name I pray, amen.*

The pain had grown more intense, but being a healthy twenty-eight-year-old,
I ignored it—until one day I could ignore it no longer. Two weeks later I sat
in Dr. Barham's office and listened in disbelief as he told me I needed to immediately check in to the hospital to have a large mass removed. A few days
later I kissed our two-year-old son, Taylor, good-bye and left for the hospital.

I remember one morning following my surgery when my doctor was
supposed to come by and tell me that my pathology report was good. As I
lay in bed waiting, I had a distinct, overwhelming sense that all wasn't well.
God was undoubtedly gently preparing me for what was to come.

When my doctor arrived, he told me that some of the pathologists were
concerned the tumor was malignant. He released me to go home, where we
prayed and waited until M. D. Anderson sent us the results of my lab work:
I had ovarian cancer.

During the days following my diagnosis, Keith and I shared many precious moments with the Lord, praying together, listening to Christian music, reading encouraging notes and scriptures, and sometimes just holding each other as we faced the uncertainty of the future. However, one of the most memorable moments occurred when I was alone, lying in bed crying and praying. As I expressed my fears to God, He walked me through each worst-case scenario I gave Him.

"Taylor will be left without a mommy, and Lord, You know how he clings to me," I cried. The Lord Immanuel comforted me, *I'll be with Taylor. I'll watch over him and take care of him. I love him more than you do, Debbie.* "But, Lord," I continued, "Keith will be left alone, without a wife." *I'll take care of Keith. He'll be all right,* the Lord Immanuel spoke to my heart.

As tears streamed down my face, I admitted, "But, Lord, I don't want to die. I don't want to leave my family." *But Debbie, if you die, you'll be with Me in heaven. Everything will be all right.*

With His final comforting words, calm like I had never before experienced flooded my soul. The Lord Immanuel lavished me with the peace He promises in John 14:27: "Peace I leave with you; My peace I give to you; not as the world gives do I give to you. Do not let your heart be troubled, nor let it be fearful."

Surgery isn't fun. Being told you have cancer is devastating. Waiting for reports is heart-wrenching. But having Immanuel and His peace is an indescribable blessing. If you've had a similar experience, I know that you're echoing a hearty "Amen!"

We can look to Immanuel, God with us, in any situation and experience the blessing of His presence.

IMMANUEL IS A PROMISED BLESSING

The Hebrew word `*Immanuw'el* is a symbolic and prophetic name of the Messiah, the Christ, meaning "God with us."[1] God planned Christ's birth and named His Son long before He was born. Isaiah 7:14 prophesied, "Therefore the Lord Himself will give you a sign: Behold, a virgin will be with child and bear a son, and she will call His name Immanuel." When Mary conceived, an angel of the Lord told Joseph to take Mary as his wife, explaining that His birth and name were in fulfillment of Isaiah's prophecy.[2]

The fact that God sent His only begotten Son to earth to be with us and save us from our sins is incredible! If you ever feel alone or if feelings of low self-worth ever wash over you, take comfort in this thought: God sent Jesus, Immanuel, from heaven to be with you. You are not alone, nor will you ever be separated from God's love. May our faces reflect the incredible assurance Paul penned in Romans 8:38–39, "I am convinced that neither death, nor life, nor angels, nor principalities, nor things present, nor things to come, nor powers, nor height, nor depth, nor any other created thing, will be able to separate us from the love of God, which is in Christ Jesus our Lord." Nothing, my friend, can separate you from Immanuel's love and presence.

IMMANUEL IS WITH US AS HE WAS WITH THE SAINTS OF OLD

The God who created us planned that we live in a dynamic, interactive relationship with Him. As you read the following ways in which God has been with people, consider how Immanuel might be calling you to live more purposefully aware of His presence. Ponder how He might want to help you, encourage you, counsel you, guide you, help you fight your battles, and stand with you in your lions' den.

Immanuel was with Abraham, starting a nation.[3] God called Abraham to the awesome task of leaving his country and starting a new nation. Perhaps you are called to the awesome task of raising children in an ungodly society or being the caregiver to a loved one. Immanuel may have called you to a ministry or job that requires more than you feel equipped to do. Read Genesis 18:16–33 and consider how Immanuel walked with and talked to Abraham. Notice how Abraham responded: he walked and talked with God. Abraham listened to and learned from Him. Are you purposefully

[handwritten margin note: stand up for truth in a church that doesn't address sexual sin 10/24/15]

walking with God to learn more about Him? Do you listen to and follow His counsel?

Immanuel was with Moses, leading Israel out of Egypt.[4] Although God called Moses to be His visible spokesman, Immanuel's continuous promise was that He would be with Moses and empower him. "I will" was Immanuel's promise to Moses[5] just as it was to Abraham.[6]

Moses understood the necessity of God's presence to such a great extent that he refused to go forth without Him. Listen to his prayer: "If Your presence does not go with us, do not lead us up from here" (Exodus 33:15). Later Moses prayed, "I pray You, show me Your glory!" (Exodus 33:18). Do you, like Moses, yearn for Immanuel to fill you and lead you? Do you crave His glorious presence?

Exodus 33 also tells us that "the LORD used to speak to Moses face to face, just as a man speaks to his friend" (vv. 9, 11). As with Moses, the Lord invites us into His presence to speak with us! Are we so overscheduled that we don't have time for God? If so, let us get on our knees, confess the foolishness of our overcrowded lives, and make time with Immanuel a nonnegotiable!

Immanuel was with Joshua, conquering enemies and taking possession of the Promised Land.[7] Moses's servant Joshua often lingered at the tent of meeting after Moses met with God.[8] Do you think God noticed Joshua? Of course He did! Immanuel sees who lingers in His presence, who yearns for a glimpse of His glory. He also notices who lingers in bed or in front of the computer or television, not valuing His presence enough to seek Him in worship and the Word.

After the death of Moses, the Lord spoke to Joshua. Imagine Joshua's thrill when he heard God call his name! When you read the account of their first conversation in Joshua 1:1–9, notice Immanuel's promise to Joshua, the greatest promise any of us can hear: "Just as I have been with Moses, I will be with you; I will not fail you or forsake you" (v. 5).

Did Joshua fall on his face? I would imagine he was already on his face!

Perhaps the reason more of us do not have the assurance of God's presence as we lead in our homes, battle against sin, or encounter difficult situations is because we do not initiate encounters with God. We do not still our hearts and quiet our minds to listen to Him. If we did, I'm sure we would hear and take to heart, as Joshua did, God's encouraging words, "Be strong and very courageous; be careful to do according to all the law . . . do not turn from it to the right or to the left, so that you may have success wherever you go" (v. 7). *church needs a response time – to the message + what God's saying*

The Bible is filled with examples of Immanuel being present with men and women. He walked and talked with Adam and Eve in the Garden.[9] He protected righteous Noah from judgment in the flood.[10] He was with Samuel, judging a nation;[11] with David, overcoming Goliath;[12] with Daniel, in the lions' den;[13] with Peter, walking on water;[14] with the adulterous woman, forgiving her sin;[15] with the dead, raising them to life.[16]

Are you dismayed? Does life seem too hard? Do you face overwhelming battles? Please hear Jesus's encouraging words to you today: "I am with you always, even to the end of the age" (Matthew 28:20). Be with Him! You'll find comfort in His presence.

Immanuel Is with Us in the Person of the Holy Spirit

People may ask, "How do you know God is with you?" Our answer is based on historical facts and a present reality.

Fact One: There was a historical Jesus who performed mighty works by the power of God.

Fact Two: This same Jesus, knowing that the time of His death, resurrection, and ascension to heaven was near, promised not to leave His followers as orphans. "I will ask the Father, and He will give you another Helper, that He may be with you forever; that is the Spirit of truth, whom the world cannot receive, because it does not see Him or know Him, but you know Him because He abides with you and will be in you" (John 14:16–17). Jesus promised that His presence would not only be *with* believers but *in* them.

Jesus paints a portrait of the Holy Spirit smack dab in the middle of our souls! Could we ask for the Lord Immanuel to be any more present? Rather than only walking beside us, behind us, and before us, *the Lord Immanuel abides in us!*

Fact Three: Interestingly, Jesus did not make a brash promise that God the Holy Spirit would be in every single person. As a matter of fact, Jesus stated that the world at large would *not* have God's Spirit and presence. Why? Because the world does not know Jesus and keep His commandments.[17] In other words, to receive the gift and blessing of the indwelling presence of God the Holy Spirit, one must have a genuine relationship with God the Father through Christ the Son.

Fact Four: A significant event following Jesus's ascension birthed the early church. Acts 2 records the fulfillment of Jesus's promise to baptize believers with the Holy Spirit.[18] The word "baptize" is translated from the Greek word *baptize*, which means to "immerse, submerge, cleanse by dipping, wash, or overwhelm."[19] Believers at Pentecost were immersed with the Holy Spirit,[20] resulting in exciting changes. Imagine if you were given someone else's spirit. It would change your personality, your outlook, passions, desires, and actions. Even so, those who receive the Holy Spirit are changed.

One of the most exciting accounts of personal change brought about by the presence of the Holy Spirit is recorded in Acts 4. Peter, who had denied being a follower of Jesus during His trials, now stood in the same courtroom in which his Savior was tried and wrongfully convicted. However, having been immersed with God's presence, Peter was no longer afraid. The indwelling Holy Spirit had changed Peter's spirit and infused him with godly confidence. When questioned about Jesus, rather than shrinking back, this time he boldly proclaimed, "There is salvation in no one else; for there is no other name under heaven that has been given among men by which we must be saved" (Acts 4:12). The next verse describes the outcome of his boldness, "Now as they observed the confidence of Peter and John and un-

No one I'd rather impress or show off for — yet the stress of maintaining perfection is killing me. 4/7/15

He sees the worst — nay, even brings out the worst in me. I can't keep up the mask for him.

derstood that they were uneducated and untrained men, they were amazed, and began to recognize them as having been with Jesus" (Acts 4:13).

Who in your family or at work or perhaps in your church ministry is amazed at what God is doing through you? Are those closest to you, those who know you best, amazed as they recognize Jesus in you? Immanuel, God with us, should make a difference in our lives. If not, we need to ask ourselves why the One who put the stars in place is not given a place in our lives. Those who are being used powerfully of God in their homes, schools, offices, and factories are not those who have the most money. They are those who recognize that God is in them and who open their hearts and minds to His wonder-working power.

? Is E? I feel the closer he gets the less good he sees.

Immanuel in us is able to teach us,[21] bear fruit through us,[22] give fullness of joy,[23] love others through us,[24] and empower us.[25] Are you experiencing the blessing and fullness of His presence?

I've been a believer for 25+ years — why am I not more sanctified?

Meditation Moment

Immanuel, God with us, is a cherished blessing, who provides comfort in illness and sorrow, strength when you are weak, wisdom and empowerment to live day-by-day. He will never leave you. He is with you in life and will be with you in death. Meditate on the bountiful blessings of His presence.

KNEEL *and* PRAY

WORSHIP THE LORD IMMANUEL

P *Praise* the Lord Immanuel for being with you in the person of the Holy Spirit. Thank Him for the blessing of His presence, for providing strength in your weakness and peace in the midst of turmoil. _____

Wanna run away + be clothed + hidden + OK in my sin. No one to bug me about it or rub me the wrong way.

_____ at me on Wed (poor stomach 7-8 am) _____
_____ Q's prayrs — desire to bear trial together. _____

R *Repent* and confess if you have failed to appreciate His presence, if you have ignored His empowerment, gifts, and bountiful blessings. _____

_____ been unforgiving + bitter — don't want Sanctification _____

Scared hell... next minute hoping he will

Am I weary of yucky b/c I am not letting it go?

Left margin (vertical): *What if the graciousness + spirit Jesus saw in the raw version — the real me? — doesn't exist in me at 1st at all? how am I going to keep it? If I can't earn his ♡, how am I (like w/ dad?)*

Right margin (vertical): *Is God working on him too, or am I the only one w/ issues?*

A *Ask* the Lord Immanuel to give you a hunger for His presence and a heightened sensitivity to His will. Ask Him to make His presence known to you through the Holy Spirit's promptings. Pray for those who do not know Christ to hunger for His presence as they see the difference He makes in you. *on "show" all wk @ school — takes alot out. on "show" @ church — no transparency*

Y *Yield* to the Holy Spirit's leading. When the Lord Immanuel puts a halt on your words or actions, stop and consider how He is guiding you. When He nudges you to speak, speak. When you feel alone or troubled, remember Immanuel is with you, a very present help in time of need! _____

-see good deeds → praise Father

- reason for hope they have.

If und. cross wouldn't want to sin any longer.

CHAPTER 15

LORD, YOU ARE JUST

WHEN I WITNESS INJUSTICE,
I KNOW THAT YOU ARE RIGHT, FAIR, AND TRUE

*The Rock! His work is perfect, for all His ways are just; a God of
faithfulness and without injustice, righteous and upright is He.*
DEUTERONOMY 32:4

*Lord, You are Just, equitable in all Your ways. When I fail, You are merciful.
When others wrong me, You judge with fairness. You watch over my family in
love. You teach us to leave vengeance to You. Praise, honor, and glory belong to
You! Help me live in honor of Your just, righteous name, amen.*

Daily we read or hear reports of gruesome injustices. A mother amputates
her eleven-month-old daughter's arms. An eighteen-year-old survives a tsunami only to suffer the brutality of being raped by her rescuer. Police find
an eight-year-old girl buried alive in a Dumpster after being abducted from
her home. You surely have your own stories of injustices you've witnessed or
experienced. In a world that sometimes seems to have gone mad, where is
God? Is He just? Will He exercise vengeance and justice?

Although the courts may not always be just, although moms and dads
may fail to parent with equity, and although justice may not prevail in business, we can trust God to be just.

GOD'S LAWS AND WAYS ARE JUST

Listen to the words of Moses as he described God to Israel before his death:
"The Rock! His work is perfect, for all His ways are just; a God of faithfulness

and without injustice, righteous and upright is He" (Deuteronomy 32:4).

Moses, who knew God intimately, said that God is right in His cause, righteous in His conduct and laws, and righteous in the way He governs man. The Hebrew word for "just" is *tsaddiyq* and means "lawful, righteous in conduct and character, vindicated by God, correct."[1] Moses then reviewed Israel's past, her faithlessness toward God and how God justly allowed Israel's enemies to prevail when she rebelled against His laws.

> *You neglected the Rock who begot you,*
> *And forgot the God who gave you birth.*
>
> *The LORD saw this, and spurned them*
> *Because of the provocation of His sons and daughters.*
> *Then He said, "I will hide My face from them,*
> *I will see what their end shall be;*
> *For they are a perverse generation,*
> *Sons in whom is no faithfulness. . . .*
> *They have provoked Me to anger with their idols."*

DEUTERONOMY 32:18–21

After reminding Israel of the consequences they experienced when they did not honor God and observe His laws, Moses reminded them of God's just reaction to enemy nations that rose against Israel when she was serving Him:

> *The LORD will vindicate His people,*
> *And will have compassion on His servants,*
> *When He sees that their strength is gone. . . .*
> *And He will say, "Where are their gods,*
> *The rock in which they sought refuge? . . .*
> *See now that I, I am He,*
> *And there is no god besides Me;*
> *It is I who put to death and give life.*

I have wounded and it is I who heal,
And there is no one who can deliver from My hand. . . .
If I sharpen My flashing sword,
And My hand takes hold on justice,
I will render vengeance on My adversaries,
And I will repay those who hate Me. . . ."
He will avenge the blood of His servants,
And will render vengeance on His adversaries,
And will atone for His land and His people.

DEUTERONOMY 32:36–37, 39, 41, 43

Have you or a loved one been treated unjustly? Have you been to court and felt the judge was unfair? Have you appealed to a higher court but found the procedure lacking? Do you seek to rule your home justly but often fail to do so? Some people think that God is sitting back, not paying attention when injustice is done in our courts, in our homes, businesses, and relationships. However, God neither slumbers nor sleeps.[2] He is ever watchful, and He will maintain justice for those who serve Him.

How can we pray in relation to God's being just? First, we can praise Him. We can recognize that He alone is perfect in justice. Second, we can repent and ask forgiveness for times we've rebelled like Israel and forgotten the God who birthed us. Third, we can purposefully ask God to act justly on our behalf and on behalf of others. If someone is going to court or involved in a mediation, we can pray for the judge, lawyers, and jury to be just. We can pray for the courts of our land to be equitable and fair. We can pray that God would fill our nation's courts, from the Supreme Court to the lower courts, with holy judges, people of integrity who love, honor, and heed God's leading as they rule. We can ask God to help us be just in our dealings with others. We can pray for our children to love justice and to treat others fairly. We can ask God to forgive us for harboring resentment toward those who have wronged us and for taking vengeance into our own hands. We can rest in His justice, knowing that He will repay.

GOD REIGNS IN JUSTICE AND SOVEREIGNTY

Lessons in God's justice are difficult, whether we are the ones learning the lesson or we have to stand by and watch someone fail miserably in the process of learning that God alone is God and due our honor.

Daniel 4 records how Nebuchadnezzar, king of Babylon, learned this lesson in a particularly difficult way. The first part of his life he lived praising himself, not God. One night he had a disturbing dream and called Daniel to interpret it. Daniel had the assignment of telling the king that God would humble him in order to show that He alone was God. Daniel urged Nebuchadnezzar, "Break away now from your sins by doing righteousness and from your iniquities by showing mercy to the poor, in case there may be a prolonging of your prosperity" (v. 27).

Nebuchadnezzar didn't listen to Daniel's warning, even though he recognized "a spirit of the holy gods" in him (v. 18). He, like many, recognized godly counsel but ignored it.

Twelve months later Nebuchadnezzar declared, "Is this not Babylon the great, which I myself have built as a royal residence by the might of my power and for the glory of my majesty?" (v. 30). While the words were still in his mouth, a voice from heaven announced, "King Nebuchadnezzar, to you it is declared: sovereignty has been removed from you, and you will be driven away from mankind, and your dwelling place will be with the beasts of the field. You will be given grass to eat like cattle, and seven periods of time will pass over you until you recognize that the Most High is ruler over the realm of mankind and bestows it on whomever He wishes" (vv. 31–32).

Immediately the prophecy was fulfilled. Nebuchadnezzar was driven into the wilderness and began eating grass like a cow. He remained alone in the wild "until his hair had grown like eagles' feathers and his nails like birds' claws" (v. 33). At the end of that period, Nebuchadnezzar at last raised his eyes toward heaven. Listen to his testimony:

My reason returned to me, and I blessed the Most High and praised and honored Him who lives forever;

For His dominion is an everlasting dominion,

And His kingdom endures from generation to generation.

All the inhabitants of the earth are accounted as nothing,

But He does according to His will in the host of heaven

And among the inhabitants of earth;

And no one can ward off His hand

Or say to Him, "What have You done?"

At that time my reason returned to me. And my majesty and splendor were restored to me for the glory of my kingdom, and my counselors and my nobles began seeking me out; so I was reestablished in my sovereignty, and surpassing greatness was added to me. Now I, Nebuchadnezzar, praise, exalt and honor the King of heaven, for all His works are true and His ways just, and He is able to humble those who walk in pride.

vv. 34–37

What an awesome message for us to take to heart. Though we may not rule a nation, we do reign, or have control, over our bodies, minds, and hearts. We also have some control over how we rule our homes, businesses, ministries, commitments, calendars, and money. Have we submitted our reign to God, who is just and sovereign? Or have we, like Nebuchadnezzar, forgotten that the sovereign Lord has entrusted to us all that we possess and it is to be used for His glory?

If you have not humbled yourself in God's presence and recognized that He is just in giving and in taking away, will you kneel at His footstool today? Let us humble ourselves in the presence of God, who justly rules over all.

GOD, WHO IS JUST, HAS JUSTIFIED BELIEVERS

In the Old Testament we read Zechariah's prophecy, "Rejoice greatly, O daughter of Zion! Shout *in triumph*, O daughter of Jerusalem! Behold, your king is coming to you; He is just and endowed with salvation" (Zechariah 9:9).

Oh, how the people yearned for a just king! Desperately they prayed for one who would rule with equity and govern in righteousness! In the New Testament we see that God sent just such a King, His own Son. As Peter explained, "Christ also died for sins once for all, the just for the unjust, so that He might bring us to God, having been put to death in the flesh, but made alive in the spirit" (1 Peter 3:18).

The Greek word for "just" is *dikaios* and means "righteous, upright, keeping the commands of God, innocent, faultless, guiltless, approved of or acceptable to God, rendering to each his due."[3] What an awesome act of royal benevolence: Christ, who is just—innocent, faultless, guiltless—died for us, the unjust. Why? So He might bring us to God.

We, who were rebellious toward God and unable to keep His righteous law, were doomed in our sin. He would have been just had He abandoned our souls to hell. But God, being rich in mercy, went beyond being reasonably just to be aboundingly just. Our sentence was paid in full, but not by us. Jesus willingly laid down His life in order to justify us, to bring us to God. Christ's death on the cross paid our sin debt, and we who believe in Christ for the forgiveness of sin pass out of condemnation into life eternal. That's justice! God has ruled in our favor in an extraordinary way while at the same time executing just judgment on our sin.

How do we say thank you and live passionately for the One who sent His Son to die for us? We pray to act justly as we counsel others and make decisions in our homes, marriages, and businesses. When we are wrongfully accused, we kneel before God's throne to find comfort, knowing that He will justly judge the one who is wrong. If we are cheated, we remember that "a just balance and scales belong to the LORD; all the weights of the bag are His concern" (Proverbs 16:11). Knowing that wrongs are not hidden from God's sight and that He will deal justly with those who do wrong, we rest in Him. If we have done wrong, we seek His forgiveness.

God is just. Let us rest in His justice and reflect His justice as we look to Him in praise!

Meditation Moment

You can rejoice in God's justice, knowing that He is right, fair, and just. You can release vengeance to Him who renders justice with equity. Are you living passionately for God, who in His mercy justified you?

Kneel *and* PRAY

Worship God, Who Is Just

P *Praise* God, who is just and equitable in all His dealings. Praise Him who judges you not according to your sins but according to Christ's righteousness! _____

_____

R *Repent* and confess any vengeance you have held rather than entrusted to God, who is just. _____

_____

_____

A *Ask* the Lord to give you a forgiving spirit toward those who have wronged you, knowing He is just in all His dealings. Pray that He will give you a keen sense of His justice so you can model His equity. Pray for others to acknowledge God as the Most High and worship Him, so that they won't come under His wrath but rather experience His justice and mercy.

_____

_____

Y *Yield* to God, who is just. What He says, do. _____

_____

_____

CHAPTER 16

Lord, You Are *the* King *of* Kings

When I Am Pulled by the World, I Look to Your Glorious Reign

Heed the sound of my cry for help, my King and my God, for to You I pray. In the morning, O Lord, You will hear my voice; in the morning I will order my prayer to You and eagerly watch.
Psalm 5:2–3

Lord, You reign in glory, power, and majesty. I praise You, King of kings! Thank You for the promised blessing of living in Your glorious presence and kingdom for eternity. Forgive me when I resist Your reign in my life. Fill me with Your Spirit and use me as a faithful servant in Your kingdom. In Jesus's name, amen.

The marriage of Prince Charles and Lady Diana in 1981 captured the attention of 600,000 people in London and 750 million people by television. Diana was the first English woman to marry an heir to England's throne in more than 300 years! It was the wedding of the century.

The fairy-tale princess rode to St Paul's Cathedral in the royal carriage, escorted by the Royal Guard. Following their vows, the prince and princess left the church to the refrain of Elgar's "Pomp and Circumstance." The couple's kiss on the balcony at Buckingham Palace was the grand finale to the day.

Although the fairy tale crumbled due to the couple's marital troubles and Princess Diana's tragic death, the world's response to the royal wedding revealed how deeply we long for a "happily ever after" kingdom.

Will we ever experience such a time? Will we ever know what it's like to live in a beautiful kingdom, under a good king? Yes, if we're Christians, we will. The Bible describes God's kingdom as glorious and God as a good King.

WE HAVE BEEN RESCUED BY THE KING OF KINGS

"Are You the King of the Jews?" Pilate asked, staring at the Jewish rabbi before him (John 18:33). Jesus certainly didn't look like a king after being beaten by the Roman soldiers.

Jesus affirmed, "You say correctly that I am a king, For this I have been born, and for this I have come into the world, to testify to the truth. Everyone who is of the truth hears My voice" (John 18:37).

"What is truth?" Pilate asked, as he brushed past the King of kings without waiting for His reply (John 18:38).

> *No guilt in Him, Pilate announced.*
> *No guilt, yet crucified*
> *My Savior hung upon the cross*
> *By whom I'm justified.*
> *No guilt in Him, the Lamb so pure*
> *No guilt in Him, but me.*
> *He gave His life so pure and true*
> *For my eternity.*
> *No guilt in Him, the King so pure*
> *His crown He set aside*
> *So I could live eternally*
> *His pure and spotless bride.*[1]

What kind of King do we worship? Dear friend, we worship the King of kings who "rescued us from the domain of darkness, and transferred us to the kingdom of His beloved Son, in whom we have redemption, the forgiveness of sins" (Colossians 1:13–14). He is the King of the universe, the King of worlds. To Him all praise and glory belong.

We Are Invited to Pray to the King of Kings

The Greek word for "king" is *basileus* and means "prince, commander, lord of the land."[2] I don't know about you, but I would quiver in my boots at the opportunity to meet a king. Or imagine if the president called and said, "Please feel free to call me any time. If there's something I can do to help with your finances, children, or work, let me know. Also, I have some thoughts on how I could use you to impact our nation. I'd like to visit with you about my ideas."

You're probably shaking your head and thinking, *Now just how realistic is that?* Actually, I met our president several years ago. But I assure you, he did not offer his phone number or extend to Keith and me an invitation to call him. However, the King of kings has extended such an invitation to me—and to you: "Until now you have asked for nothing in My name; ask and you will receive, so that your joy may be made full" (John 16:24).

Are we wisely responding to our God and King's invitation to come to Him in prayer? The psalmist David took our King seriously. Listen to his prayer: "Heed the sound of my cry for help, my King and my God, for to You I pray. In the morning, O Lord, You will hear my voice; in the morning I will order my prayer to You and eagerly watch" (Psalm 5:2–3).

What confidence David had that he could pray to his King and He would hear! Have we yet grasped that God hears our voice? Does the King hear your voice in the morning as He did David's?

David not only expressed his needs in prayer, he eagerly watched for how his God and King would respond. Are you confidently watching to see how your King answers your prayers?

The King to Whom We Pray Is the King of Glory

Psalm 24:10 describes our King: "Who is this King of glory? The Lord of hosts, He is the King of glory." The word "glory" in this passage is translated from the Hebrew word *kabowd* and means "honor, glorious, abundance, splendor, dignity, and reputation."[3] Jesus's incarnation, His time on earth, revealed His kingly love and power but not the fullness of His glory. John captured more of the essence of our King's glory: "Behold, a throne was standing in heaven, and One sitting on the throne. And He who was sitting was like a jasper stone and a sardius in appearance; and there was a rainbow around the throne, like an emerald in appearance" (Revelation 4:2–3). Our King's glory is beyond our imagination!

The King who hears our prayers is full of glory and honor. Abundance and splendor are at His fingertips. Dignity and reverence embrace His essence. Let us run to our King, knowing that there is no more glorious One to whom we can go.

The King to Whom We Pray Is the Great King

The King to whom we pray is not only King of kings, glorious and eternal, He is great. Psalm 47:2 says, "The LORD Most High is to be feared, a great King over all the earth." The Hebrew word for "great" is *gadowl* and means "large in magnitude, extent, intensity, importance."[4]

In other words, we can pray great big prayers because we have a great big King, who is large in magnitude, whose extent is all-reaching. Are you the target of the Enemy? Take confidence! Our King is the Lord Most High, able to extinguish the Enemy's fiery darts. Need a little mercy but hate to ask? He has basketfuls! Need a little fruit of His Spirit for your spirit? His bin is overflowing! Take some love, joy, peace, patience, kindness, goodness, gentleness, faithfulness, and self-control. Our King has more where that came from.

The King to Whom We Pray Is the King above All Gods

We tend to set up all sorts of little idols around our homes and hearts: sports, money, clothing, car, house, yard, children, work, pornography, bitterness, religiosity, food, pleasure, leisure, and more. Our gods are the things to which we give ourselves, the things that control us and have power over us. The wonderful news about our King is that He is above all gods.

Psalm 95:3 declares, "For the LORD is a great God and a great King above all gods." The word "above" is translated from the Hebrew preposition "`al, which means "beyond or over."[5] The King to whom we pray is over all gods. If we have a problem, an addiction, a need or necessity, we can go to the top God, the One who has control over all other people, powers, and principalities!

If life is getting you down, if you've been feeling the heat of the Enemy, if your sin is raging out of control, or if you're worried about your children, finances, or relationships, look up! The King above all gods is seated on the throne. Throw yourself and your situation at His mercy. You'll find help in time of need.

WE CAN PLAY A ROLE IN THE KINGDOM OF OUR GLORIOUS KING

We can ask the King of kings for our needs, for the needs of others, and for the needs of His kingdom on earth. He will hear and answer. But He also wants to use us as servants in His kingdom!

While I used to rebel at the thought of being anyone's servant, I have come to understand that we all serve someone or something, even if it is ourselves. I have discovered that the highest purpose and most noble person I can serve is Christ, my King. His purposes will live for eternity.

How then do we passionately live as servants of our King? The parable of the talents in Matthew 25:14–30 provides the answer.

First, recognize that Jesus, our Master and King, has entrusted us with gifts and talents to be used for His kingdom. We must understand that we are God's servants by nature of the fact that we are not our own. He bought us with His Son's blood. If we think we exist for ourselves, we are greatly deluded and will be most sorrowful when we meet the King eternal and try to explain why we squandered our days.

Second, recognize that how we live in our King's absence is important. Are we like children who, when their parents leave, take the opportunity to do that which displeases the parents? Or are we taking advantage of the time to develop and use that which God has entrusted to us?

Third, recognize that there is a day of reckoning coming. The master will return and call upon his servants to give an account of how they used the talents he had entrusted to them. Our King has given us the greatest of gifts: His Holy Spirit. Along with the gift of His Spirit, God gives each believer a spiritual gift.[6] Let each of us discover our spiritual gift and use it for the furtherance of God's kingdom.

Fourth, recognize that faithfully serving the King leads to joy. The faithful servants are invited to "enter into the joy of your master!" Joy, that elusive gift for which so many long, is not found in a bar or the refrigerator. It is not found in marrying the most beautiful woman or handsome man. Joy is not found in a bank account, possessions, or business success. Where is joy found? In serving our King.

Are you purposefully praying to serve your King? Are you passionately living, using your God-given talent, your spiritual gift, to build up the kingdom of God?

WE CAN TRUST THE KING OF THE NATIONS TO BRING JUSTICE

The United Nations held its first opening session in London on January 10, 1946. It was conceived as an organization of peace-loving nations who were joining forces to prevent future aggression and for other humanitarian purposes. However, in recent years corruption has infiltrated the United Nations, and it has been unable to prevent terrorist attacks and other global tragedies. Beheadings, rapes, murders, abuses, kidnappings, car bombs, and more are highlighted daily on the evening news. In dismay we may wonder who's watching over the world. Who's keeping an eye out for all the nations of the earth? The answer is found in Jeremiah 10:6–7: "There is none like You, O LORD; You are great, and great is Your name in might. Who would not fear You, O King of the nations? Indeed it is Your due! For among all the wise men of the nations and in all their kingdoms, there is none like You."

When wars rage and tragedy strikes on the national level and evil seems to prevail, let us look up. Let us praise the King of the nations and pray for His sovereign will. Realizing we do not have the benefit of our King's heavenly perspective, let us trust Him to protect that which is good, stand against evil, and bring justice to whom it is due.

We may not see justice and equity in our lifetime, but our King will render it. Therefore, in troubling times, let us go to the King of the nations, our King who loves justice.

Meditation Moment

You are invited to enter God's kingdom, to kneel at His throne, to look upon His face, and to be empowered by His Spirit. As you prayerfully enter His throne room, be still and quiet. You'll hear angels singing "Holy, Holy, Holy." You'll hear thunder coming from His throne. Walk closer. You'll see the radiance of the King's holy face. Fall at His feet. Worship and serve Him. His kingdom is at hand!

Kneel and PRAY

Worship the King of Kings

P *Praise* the King of kings, the King above all gods, the King who loves justice, the King of glory, the King who hears your voice. Praise Him who has rescued you from the domain of darkness and transferred you to His kingdom of light. _____

_____

_____

R *Repent* of any ways you fail to worship and serve the King of kings, that you live for yourself or do not use the spiritual gift He has entrusted to you to use for His kingdom. Confess any worry that keeps you from trusting the

King of the nations. _____

_____

_____

A *Ask* the King of glory to infuse you with passion for His kingdom. Ask Him to reveal the spiritual gift He has entrusted to you and to show you where and how to use it for the glory of His kingdom. _____

_____

_____

Y *Yield* your body, mind, and heart to the King of kings. Yield your time to His kingdom work. _____

_____

_____

CHAPTER 17

LORD, YOU ARE LIGHT

WHEN DARKNESS SURROUNDS ME, YOU LIGHT THE WAY

Then Jesus again spoke to them, saying, "I am the Light of the world; he who follows me will not walk in the darkness, but will have the Light of life."
JOHN 8:12

Lord, I praise You, the Light of the World! Forgive me when I walk in darkness rather than turning to the light of Your counsel. Enlighten my mind to increasingly know You. Help me be a reflection of Your light, pointing others to You. In Jesus's name, amen.

On August 14, 2003, a massive power outage left New York, Cleveland, and Detroit in the dark, along with Toronto and Ottawa, Canada. In just three minutes, twenty-one power plants shut down, halting trains, subways, and elevators and affecting water supplies and airports.

In its coverage of this "cascading blackout" that affected millions of people, one media report explained, "The 21 plants went off line because when the grid is down there is no place for the power output to go. Power is generated as it is used."[1]

The fact that power needs an outlet and that more power can only be generated as power is used presents a compelling image for believers. Jesus manifested Himself as the Light of the World, a never-ending power source. However, His power is given to those who use it. If we aren't experiencing God's power and light in our lives, could it be because we aren't using the power the Holy Spirit has given us?

When Christians walk by the light of God, it's obvious that He continues to pour more of His power into their lives. However, there is little need for God to generate spiritual light and power in the one who doesn't intend to use it but instead walks in the flesh.

Are you a source through whom Jesus radiates His power and light?

WALK IN GOD'S LIGHT BY RECEIVING THE TRUE LIGHT: CHRIST

God has given light—both physical and spiritual—to the world since creation. As a matter of fact, James 1:17 identifies God as the "Father of lights, with whom there is no . . . shifting shadow." Just as God placed the sun in the sky to give light and life to the earth, He has placed His Son in the hearts of those who receive Him. His light dispels darkness and gives light and life. Those who receive the Light of Christ have the opportunity to be daily illumined and bear fruit for God.

Those who refuse the true Light often gravitate to artificial light forms. In a recent Internet search, I found a religious Web site that offered a cafeteria of light forms from which the browser could choose: Buddhist, Hindu, and Muslim philosophies, angel wisdom, Bible passages, and Torah readings. However, intriguing as other light forms may be, there is only one True Light. The word "light," in reference to Jesus, is from *phao*, which means "to shine or make manifest, especially by rays, brightness."[2] Jesus is the True Light that was "in the beginning" and in whom is life. He is "the Light of men" (John 1:1, 4).

If you are a Christian, regularly spending time in God's presence is the means by which He will illumine you. Such a commitment is well worth your investment of time, as it helps keep the wick trimmed and the oil of the Holy Spirit flowing in your heart so others can see the Light in you. If you're not a Christian, you can ask the True Light to come into your life and illumine your heart.

WALK IN THE LIGHT BY FOLLOWING GOD'S WILL

At various times we'll confront frustrations, turmoil, indecision, heartaches, and challenges. In the midst of it all, Jesus invites us to follow Him: "I am the Light of the world; he who follows me will not walk in the darkness, but will have the Light of life" (John 8:12).

John painted a vivid word picture to contrast walking in God's Light with walking in darkness: "God is Light, and in Him there is no darkness at all. If we say that we have fellowship with Him and yet walk in the darkness, we lie and do not practice the truth; but if we walk in the Light as He Himself is in the Light, we have fellowship with one another, and the blood of Jesus His Son cleanses us from all sin" (1 John 1:5–7).

Perhaps we can best envision God's invitation to walk in His light by considering a scene in a play. A lead actor is spotlighted on stage. Soon an actress joins him in the spotlight, and they walk and talk together. As long as she follows him, she is in the light as he is in the light. However, if she moves away from him, she will be out of the spotlight and in the darkness.

God, who is Light, invites us to join Him, to walk with Him in the light of His will. But how can we do so, especially when we are presented with difficult decisions, conflicting emotions, and contradictory demands from other people? "Go. / Stay." "Get him out of jail. / Let him stay." "Loan the money. / Say no this time." "Forgive for the umpteenth time. / Forgive, but change the locks on the doors." "Go back to work. / Stay home with the children." "Stop life support. / Continue life support."

How do we know when to say yes and when to say no, when to go and when to stay? Jesus showed us how, through His response to events recorded in John 11.

The decision must have been hard. Mary and Martha sent word to Jesus that Lazarus, His friend, was sick. One would have expected Jesus, the Great Physician, to hop on the first donkey, hightail it to Bethany, and heal Lazarus. However, Jesus didn't leave right away. Undoubtedly, Martha and Mary, who had sent word to Jesus, were disappointed when He did not immediately respond.

Two days later Jesus announced, "Let us go to Judea" (v. 7). Jesus's decision took the disciples by surprise. They quickly reminded Him that the Judeans had tried to stone Him. Clearly, their choice would have been to stay out of Judea! Jesus simply replied, "If anyone walks in the day, he does not stumble, because he sees the light of this world. But if anyone walks in the night, he stumbles, because the light is not in him" (vv. 9–10).

What did Jesus mean? Were His words some encrypted message? No. He simply pointed out that people don't stumble if they walk in the daylight. However, if they walk at night, with no light, they stumble. Jesus wasn't worried about stumbling into trouble in Judea, and He didn't stumble over his decision, because He walked in the light of God's will. He spent time in prayer. He subjected His will to His Father.

In the same way, when we kneel in prayer and yield our hearts and hands to God, we will discover the peace and confidence of walking in His light.

WALK IN THE LIGHT BY FOLLOWING THE BIBLE

God enlightens us to His will not only through prayer but also through the Bible. The psalmist wrote, "Your word is a lamp to my feet and a light to my path" (Psalm 119:105). What a precious promise!

If we want to walk in the light of God's will and not stumble through life, we can experience God's light being "turned on" in our hearts and minds by meditating on God's Word. Why meditate on God's Word? Quickly skimming a chapter is certainly better than nothing, but unless we sit and absorb God's light, our souls will not be changed any more than our skin would be tanned by a quick dash in the sunlight.

In order to get the most light out of your reading, bow your head and ask God to enlighten the eyes of your heart.[3] Ask Him to transform your mind by the light of His counsel so you can walk in His ways. Slow down as you read. Put yourself into the passage. Read as if the words were directed to you personally. Knowing God's Word will brighten your day. Walking in God's light will keep you in fellowship with God, prevent you from stumbling in the dark, and empower you to be a source of His light to others.

Walk in the Light by Kindling the Holy Spirit in You

Our lives have greater meaning and purpose when we understand that God has made us to be His lights on earth. In Matthew 5:14–16 Jesus told His followers: "You are the light of the world. A city set on a hill cannot be hidden; nor does anyone light a lamp and put it under a basket, but on a lampstand, and it gives light to all who are in the house. Let your light shine before men in such a way that they may see your good works, and glorify your Father who is in heaven."

As the moon reflects the sun, so we are to reflect the Son. We have no light in and of ourselves. Yet our lives can penetrate the world with Christ's Light when the Holy Spirit burns within our hearts.

Just as Paul urged Timothy to "kindle afresh" the gift within him (2 Timothy 1:6), we can kindle afresh the flame of the Holy Spirit within us. Throw a log on the fire of Christ's Spirit! Praise Him A to Z with your whole heart. In repentance, remove the dirt, and confess the sin that smothers Christ's light in your soul.

Why kindle the gift of the Holy Spirit? Some of us have let the fire dwindle. The passion we once had for Christ has died down. Our hearts have grown cold through neglect. We become busy and don't fan the fire of Christ's Spirit through the study of His Word, prayer, and service. Or perhaps we quench the Spirit, which 1 Thessalonians 5:19 warns us not to do. The word "quench" is the Greek word *sbennumi* and means to "extinguish, suppress, stifle."[4] When we continue to sin, we become like those whose lamp is "under a basket." Christ did not save us and baptize us with the Holy Spirit so that His light would be hidden. He ignited us with His Spirit so that we would be light drawing others to Him. "Let your light shine before men in such a way that they may see your good works, and glorify your Father who is in heaven" (Matthew 5:16).

Recently I shared this verse at a conference. Afterward a woman came up to me. Her face beamed as she shared, "I memorized this verse when I first became a Christian and have lived by it ever since!" The joy and light of her countenance substantiated her words. Do your countenance and words substantiate that Christ is the burning passion in your life? Do others see Christ's light in you and glorify God?

Meditation Moment

God is the Father of Lights. Christ is the Light of the world. God, in whom there is no darkness, invites you to walk in His light, follow His will, and let your light shine before men so that they will see your good works and glorify your Father in heaven.

Kneel *and* PRAY

Worship God, the Father of Lights, and Christ, the Light of the World

P *Praise* God for shining the glory of Christ in your heart through the Holy Spirit and for lighting your way through the Bible and prayer.

_____

_____

R *Repent* of ways you've quenched the fire and light of the Holy Spirit. Confess if you miss Christ's daily enlightenment and stumble in darkness because you do not spend quiet time in the light of His presence and follow His Word and will._____

_____

_____

A *Ask* Jesus to shine in your heart, to dispel any darkness, to reveal any sin, and to show you His way, will, and works He wants you to do. Ask Him to make the light of His presence burn passionately in you so that you will be a source of His light to others. _____

_____

_____

Y *Yield* your mind, heart, and will to Christ, the Light of the world. Prayerfully follow the illumination God gives you. Live in the light of His presence. _____

_____

_____

CHAPTER 18

LORD, YOU ARE MAJESTIC

WHEN I AM DOWN,
I AM UPLIFTED BY YOUR SPLENDOR

O LORD, our Lord, how majestic is Your name in all the earth,
who have displayed Your splendor above the heavens!
PSALM 8:1

Lord, You are majestic, glorious in all Your ways. Your majesty is seen in the clouds, the sun, the moon, the ocean waves. Forgive me for not worshiping Your Majesty more often. Teach me to look beyond the daily grind to You. May each sunrise and sunset, blooming flower, and gentle breeze remind me to praise You, the Majestic Lord! In Jesus's name, amen.

Bundled as warmly as possible, Keith and I walked through the darkness toward the hum of the floatplane warming on the Alaskan shoreline. One of the guides greeted us with a rugged smile. "Morning! Ready for another great day?" Excited at the thought of another day of fishing in some of the most spectacular and remote wilderness fishing sites, I chuckled at how I had at first dragged my feet at the idea. Not being a fisherman, I'd been hesitant when Keith insisted I be included. Now, as I gazed at the water gently lapping the peaceful shoreline, I was sure this was the most remarkable trip we had taken. One of the guides broke into my thoughts by gesturing for me to look up into the black morning sky. There I saw the aurora borealis, a phenomenal display of lights that appears in the Alaskan sky. The resplendent greens, blues, purples, yellows, and reds of the Northern Lights, as they are called, create majestic streaks, showers, curves, and arcs against the northern black sky. On this particular morning I looked up to see a luminous arch of emerald green sweeping across the sky. I was in awe of God's majesty!

What comes to your mind when you think of God's majesty? A newborn's tiny finger wrapped around yours? The radiance of colorful spring flowers? The clean fresh smell of the air after a rain? The roar of the ocean as waves crash one upon another?

When you think of God and His majesty, do you look up into the heavens in wonder at how He holds each star in place? Is your heart renewed each day as the sun rises? Or do you wake to the sound of the alarm, hit the shower, throw on your clothes, and start your home responsibilities or grab your keys and head out the door to work?

Current circumstances may seem to be turning your life into a tragedy, comedy, drama, or even a soap opera. But regardless of what is happening, we can learn to purposefully, prayerfully walk through each day with our eyes on God, who displays His splendor above the heavens and His majesty in all the earth.

THE LORD'S RIGHT HAND IS MAJESTIC IN POWER

Are you in need of deliverance from a habit, attitude, or lifestyle that is not glorifying to the Lord? Perhaps you need deliverance from being spiritually stagnant or from feeling like you can't move forward after the loss of a loved one or a divorce. If so, you can turn your eyes upon the Lord, whose right hand is majestic in power. Moses spoke of God's right hand, praising Him, "Your right hand, O LORD, is majestic in power. Your right hand, O LORD, shatters the enemy" (Exodus 15:6). The Hebrew word for "majestic" is *'addiyr* and means "great."[1] Why could Moses write those words? Because he had experienced the greatness of God's majestic right hand. He had walked through the Red Sea on dry ground. He had seen the Majestic God defeat the powerful Egyptians. He had been part of God's majestic work!

Listen to Moses's song of praise after God majestically parted the Red Sea:

I will sing to the LORD, for He is highly exalted;
The horse and its rider He has hurled into the sea.
The LORD is my strength and song,
And He has become my salvation;
This is my God, and I will praise Him;
My father's God, and I will extol Him. . . .
Who is like You among the gods, O LORD?
Who is like You, majestic in holiness,
Awesome in praises, working wonders?
You stretched out Your right hand,
The earth swallowed them,
In Your lovingkindness You have led the people whom You have redeemed;
In your strength You have guided them to Your holy habitation.

EXODUS 15:1–2, 11–13

God knows that we are but flesh. Therefore, He empowers those who seek His majestic right hand.

THE LORD'S HOLINESS AND WONDERS ARE MAJESTIC

The Bible is replete with the testimonies of those who have experienced God working majestically through their lives. Moses was not the only one to write of God being majestic in holiness, awesome in praises, and working wonders. Listen to David's psalm of praise:

O LORD, our Lord,
How majestic is Your name in all the earth,
Who have displayed Your splendor above the heavens! . . .

When I consider Your heavens, the work of Your fingers,
The moon and the stars, which You have ordained;
What is man that You take thought of him,
And the son of man that You care for him?

Yet You have made him a little lower than God,
And You crown him with glory and majesty!
You make him to rule over the works of Your hands;
You have put all things under his feet. . . .

O LORD, our Lord,
How majestic is Your name in all the earth!

PSALM 8:1, 3–6, 9

God has not changed. He who was awesome in majesty, power, and holiness in Moses's and David's day is awesome in majesty, power, and holiness today. Are you in need of a little wonder-working power? Are you backed into a corner at work and see no way out? Are your financial troubles bearing down upon you? Are you drowning in a sea of commitments and don't know how to pull out? Is your family or marriage in a threatened position? Do you feel as if you could die of heartache?

My friend, look up. God is majestic in holiness and able to work wonders in our homes, lives, relationships, and areas of service. Kneel down and, with hands lifted in praise, worship the Majestic Lord who has placed the stars in the sky and keeps the sun and moon in their places. Repent of trying to part waters through your own ability, mend relationships in your strength, manipulate situations by your wit, or control people by your power. Ask the Majestic God to lavish you with His Holy Spirit, to give you His mind and empower you to walk in His ways. If you do, you'll see His holy, powerful majesty displayed in and through you.

THE LORD'S VOICE IS MAJESTIC

Do you ever get tired of all the noise in the world, of all the voices? They come to us not only in face-to-face encounters but also through the television, radio, and our phones. We sometimes even hear voices in our heads as we replay conversations.

One voice that is like no other and to which we can learn to be attuned is the Lord's voice. The psalmist said: "The voice of the LORD is powerful, the voice of the LORD is majestic" (Psalm 29:4). We are able to hear the Lord's majestic voice in our souls when He speaks to us in prayer; in our minds when He speaks to us through the Bible; and in our hearts when the Holy Spirit speaks words of both comfort and conviction. John describes God's voice as "the sound of many waters" (Revelation 1:15).

Keith and I love rain because it means our dry Texas creeks will once again flow with the sound of rushing water. How awesome it is to think of the Lord's voice as flowing and powerful! Did the Majestic Christ not say, "If anyone is thirsty, let him come to Me and drink. He who believes in Me, as the Scripture said, 'From his innermost being will flow rivers of living water'" (John 7:37–38)?

If we're thirsty for God's voice, we can go to Him in prayer. We can pray for the filling of the Holy Spirit to gurgle and flow through us. The Lord's majestic voice flows powerfully in us as we kneel in His presence and read the Scriptures. As we go through our day, we can ask the Majestic Lord to help us be increasingly sensitive to His voice in the midst of other voices. The Majestic God speaks to the one who is listening!

Years ago when I began praying that God would teach me to be sensitive to His voice, I started keeping my pen and journal close at hand when I prayed. As a secretary who takes dictation from her employer, I discovered that when I enter God's presence with my journal open and pen in hand, He speaks to me and guides me. He directs me how to pray for my family, friends, ministry, church, nation, and the unsaved. When I face decisions or am preparing to teach, I kneel and ask God to divinely lead me. Then I listen to His voice.

If you're hungry to be led by God's majestic voice, plan time each day to be silent in His presence, neither speaking nor acting but simply listening. Keep your pen and paper handy!

God's majestic voice is not limited to being heard in the quiet of our prayer time. It can also be heard throughout the day as we tune our ears and hearts to Him. Ask Him to teach you to be sensitive to His voice. When He speaks, yield to Him. You'll be amazed by His majesty, enthralled by His love, attention to you, and empowerment. Your passion to live for Christ will grow as you hear and respond to the Majestic Lord!

We Are to Magnify the Majestic Lord and Point Others to Him

As believers we have both the privilege and responsibility to magnify the Majestic Lord and point others to Him. Just as the Alaskan guide directed me to look up and see the majesty of the aurora borealis, we can direct others—by our countenances, words, and actions—to look to our Majestic Lord.

Prior to His death, Jesus assigned believers the responsibility of pointing others to God. "All authority has been given to Me in heaven and on earth. Go therefore and make disciples of all the nations, baptizing them in the name of the Father and the Son and the Holy Spirit, teaching them to observe all that I commanded you; and lo, I am with you always, even to the end of the age" (Matthew 28:18–20).

After He rose from the dead, Jesus reaffirmed that we are to continue His work of pointing others to God: "As the Father has sent Me, I also send you" (John 20:21). There is no question but that the Father and Son planned for believers to bear Their majestic power and name to each generation. How do we magnify the Lord and point others to His majesty? As 2 Corinthians 3:18 states, when we behold Christ as in a mirror, we are transformed into His glory. Therefore, the more we purposefully focus on knowing God and the more we pray that His divine attributes will bear upon our lives, the more we will magnify the Lord and point others to Him.

In a world in which people often walk in discouragement, are you pointing them to the Majestic God?

Meditation Moment

Who is like your God, majestic in holiness, in power, in wonders, who has crowned you with His majesty? He invites you to come to Him in prayer, and He speaks to you as you kneel in His presence and listen to His voice.

Kneel *and* PRAY

Worship the Majestic God

P *Praise* God for His majestic right hand, holy wonders, and voice!

_____

_____

R *Repent* and ask forgiveness for failing to look up and worship His Majesty, for settling for the mundane, and forgetting that He has crowned you with His majesty and charged you to go into the world and point others to God. _____

_____

_____

A *Ask* God to renew your sense of appreciation for His majesty, as seen in the splendor of His hand, wonders, and voice. Pray to live in a way that will bring glory to Him. Ask God to use you to point others to His majesty through your countenance, words, and actions. _____

_____

_____

Y *Yield* your life to the Majestic God's power, holiness, and voice through the day. _____

_____

_____

CHAPTER 19

LORD, YOU ARE *the* GOD *of* NEW LIFE

WHEN MY OLD WAYS PULL AT ME, I PUT ON MY NEW SELF IN CHRIST

Therefore if anyone is in Christ, he is a new creature;
the old things passed away; behold, new things have come.
2 CORINTHIANS 5:17

Lord, I praise You for the New Life You have given me in Christ Jesus. Thank You for the new heart and new spirit You have given me so that I might walk in newness of life. Forgive me when I walk in my old nature rather than as the new creation You have made me. Help me live passionately for You in light of the new heaven and earth, where I will sing a new song to You! In Jesus's name I pray, amen.

Q. B. Taylor was the hard-working general manager at Fenner Tubbs Company Chrysler Dealership. His face and arms were tan from spending his days on the car lot and the golf course. Although a church member, he rarely could be found there; Sunday was his day for golf.

Then one day God "got hold of him." At the age of forty-six, Q. B. gave his life to Christ. People told his daughters that Q. B. was a changed man, but they didn't have to. His daughters saw it for themselves. They saw him walk down the aisle and take the preacher's hand. They saw him walk through the baptismal waters. They heard the change in his voice when he prayed. They saw him reading his Bible at night. They saw that, while they used to beg him to go to church, now he was the first one out the door on Sunday mornings.

People started saying that if you went to see Q. B., he'd either sell you a car or lead you to the Lord—or both. He truly was a new man.

How do I know?

He was my father.

CHRISTIANS ARE NEW CREATIONS WITH NEW HEARTS AND NEW SPIRITS

The Bible says that when we become Christians, we are given new hearts and new spirits, which makes us new creations! Christians are internally and eternally different from non-Christians. Second Corinthians 5:17 explains, "Therefore if anyone is in Christ, he is a new creature; the old things passed away; behold, new things have come." The Greek word for new is *kainos* and means "recently made, fresh, unused, unworn, of a new kind, unprecedented."[1]

Through Christ, God did a new, unprecedented thing. He inaugurated a new and living way by which we come to Him.[2] He sealed believers with His Holy Spirit *in* their spirits. Unlike Old Testament believers with whom the Holy Spirit would reside, New Testament believers received the Holy Spirit in their innermost being. The Holy Spirit takes up permanent residence in us. Thus, God transforms who we are in our innermost being. In the same sense that a cardiologist transplants a healthy heart into a dying person, so God transplants a new heart and a new spirit—Jesus's heart and the Holy Spirit—into those who admit they are dead in their sins and call on Him for salvation. Our becoming new creations through the gift of the Spirit is a fulfillment of Ezekiel 36:26: "Moreover, I will give you a new heart and put a new spirit within you; and I will remove the heart of stone from your flesh and give you a heart of flesh."

We may not feel the spiritual surgical procedure any more than a person under anesthesia feels the surgeon's knife. However, we should experience the aftereffects. A new heart and new spirit create new energy, new desires, new tastes, and new hope.

Christians Walk, Love, and Serve in Newness of Life and the Spirit

As new creations, with new hearts and new spirits, we are able to walk, love, and serve in newness of life, as the following scriptures point out:

We have been buried with Him through baptism into death, so that as Christ was raised from the dead, . . . we too might walk in newness of life. (Romans 6:4)

But now we have been released from the Law, . . . so that we serve in newness of the Spirit and not in oldness of the letter. (Romans 7:6)

"A new commandment I give to you, that you love one another, even as I have loved you." (John 13:34)

The good news of our new life is that as Christ was raised from the dead by the glory of God, so we are raised by the glory of God to walk in newness of life. In other words, if we sing praises at church because our sins are forgiven but then get into the car and start bickering, we're not walking by the Spirit in newness of life. What do our lives look like when we walk, love, and serve in "newness of life"? They look like Jesus.

We have new priorities. Jesus's priorities were clear. He came to serve God. He "came to seek and to save that which was lost" (Luke 19:10). His walk with God affected His walk with others. He taught people the way to God and the ways of God. We walk in newness of life when we purposefully allow God to use us. We serve the body of Christ not because we have to but because He has gifted us to do so and it is where we find our greatest joy.

We have new power. Jesus demonstrated God's power in His life, and we are to do the same. Paul explained the hope we have for overcoming sin, walking in love, and serving Christ: "Christ in you, the hope of glory" (Colossians 1:27). As a car with a new engine runs differently, so our lives should reflect our new power source as we strive "according to *His* [Christ's] *power*, which mightily works within" (Colossians 1:29). If we're Christians but have been bound in sin or spiritually sluggish, let us go to God for a tune-up. Let us take to heart that Christians have not been given "a spirit of timidity, but of power and love and discipline" (2 Timothy 1:7).

We produce new fruit. Jesus told His followers to be fruitful. How can we be fruitful for God? We produce spiritual fruit by remaining "on the Vine,"[3] by abiding in Christ in prayer, His Spirit, and Word. When we are grafted into Christ, rooted in His Word, and have His Spirit flowing through us, we bear the fruit of His presence. Therefore, let us not walk in the flesh and produce only that which is here today and gone tomorrow. Instead, let us offer our bodies as living and holy sacrifices. Let us purposefully pray, "Lord, use me for eternity. Help me plant seeds of faith, hope, and love today. Help me be sensitive to souls whom You desire to touch for eternity. Give me opportunities to speak for You and serve others in Your name."

CHRISTIANS HAVE A "NEW SELF"

How do we walk in newness of life on a daily basis? Ephesians 4:17–32 offers practical guidance, specifically telling us in verses 22–24 to "*lay aside the old self,* which is being corrupted" and "be renewed in the spirit of your mind, and *put on the new self,* which in the likeness of God has been created in righteousness and holiness of the truth."

We choose every day with what to clothe our spirits, just as we decide with what to clothe our bodies. We can put on yesterday's old, dirty clothes, or lay them aside in the clothes hamper and put on new, clean clothes. In like manner, we can choose to *put aside* our old self, our old mind, our old emotions, and old will and to *put on* our new self, which is in the likeness of God.

Are you walking around in old clothes? Is your head covered with a worry hat? Does a shirt of unforgiveness cover your chest? Are you carrying a sin-stained wallet of selfishness? Are your shoes dirty from walking in self-indulgence? Or have you laid aside your old self and put on your new self?

If you have not yet laid aside the old and put on the new, use Ephesians

4:25–32 to jumpstart your prayer: "Lord, You are the God of New Life. Help me daily lay aside my old self. Clothe my mind, emotions, and will with Your mind, emotions, and will. Help me discard falsehood and speak only the truth today. If I become angry, help me lay my anger aside and not sin. Clothe my heart with love and a desire to share with those in need. I see now that I have been walking around with unwholesome thoughts and words on my mind. Forgive me and put on my heart and tongue words that will edify and encourage others. Forgive me for the ways I have grieved Your Holy Spirit. I lay aside my bitterness, wrath, anger, and slander. Clothe me with Your Spirit of kindness, tenderness, and forgiveness."

If we wait until heaven to put on our new self, we'll miss the joy of the Spirit-filled life today.

Christians Can Look Forward to New Heavens and a New Earth

Although we've been given a new heart and new spirit through Christ, as long as we remain on earth, we'll experience the effects of sin. Therefore, as Christians, let us purposefully pray to live passionately in anticipation of the new heavens and earth that await us. Let us be encouraged by God's comforting promise, "For behold, I create new heavens and a new earth; and the former things will not be remembered or come to mind" (Isaiah 65:17).

Let us cling to Peter's affirmation of Isaiah, "According to His promise we are looking for new heavens and a new earth, in which righteousness dwells." Let us repent if we have not taken seriously the admonition to "be diligent to be found by Him in peace, spotless and blameless" (2 Peter 3:13–14).

New heavens and a new earth await those who have entered into a New Covenant relationship with God. When life becomes overwhelming, when your days are boring, or when the battle with sin is exhausting, look up! Rather than trudge through life, live joyfully and passionately as you look forward to the new heavens and earth that await you! Let your countenance, commitments, and conversations reflect your faith as you live in anticipation of the new name you'll receive[4] and the new song you'll sing[5] when "He who sits on the throne" makes "all things new" (Revelation 21:5).

Meditation Moment

Praise the God of New Life, who gives you a new spirit and a new heart by which you have become a new creation. Rejoice that you can serve, love, and walk in newness of life as you look forward to the new heavens and earth that await you!

KNEEL *and* PRAY

WORSHIP THE GOD OF NEW LIFE

P   *Praise* God for your new life, new spirit, and new heart, for making you a new creation! _____

_____

_____

R   *Repent* and confess ways in which you fail to put on the new self and walk as a new creation. _____

_____

_____

A   *Ask* the Lord to fill you with His Holy Spirit so that you walk, love, and serve in newness of spirit. _____

_____

_____

Y   *Yield* your new heart to God. Give Him your ear and hand and walk in newness of life. _____

_____

_____

Chapter 20

Lord, You Are *the* Overcomer

When I Feel Defeated,
You Help Me Triumph in Christ

*These things I have spoken to you, so that in Me you
may have peace. In the world you have tribulation,
but take courage; I have overcome the world.*
John 16:33

*Lord, You are the Christ, the One who has overcome the world. Forgive me
when I forget the hope I have in You. Fill me with Your presence and help me
look to You to overcome darkness, temptation, and discouragement. In Jesus's
name, amen.*

Problems, temptations, enemies—we don't ask for them. They simply happen. They appear at our doorsteps. They even slip into the church. They attack the happiest of marriages and the best of children. They disillusion teachers, provoke law-enforcement officers, keep the political wheels moving, and send family members to their knees in prayer.

Problems, temptations, enemies—what do you do with them? Try running from them and they'll sneak up behind you. Try avoiding them and they'll trip you up. Try sticking your head in the ground and pretending they are not there, but sooner or later you'll have to come up for air.

Where do problems, temptations, and enemies come from? Whether they originate with others or with us, Jesus puts them under the umbrella of the "world." And He tells us He has overcome the world.

The Overcomer, Who Is from Above, Has Conquered Evil

The God to whom we pray makes black-and-white statements in a "gray" world that resists absolutes. The Bible identifies Satan as the ruler of the world: "We know that we are of God, and that the whole world lies in the power of the evil one" (1 John 5:19).

What does the Bible mean when it refers to the "world"? In Scripture, "world" is often used as a reference to "the whole mass of men alienated from God, and therefore hostile to the cause of Christ, the whole circle of earthly goods, endowments, riches, advantages, pleasures, etc, which . . . seduce from God and are obstacles to the cause of Christ."[1]

Jesus distinguishes Himself from the world by making it clear that He is from above and not of the world:

> *"You are from below, I am from above; you are of this world, I am not of this world."* (John 8:23)

> *"I came forth from the Father and have come into the world; I am leaving the world again and going to the Father."* (John 16:28)

> *"My kingdom is not of this world. . . . For this I have come into the world, to testify to the truth."* (John 18:36–37)

Jesus makes a distinction between the world and Himself and between the world and heaven. Then He states with authority, "I have overcome the world" (John 16:33).

The word "overcome" is translated from the Greek word *nikao* and means "to conquer, to carry off the victory, to win the case, maintain one's cause."[2]

Jesus overcame the world by conquering Satan. He said to His disciples, "Now judgment is upon this world; now the ruler of this world will be cast out" (John 12:31). Jesus came into the world to overcome evil. He did so, and He victoriously returned to heaven to prepare a place for those who believe in Him. If you are struggling or feel defeated, take courage. Look in faith to Christ who has overcome the world!

THE OVERCOMER CALLS AND EMPOWERS US TO OVERCOME THE WORLD

What gets you down? What presses on you and causes you to be out of sorts or out of fellowship with God? What things of the world, which may not be evil in and of themselves—such as nature, hobbies, or work—distract you from being more committed to Christ? What in the world do you give your time, money, and energy to in place of giving them to the Lord?

Prior to Jesus's death, He warned the disciples about their relationship to the world. He explained that just as He was not *of* the world, neither were they *of* the world. He encouraged them that as He had overcome the world, so they were to overcome the world by their faith.

Then, Jesus prayed to His heavenly Father for us: "I do not ask You to take them out of the world, but to keep them from the evil one" (John 17:15).

JESUS CALLS US TO BE SEPARATE FROM THE WORLD

Jesus, in praying to God about our relationship to the world and evil, did not pray that we be removed from the world but rather that we remain in the world serving Him. However, He warned that by living as His followers, we would evoke hate from the world: "I chose you out of the world, because of this the world hates you" (John 15:19).

Speaking from experience, Peter wrote: "Do not be surprised at the fiery ordeal among you . . . as though some strange thing were happening to you. . . . If you are reviled for the name of Christ, you are blessed, because the Spirit of glory and of God rests on you" (1 Peter 4:12, 14). In other words, if you're living separate from the world and following the tenets of Christ, you will experience tension, tests, and persecution. There will be people who hate you as they hated Christ.

Perhaps no person better exemplifies being reviled for the name of

Christ than Stephen. Acts 6:15 tells us that when Stephen defended his faith before the leaders who had crucified Jesus, all who were sitting in the Council saw his face like the face of an angel. After Stephen testified that Jesus, whom they crucified, was the Christ, they were cut to the quick and began gnashing their teeth. What was the worldly Council's response to the truth? They stoned him.[3]

Today few of us will experience physical persecution as Stephen did. However, we will be called to stand for our faith when we go to the polls. We will attend meetings and social functions where we would be remiss in going along with the crowd if the opinions or actions are contrary to God. We have a responsibility to train our children in God's ways and to make an impact on our generation for Christ. When we do, we will often stand opposed to the world's political, social, educational, and religious agendas. However, like Stephen, we can overcome, even in the midst of being verbally stoned for our faith. As Stephen overcame by faith, we can overcome by faith: "For whatever is born of God *overcomes* the world; and this is the victory that has *overcome* the world—our faith. Who is the one who *overcomes* the world, but he who believes that Jesus is the Son of God?" (1 John 5:4–5).

Rather than live as spiritually placid or defeated Christians, let us turn our faces in praise to Him who has overcome the world! May our hearts' desire be for the Spirit of glory and God to rest on us!

Jesus Calls Us to Overcome Evil

God's Word instructs us, "Do not be overcome by evil, but *overcome* evil with good" (Romans 12:21).

The "good" through which we are able to overcome the world's evil is "Christ in [us], the hope of glory" (Colossians 1:27). Jesus overcame the world. He overcame evil. Because He is in us, we can overcome the world's temptations and evil.

Living in the world but not being *of* it—holding different values and serving a different Master—affects our relationship with the world. We are not friends of the world but rather friends of Jesus.[4]

The fact that Christians are not of this world may help explain why we struggle so greatly if we are not fully committed to Christ. We may feel torn because we have one eye on the things of the world and one eye on Christ.

We may need to pray about our lives, in regard to Jesus's teaching, that we are not of the world. We can ask Jesus to fill us with His Spirit and make us distinct from the world. We might pray, "Lord, You are the Overcomer! I praise You for not being of the world but being distinct from the world, holy, pure, and righteous. I confess that too often I act as if You have not redeemed me out of the world. I walk around defeated. Other times I am entangled in the world's trappings. Lord, forgive me. I yield my mind, heart, and spirit to You, who have overcome the world and bought me for Your kingdom."

In addition, we can triumph over the lure of sin as the Overcomer did. With the sword of the Spirit, the Word of God, we can be triumphant! By hiding Bible verses in our hearts and minds, we can overcome evil through Christ in us.

Jesus Helps Us Overcome Worldly Tribulations

Many things in the world can cause us affliction and distress, to feel oppressed, or as the Bible refers to it, to experience "tribulation."[5] Jesus states that although we have tribulation in the world, we can take courage. Why? Because He has overcome the world.

When you or a loved one faces physical, emotional, or spiritual tribulations, the Bible offers these comforting words. "You are from God, little children, and have overcome them; because greater is He who is in you than he who is in the world" (1 John 4:4).

Prayerfully meditate on the words "greater is He who is in you than he who is in the world." Let the joy of that truth fill your soul. Christ, the Overcomer, is in you. Christ, the Overcomer, is greater than the world! Praise and rejoice in Him. Ask Him to overwhelm you with His fullness so that you can overcome any tribulation or discouragement through Christ in you. Remember, "in all these things"—tribulation, distress, persecution, famine, nakedness, peril, sword—"we overwhelmingly conquer through Him who loved us" (Romans 8:35, 37).

Jesus Gives Peace That Overcomes the Stresses of This World

As Christians we are distinct from the world, even as Jesus is distinct from the world. One blessed distinction we have is the peace the Overcomer gives, a peace that "transcends all understanding" (Philippians 4:7 NIV). Jesus said, "My peace I give you; I do not give to you as the *world* gives. Do not let your hearts be troubled and do not be afraid" (John 14:27 NIV). When we're troubled, grieved, or worried, let us remember that the Overcomer gives peace that overcomes the world's stresses. Let us praise His holy name, knowing that He will work all for good to those who love Him.[6] Let us claim His peace as we open our hearts and minds to Him.

The Overcomer Promises Rewards to Those Who Overcome

Jesus states that being a believer in the world is a challenge. He minces no words when He tells us that the struggle against Satan and temptation is real. However, He encourages us by telling of the rewards that await those who overcome. Jesus has promised:

"To him who overcomes . . .

- *I will grant to eat of the tree of life which is in the Paradise of God."* (Revelation 2:7)

- *he . . . will not be hurt by the second death."* (Revelation 2:11)

- *I will give some of the hidden manna, and I will give him a white stone, and a new name written on the stone which no one knows but he who receives it."* (Revelation 2:17)

- *I will give authority over the nations.”* (Revelation 2:26)

- *[he] will thus be clothed in white garments; and I will not erase his name from the book of life, and I will confess his name before My Father and before His angels.”* (Revelation 3:5)

- *I will make him a pillar in the temple of My God, and he will not go out from it anymore; and I will write on him the name of My God, and the name of the city of My God, the new Jerusalem, which comes down out of heaven from My God, and My new name.”* (Revelation 3:12)

- *I will grant to him to sit down with Me on My throne, as I also overcame and sat down with My Father on His throne.”* (Revelation 3:21)

- *[he] will inherit these things, and I will be his God and he will be My son.”* (Revelation 21:7)

Let us praise God, the Overcomer, as we look expectantly for the reward of heaven!

Meditation Moment

The Overcomer has overcome the world, darkness, evil, sin, and tribulation. He empowers you to overcome the world and promises rewards for your faithfulness.

Kneel *and* PRAY

Worship the Overcomer

P   *Praise* God who has overcome the world, darkness, evil, and sin.

_____

_____

R   *Repent* and confess any ways you yield to the world's thinking and behavior or ways that you walk in defeat rather than overcoming the world, discouragement, and sin through Christ. _____

_____

_____

A *Ask* the Overcomer to empower you to overcome evil and walk triumphantly by faith. _____

_____

_____

Y *Yield* your body, mind, and spirit to the Overcomer's reign in your life. Give Him your hand and let Him lead you in triumph. _____

_____

_____

CHAPTER 21

LORD, YOU ARE *the* POTTER

WHEN I AM OUT OF SHAPE,
YOU MOLD ME IN YOUR IMAGE

*But now, O LORD, You are our Father, We are the clay, and
You our potter; And all of us are the work of Your hand.*
ISAIAH 64:8

*Dear Lord, You are the Potter. I am the clay. Forgive me when I rebel against
Your purposes for my life. Please mold my mind, heart, and will into Your image.
Make me a vessel of honor and holiness that brings You praise. In Jesus's name,
amen.*

Did you like playing with Play-Doh when you were young? My sister and I
did! We would roll, cut, and form the dough into cups, vases, and flowers.
From the moment we popped the red, blue, yellow, and green lids off the yellow cans and felt the cool, soft Play-Doh squish through our fingers, we had
fun—*unless* we had forgotten to securely place the lids on the cans the last
time we played. If we didn't seal the lids, the Play-Doh hardened and we
had no choice but to throw it away. Hardened Play-Doh couldn't fulfill
the purpose for which it was created: to be molded and shaped.

Just as my sister and I shaped the Play-Doh, God, as the Bible describes
Him, is a Potter who forms us into objects of glory if we stay soft and pliable
in His hand. As the master Potter sculpted and formed our earth, so He
longs to sculpt and form our earthly bodies to be carriers of His glory. He
yearns to shape our hearts to be vessels of His love. He desires to mold our
minds to be containers of His wisdom.

As I read Jeremiah 18–20, where God likens Himself to a potter and His people to clay, my heart is deeply convicted of the need to be soft and pliable in my Potter's hands. I encourage you to read at least a portion of those chapters. In them, God gives Jeremiah a message for Israel, a pronouncement of His judgment on the nation for being stiff-necked and not heeding His words.[1] It was a difficult message to communicate and to receive. Pashhur, the priest, was so angry when he heard the message that he had Jeremiah beaten and put in stocks.[2]

Jeremiah was disheartened to the point that he wished he'd never been born.[3] However, he was compelled to speak what God put on his heart.[4] Are we as pliable and useful to the Potter as Jeremiah was? When God moves us to speak, do we? When His hand is on our hearts pressing us to act, do we?

As we look further at God's Word regarding His role as the Potter and ours as the clay, let us prayerfully respond to His warning to not become hardened, unable to fulfill the purpose for which we were created.

GOD, OUR POTTER, SHAPES US ACCORDING TO HIS WILL

The word which came to Jeremiah from the LORD saying, "Arise and go down to the potter's house, and there I will announce My words to you." Then I went down to the potter's house, and there he was, making something on the wheel. But the vessel that he was making of clay was spoiled in the hand of the potter; so he remade it into another vessel, as it pleased the potter to make.

JEREMIAH 18:1–4

In this passage Jeremiah goes to the potter's house, where the potter is making something out of clay. The Hebrew word for "potter" is *yatsar* and means "to form, fashion, frame."[5] Jeremiah sees the potter fashioning an object, perhaps a cup. When it doesn't turn out like he wants, the potter remakes it into something else, perhaps a bowl. That is his prerogative.

"Then the word of the LORD came to me saying, 'Can I not, O house of Israel, deal with you as this potter does?' declares the LORD. 'Behold, like the clay in the potter's hand, so are you in My hand, O house of Israel'" (Jeremiah 18:5–6).

At this point God speaks to Jeremiah and compares the potter to Himself and the clay to Israel, declaring His eternal purpose and prerogative to shape and mold the nation as He pleases. He continues by stating that Israel has forgotten Him; the people are not fulfilling the purpose for which He formed them. God then speaks a word of warning to Israel. He states that He is devising a plan against them if they do not soften their hearts and turn back to Him.

What word does God have for us in regard to His being the Potter and our being the clay? First, we are not our own. We have been created by God, for God. Second, it is God's prerogative to make out of our lives what He wishes. God may use us as His vessels whenever and however He wants. He may use us as corporate executives or on an assembly line, in a day care or caring for an elderly parent.

How do you respond when God fashions you first for one purpose and then for another? For instance, if you've been a career woman and then God calls you to be a stay-at-home mom, do you argue with your Potter? Or do you prayerfully consider how He wants to use your days of changing diapers and driving carpool? Do you submit yourself every day to God so He can fill you with His love? Do you pour forth the knowledge of God into your little ones' hearts and minds with Bible stories and music?

Or if you're used to being healthy but now battle a health problem, are you continuing to look in the face of your Potter to see how He wants to use you as a vessel at the hospital, with your doctor, or as a witness to your friends and family? When my mother was terminally ill, she used her days to speak to others about God. Even though she was a physically weakened vessel, her spirit remained strong. As God's vessel she faithfully prayed for her family, friends, church, and others. We can be vessels, useful to our Potter, even when the shapes of our bodies or lives take different forms.

When you get bent out of shape over where you are or what's happening to you, stop and look up into the face of your Potter. Remember, He has not forgotten you. In fact, He may be shaping you to be a vessel to further His kingdom or to be a vessel of His mercy. Will you pray to faithfully carry out His divine design?

GOD, OUR POTTER, NEEDS US TO REMAIN PLIABLE

God, the Potter, warned Israel that if they became hardened against Him, they would be broken. "Just so will I break this people and this city, even as one breaks a potter's vessel, which cannot again be repaired" (Jeremiah 19:11).

If you've ever worked with clay or used a potter's wheel, you understand God's message: hardened clay cannot be reshaped. I've worked with clay only once, but I learned that the clay can be worked only if it is moist. Therefore, the potter must continually apply water to the clay to keep it soft and pliable. If it becomes hard, it can no longer be made into anything and must be tossed aside. Clay is only valuable in the potter's hand when it is pliable to the potter's touch.

The point could not be clearer. Are we hard-headed, hard-hearted, hardened in sin, hardened in our old way of doing things, hardened to the conviction of the Holy Spirit? Or are we soft in our Potter's hand, letting Him mold our lives through the Holy Spirit as we study His Word and pray?

Dear friend, our Potter's words warn us. We are hypocrites if we say, "Lord, You are my Potter," but we're always climbing off the Potter's wheel! We're giving lip service to the Lord if we say He is our Potter but do not pray for the anointing flow of the Holy Spirit to keep us soft and pliable in His hands. Just as God re-created the earth with a flood, so He can re-create us when we pray for the Holy Spirit to flood us with His life, cleansing, and power.

Feeling dry? Cracking up? Are you bent out of shape? Do you feel like your life is spinning out of control? Crawl back to the Potter's wheel. Pray for the Holy Spirit to flood your heart, mind, emotions, and will. Remain in God's hands as He molds you and shapes you into a vessel of honor, useful for His purposes.

GOD, OUR POTTER, MOLDS OUR LIVES FOR HIS PURPOSES

Have you ever looked at someone and wished you were in that person's shoes? Perhaps you've admired a vocalist and wished you could sing as beautifully as she does, or you've listened to a musician and wished you could perform as flawlessly. Perhaps you've wished you had a different job, lived in a different place, looked different, or had perfect children. Often there is nothing wrong with our desires. As parents we want what's best for our children. As employees and employers we want our business to be successful. As spouses we desire to have a good marriage. As friends we want deepening relationships. In ministry we want God to be glorified and for our service to be effective.

What happens, however, when the bottom drops out? What happens when a spouse walks out the door and doesn't come home? What happens when a child turns and says, "I hate you"? What happens when we sit alone on Christmas Day? What happens when the "good folk" at the church are the ones who cause us so much pain? What do we do then?

I think those can be some of the most difficult times. However, in those experiences, when we don't like the shape of our lives or days, God warns us, "Woe to the one who quarrels with his Maker—an earthenware vessel among the vessels of earth! Will the clay say to the potter, 'What are you doing?' Or the thing you are making say, 'He has no hands'?" (Isaiah 45:9).

At times it is only natural to wonder what in the world is happening to us and why. In those times we can look up. Rather than sit and stew, let us stop, drop to our knees, and pray. As Jesus did in the Garden of Gethsemane, let us prayerfully relinquish our will and future to God. Jesus did not argue with God, the Potter, about how His life was taking shape. However, He did reverently, honestly pray. He expressed His true feelings, making it

171

clear that He desired a different way than the cross. Then Jesus accepted the Potter's shape and purpose for His life, though it meant being left friendless when the disciples fled. He submitted to humiliation, bodily injury, and pain when He hung on the cross. He yielded to God's purpose for His life, even when it meant death.

The questions for us to seriously contemplate are these: Are we arguing with our Potter or reverently praying and submitting to His hand and will? When bad things happen to us,[6] or perhaps we are spiritually dry, do we prayerfully remain in the Potter's hand? Do we daily allow Him to fill our earthen vessels with the treasure of His surpassing greatness?[7]

Meditation Moment

God, the master Potter, is molding your life according to His divine design and for His eternal purposes. Pause to consider how His hands are shaping and fashioning you into a vessel fit for His use.

KNEEL and PRAY

WORSHIP YOUR POTTER

P   *Praise* your Potter for molding and shaping you according to His divine design, for desiring to manifest His presence in and through you.

_____

_____

R   *Repent* if you have rebelled against God's shape and purpose for your life. Confess if you have been trying to crawl off the Potter's wheel.

_____

_____

A   *Ask* your Potter to mold your mind and heart into a vessel of honor that brings Him praise. Ask Him to fill you, an earthen vessel, with the surpassing greatness of His power, even as a pitcher is filled with water. Pray for others to submit to the Potter and to be pliable in His hands.

_____

Y *Yield* to the Potter's touch today. Where He presses, yield. How He shapes you, conform. Keep the Holy Spirit, His Living Water, flowing through you so you remain soft and pliable in His hand, a vessel that is useful to the Potter. _____

_____

_____

Chapter 22

Lord, You Are *the* Quickening Spirit

When I Am Dull, You Revive and Guide Me

Quicken us, and we will call upon thy name.
Psalm 80:18 KJV

Lord, You are the Quickening Spirit. You quicken my heart and prompt me to speak, act, go, and do. At other times You prompt me to be silent and still. I praise Your name and pray to be ever sensitive to Your Quickening Spirit, who guides, instructs, convicts, and draws me to You. In Jesus's name, amen.

Does God still speak to people as He did in biblical days? Does He direct people to their professions and where they are to live as He did Abraham? "Go forth from your country, . . . to the land which I will show you" (Genesis 12:1).

Does God still speak as He did to Moses, "just as a man speaks to his friend" (Exodus 33:11)?

Does God still direct people as He did Jesus, who said, "I do nothing on My own initiative" (John 8:28–29)?

Does the Holy Spirit speak as Jesus said He would and convict "concerning sin and righteousness and judgment" (John 16:8)?

Yes, God still speaks. The question is: are we listening? Have we offered ourselves as living and holy sacrifices to Him? Are we daily renewing our minds and actively being transformed into His image so we hear and discern His voice?[1]

The Quickening Spirit Is a Gift to Cherish

God's Spirit is alive. The Holy Spirit lives within each believer, prompting us to both large and small tasks as we yield to Him moment by moment. God's quickening is something to which I continually yearn to be more sensitive and responsive. Why? Because nothing is more awesome and exciting than being in God's will and doing His work, His way.

The Holy Spirit is a gift from God to the believer, and His prompting is a gift to honor, cherish, and nurture by developing a loving, passionate relationship with the Lord.

If the Quickening Spirit were to look for someone to act in your city on His behalf, would you be His contact person, His "go to" guy or gal? Are you "seeking the things above, where Christ is," setting your mind "on the things above" (Colossians 3:1–2)? Or are you earthly driven, worldly minded, and closed to His higher calling, insight, and wisdom?

Do you honor God's presence, recognize His righteousness, and confess when you grieve or quench Him?[2] Do you offer yourself to His service and respond to His promptings? If not, you can pray along with the psalmist, "For the sake of Your name, O LORD, revive me, in Your righteousness bring my soul out of trouble" (Psalm 143:11). Or as the *King James Version* says, "Quicken me, O LORD, for thy name's sake: for thy righteousness."

The psalmist acknowledged that his soul was in trouble apart from God. He knew that apart from God he would not be spiritually revived. His prayer was not for money or gain but rather for God to quicken him on the basis of God's righteousness and for God's name and sake.

The Hebrew word for "quicken" is *chayah*. It is a primitive root word that means "to live, revive, refresh, cause to grow."[3]

If our walk with God is dull, boring, or inactive, if He is not using us to impact others for His kingdom, we need to consider why. If our spiritual life is unlively, we need to ask God to show us what is preventing His Quickening Spirit from flowing into our hearts and minds. Are we not spending enough time with Him? Have things of the world created a dam between us? Has sin dulled our minds to His Quickening Spirit?

The Holy Spirit is alive and active. He is able to revive, refresh, and stimulate us to grow. He enables us to have a thriving spiritual life when we open our hearts and minds to His will, when we walk in faith as He prompts.

If you are spiritually down, look up, into the heavens, into the face of Jesus in order to be transformed. Praise Him according to the A to Z attributes in this book.

God's Spirit Quickens Us to Exciting Work

Two years ago I was spending a lot of time on the road. On one trip, in search of something to listen to, I grabbed a new CD, one that to this day I have no idea how it got in my car. As I listened to one song, God quickened my heart to host a retreat. Not only that, He quickened me to ask a lady I'd met only once to do an interpretative dance to the song I was listening to. (I'd never seen an interpretative dance to Christian music, nor had I seen the lady dance, although I knew she was involved in the Christian arts.) He also prompted me that she was to wear a long, flowing white dress and open the retreat by dancing to the song in the light of a bonfire.

As I chuckled at the seemingly silly thoughts running through my head, I could not help but wonder if God really was prompting me to do this. When I returned home, I prayerfully approached my staff and board members of Hill Country Ministries with the idea. Everyone agreed it was a good idea.

One afternoon as I drove home after visiting several places where we might hold the conference but not feeling any of them was right, God prompted me to host the first night at our home. When I approached Keith with the idea of seating the women on a point overlooking the pond, he responded with his typical big-hearted encouragement. My next question received just as supportive a response, plus a curious look, "Can you build a bonfire on the dam for Lorraine to dance beside?"

The next major detail weighing on my mind was Lorraine and the song

God had quickened my heart that she was to dance to. I simply could not get up the nerve to approach a near stranger with what I felt was a strange idea!

One Sunday, when Keith was out of town, I felt stirred to visit a sister church. I slipped in and sat toward the back. Was I ever surprised when Lorraine slipped in beside me a few moments later. My heart raced as I contemplated sharing with her what God had impressed on my heart. However, the idea seemed too bizarre, and I quickly left after the closing prayer, deciding to put the idea totally aside. When Lorraine startled me by tapping on my car window to ask for a ride to meet her husband at a nearby restaurant, my heart leaped again as the Spirit quickened me, "Ask her!" As we rode to the restaurant, I finally yielded to the pounding in my heart. "Lorraine, you're not going to believe this, but . . ."

What was her response? "Girl! I know that song and I've got a long, white flowing dress!" I was moved beyond words when she told me that God had impressed on her heart years ago when she had visited my Bible study that she would serve Him with me one day. What had been her response to God's quickening? "How could I serve with Debbie, Lord? I'm a dancer!"

As with all God's works, the retreat was an awesome experience. At just the right moment, Lorraine and a fellow dancer appeared on the dam. I was told that they appeared as angels, poised in the light of the bonfire.

Why did God stir my heart as I drove city to city? Let me share just part of a letter from one of the 250 ladies who attended the conference:

> It was early last year when I first heard of Hill Country Ministries. I was stressed, down ALL the time, sad, bitter, and constantly angry! I thought to myself, "How in the world am I going to survive this season successfully? It's going to kill me!! When is it EVER gonna end? WHY ME?!"
>
> Well, Debbie, at the conference God shone His majestic glory of love upon this broken and discouraged woman. God showered me with His awesome mercy and love! He lifted the thick fog of darkness that surrounded me and penetrated to the depths of each pain! . . .

Honestly, I believe those heavy chains would continue to have weighed heavily on me and bound me to Satan's hold had it not been for attending your conference! The conference was God's way of confirming me—my season was then! Never in my life had I understood "for such a time as this" as when I attended the conference! The timing—God's. The anointing—God's. The season—God's. The breaking—God's. The obedience—Mine!

Whether God prompts you to leave a twenty-dollar bill under someone's windshield wiper at the gas station or to give a just-purchased carton of ice cream to a family with a carload of kids or to invite someone to church, take my word for it, it's a joy to follow the Quickening Spirit's promptings!

However, at times it can be frightening to follow the Spirit's lead. At other times we may feel silly, as I did about approaching Lorraine. Yet no matter how foolish or uncomfortable we may feel, we will never regret following God's promptings.

We Can Pray to Be Sensitive to the Quickening Spirit

The psalmist prayed, "Turn away mine eyes from beholding vanity; and quicken thou me in thy way" (Psalm 119:37 KJV). I wonder how often we waste our time doing vain, unimportant things, when we could be doing things of great joy and eternal value.[4] God is waiting for us to make ourselves available to Him. Isn't it time we prayed, "Quicken me, and I will go"?

A man by the name of Philip provides an excellent model of what it means to be sensitive to the Quickening Spirit. Let's look at how the Spirit spoke to Philip in Acts 8. "An angel of the Lord spoke to Philip saying, 'Get up and go south to the road that descends from Jerusalem to Gaza'" (v. 26). Did you notice that the Spirit prompted Philip in which direction to go, but did not reveal to him *why* he was supposed to travel that road?

Now look at the six important words that follow in the next verse: "So he got up and went" (v. 27). Philip followed the prompting of the Quickening Spirit without knowing the outcome.

179

How many of us could say we have felt God's urgings but did not get up and go? It breaks my heart to think of how often I have forfeited the opportunity to be used of God. We must not ignore the importance of quieting our hearts before God, waiting on Him, listening for His urgings and promptings, and then obeying when He quickens us to act.

Philip was sensitive and obedient to the Quickening Spirit. The road led him to a man who was in charge of the royal treasury of Ethiopia. When Philip saw him, the man was sitting in his chariot reading the prophet Isaiah.

Verse 29 says, "The Spirit said to Philip, 'Go up and join this chariot.'" This is usually where it gets tough to follow the Spirit's urging, when He calls us to invade someone's world. As long as we can sit at home and e-mail someone a sentimental poem, we feel fairly safe. But when God quickens us to move into someone else's space, it is often hard to obey. This is where I often hesitate and the Spirit has to prompt me again.

Philip, however, did not drag his heels or shuffle his sandals. Verse 30 tells us, "Philip ran." The Quickening Spirit prompted Philip, and he was quick to respond. Let our prayer be, "Please, dear God, make me a runner for You!"

What happened when Philip obeyed the Quickening Holy Spirit? He had the wonderful opportunity to explain the passage of Scripture to the man who had been struggling to understand it. Verse 35 says, "Philip opened his mouth, and beginning from this Scripture he preached Jesus to him." The result? The man believed and was baptized.

Imagine how our churches and families would be transformed if we all responded to the Quickening Spirit as promptly and willingly as Philip.

We Can Pray for the Spirit to Quicken Us through God's Word

The psalmist wrote, "My soul cleaveth unto the dust: quicken thou me according to thy word" (Psalm 119:25 KJV). The psalmist recognized that

Scripture is a tool that sharpens us and makes us alive, ready, and awakened to the Spirit. The author of Hebrews 4:12 affirmed his words, saying, "The word of God is living and active and sharper than any two-edged sword." Of course we can read the Bible hurriedly and with a distracted mind and still be dull to its quickening. Or we can meditate on it through the Spirit and discover it to be alive and powerful in our lives.

We not only want to read God's Word in the power of the Holy Spirit, we also want to obey it! The psalmist passionately prayed to be quickened to obey God's Word: "Quicken me after thy lovingkindness; so shall I keep the testimony" (Psalm 119:88 KJV). When a Christian sincerely wants to follow God's ways and prays to be quickened to obedience, the Holy Spirit will do so. However, we must be faithful to respond. How can we pray in relation to the Quickening Spirit? We can pray that God's Spirit will quicken us through the Bible to know and do His will.

In other words, if you have a sharp tongue and pray that, in obedience to Ephesians 4:29, "no unwholesome word [will] proceed from your mouth, but only such a word as is good for edification according to the need of the moment, so that it will give grace to those who hear," it's important that you respond when the Holy Spirit quickens you to hold your tongue. When we listen and respond to the Spirit's urging, we discover Him prompting us to further action. If we ignore Him, why should He continue to prompt our deaf ears?

There is great joy and potential when we pray that the Spirit quicken us according to His Word. Therefore let us read His Word for truths by which to live. A great place to practice responding to the Quickening Spirit is Ephesians. Begin by asking the Lord to enlighten the eyes of your heart as your read.[5] When a passage or verse stirs your heart, mind, or spirit, stop. Pray and ask God to accomplish His Word in you. Pray to be sensitive to and led by His Spirit and for His Spirit to quicken you throughout the day in regard to that passage.

Meditation Moment

The Quickening Spirit is alive in you if you're a Christian. Are you listening and ready to respond to Him?

KNEEL *and* PRAY

WORSHIP THE LORD, THE QUICKENING SPIRIT

P *Praise* the Lord who quickens you according to His Word in lovingkindness, to righteousness and obedience for His name's sake.

_____

_____

R *Repent* and confess ways you have grieved and quenched the Quickening Spirit, times you have not responded to God's quickening in you.

_____

_____

A *Ask* the Lord to make you increasingly sensitive to His Quickening Spirit, to quicken you to know and do His will. _____

_____

_____

Y *Yield* your body, mind, and spirit to the Quickening Spirit. When He prompts, act. _____

_____

_____

CHAPTER 23

LORD, YOU ARE RIGHTEOUS

WHEN I AM SLIPPING,
YOU SET ME ON A FIRM FOUNDATION

I will give thanks to the LORD according to His righteousness
And will sing praise to the name of the LORD Most High.
PSALM 7:17

Lord, You are righteous. There is none like You. Forgive me when I fail to seek
Your righteousness, when I settle into my sin. Help me understand that You
demand righteousness, You love righteousness, and in You I find righteousness by
which to live. In Your name I pray, amen.

I'm sure you know the importance of a good foundation. If we were to build a home, we'd want to contract with a reputable builder, one we trusted to lay a good foundation, because we know the house itself will be only as solid as the foundation.

Isn't it marvelous to know that the One to whom we pray and on whom we build our lives is the Lord our Righteousness? The psalmist proclaimed, "Your righteousness, O God, reaches to the heavens. You who have done great things; O God, who is like You?" (Psalm 71:19). "Clouds and thick darkness surround Him; righteousness and justice are the foundation of His throne" (Psalm 97:2).

The word "righteous" is translated from the Hebrew word *tsaddiyq* and means "just, right (in one's cause), righteous (in conduct and character), correct, lawful."[1] In other words, God is just, right, correct, and lawful.

Nowhere is His righteousness more clearly revealed than in His sacrificial love for us.

THE LORD OUR RIGHTEOUSNESS IS FULL OF SURPRISES!

No one expected to see Jesus in the Jordan River, waiting to be baptized, least of all John, who was understandably uncomfortable. His baptism was for repentance from sin, yet Jesus had no sin. Jesus surprised John, saying, "Permit it at this time; for in this way it is fitting for us to fulfill all righteousness" (Matthew 3:15).

Jesus wasn't baptized to be made righteous; Jesus was baptized because He *is* righteous. His baptism was a visual symbol of what happens when we choose to follow Him as our Lord and Savior. Just as Jesus died for our sin, was buried, and raised to new life, so we through Christ have died to our sin, been buried with Him, and raised to walk in newness of life.

A surprisingly wonderful switch happened when Jesus gave His life for us. Jesus took our identity and we took His. Jesus traded our sins for His righteousness. It was like playing a game of switch, but it wasn't a game. The lashes on His back ripped His flesh to the bone. The nails in His hands were real. The crucifixion was agonizing. The sword thrust into His side by a Roman executioner was real. His corpse was real.

And where were we? Standing by. We can almost hear our Savior whisper, "Take My identity and righteousness. I'll take your sin and punishment." A stolen identity? No. An identity Jesus freely gave because He loves us!

Jesus was crucified and buried for our transgressions, for our mess ups, our sins, whether they were intentional or unintentional. As 2 Corinthians 5:21 states, God "made Him who knew no sin to be sin on our behalf, so that we might become the righteousness of God in Him."

What a gracious, righteous Savior we have!

Since Jesus paid our sin debt once and for all, God accepts us as righteous. Once a crime has been paid for, the court cannot demand further payment. It is done. All we need to do is accept Christ's payment on our behalf.

When we acknowledge what a righteous God He is and fall on our knees in repentance to ask forgiveness, the "switch" occurs. His blood-stained death is applied to our sin debt. We're given His garments of righteousness. That's surprisingly good news!

THE LORD OUR RIGHTEOUSNESS HOLDS US AND WATCHES OVER US

What causes you to slip spiritually? A sin? A habit? An attitude? Worry? To whom do you look when you're about to sin? The Lord our Righteousness makes a glorious promise to which we can cling: "Do not fear, for I am with you; do not anxiously look about you, for I am your God. I will strengthen you, surely I will help you, surely I will uphold you with my righteous right hand" (Isaiah 41:10).

What an outstanding promise! Our Lord not only saves us in righteousness and helps us to build our lives on His righteousness, He also holds on to us and watches over us. He does not demand we be righteous and then leave us on our own to sink or swim. Rather, as a loving Father, the righteous Lord takes us by the hand and helps us accomplish what He calls us to be and do.

Can you remember a time when you were living in sin but the Lord your Righteousness kept nudging you to stop and turn back to Him? I can! More times than I can count, the Lord has held me when I started to fall. I felt His righteous right hand tighten when I was slipping in sin. I sensed His firm grasp when I was headed down a slippery slope, physically or emotionally.

The Lord holds on to us because He has a plan for our lives. Praise the Lord our Righteousness for holding on to you, for watching over you, and for having a plan for your life! When you start to fall away from Him, respond to the squeeze of His righteous right hand.

THE LORD OUR RIGHTEOUSNESS REVIVES US

Do you ever feel bone dry, like you have nothing left to give? As Christians we have the Holy Spirit, whom Jesus referred to as rivers of living water,[2] in our innermost being. However, there may be times when we don't sense the flow or even the trickle of His Spirit. We may wake up and not feel joyful. We may not feel like facing the day or our responsibilities. Maybe we simply aren't morning people. Or we may have sinned and grieved the Holy Spirit. When we feel drained, dry, or empty—for whatever reason—our souls crave a fresh drink of the Holy Spirit, whether we realize it or not.

When the psalmist felt that way, he knew right where to go—to God and His words: "Behold, I long for Your precepts; revive me through Your righteousness" (Psalm 119:40). The word "revive" in this passage is translated from the Hebrew word *chayah*, the same word translated "quicken." It is a primitive root word that means "to live, be quickened, restore to life or health, from sickness, discouragement, faintness, death, to refresh, cause to grow."[3]

In the same way that a person may arrive at a hospital appearing lifeless and in need of medical attention, such as CPR, we may at times need reviving. How does the Lord revive us? Through His breath, or Spirit. In intimacy, at the foot of God's throne, with our Bibles open, the Lord our Righteousness lifts the burdens of our hearts. He forgives the guilt of our sin. The Holy Spirit blows over our weary minds, refreshing and invigorating our thoughts. Christ's living Spirit flows through us, cleansing us of yesterday's debris and filling the reservoir of our hearts with His love, joy, energy, and peace. We are revived in God's presence by His righteousness. Our hollow spirits are filled with His righteous Spirit.

Feeling a little droopy? Maybe bone dry? Sin got you dragging your feet? Join the psalmist at the table of the Lord! The fresh wind of the Spirit can revive your soul. With the psalmist we can pray for others and ourselves, "Revive me through Your righteousness."

The Lord Our Righteousness Answers Our Prayers

"Yoo-hoo!" is what we used to call as we entered relatives' homes unannounced. Walking in, we continued to "yoo-hoo" until we finally saw an aunt waving us into the kitchen or an uncle walking in from the back yard. Yoo-hoo entrances were reserved for close friends and loved ones.

Are you aware that you have a yoo-hoo relationship with the Righteous Lord? In Psalm 143:1 David prays, "Hear my prayer, O LORD, Give ear to my supplications! Answer me in Your faithfulness, in Your righteousness!" In Psalm 145:17–19, David testifies that the Righteous Lord hears and answers prayers.

> *The LORD is righteous in all His ways*
> *And kind in all His deeds.*
> *The LORD is near to all who call upon Him,*
> *To all who call upon Him in truth.*
> *He will fulfill the desire of those who fear Him;*
> *He will also hear their cry and will save them.*

"Yoo-hoo! Can I have your ear, Lord? I've really messed up in my relationships at home." "Yoo-hoo, Lord! I've made a mistake at work and misled someone. OK, God, I lied." "Yoo-hoo, can You help me, Lord?"

Walk right in to prayer! The Lord our Righteousness will give an ear to anyone who draws near to Him asking forgiveness, to anyone seeking His righteousness. His throne is founded on righteousness, and His righteousness reaches to the heavens. He will hear our prayers and help us know the right thing to do. Let us listen with open hearts and receive His righteous counsel.

Relatives and neighbors greet us with a glass of tea. God greets us with His righteousness. Now that's something to yoo-hoo about!

Meditation Moment

The Lord our Righteousness is full of surprises. He takes away your sin, gives you His righteousness, and holds you tightly when your feet slip. He revives you when you feel bone-dry, and He greets your prayers with gladness.

KNEEL *and* PRAY

WORSHIP THE RIGHTEOUS LORD

P *Praise* the Lord who loves righteousness, whose foundation of righteousness rises to the heavens, who in righteousness holds you, watches over you, imparts His Spirit to you, and invites you into His presence. Give thanks and praise His righteous name! _____

_____

_____

R *Repent* and confess if you fail to live for the Righteous Lord, if you don't reach for Him when you're slipping or go to Him and His Word when your spirit needs reviving. Confess if you've been negligent to "yoo-hoo" and enter His presence in prayer._____

_____

_____

A *Ask* the Righteous Lord to revive you with His righteousness as you seek Him at His footstool in prayer and study. Pray for others to seek Christ's righteousness. _____

_____

_____

Y *Yield* your life to the Lord your Righteousness. Open the reservoir of your heart to the Holy Spirit's filling. Follow His righteous promptings through the day. _____

_____

CHAPTER 24

LORD, YOU ARE *a* SHIELD *about* ME

WHEN I AM UNDER ATTACK, YOU PROTECT ME

But You, O LORD, are a shield about me.
PSALM 3:3

Lord, You are a Shield about me. Thank You for Your love and protection, for always going before me and behind me, for guarding my way. Forgive me when I fail to acknowledge Your presence. Help me become more sensitive to Your divine guidance, covering, and protection. Be a Shield about my loved ones. I love You and praise You! In Jesus's name, amen.

Nine-year-old Genesis Estrada, a happy child who hoped to one day be a missionary or a pediatrician, was standing in the doorway of her family's apartment late one afternoon when gunfire erupted in her Las Vegas neighborhood. She and her eight-year-old sister, Heidi, rushed to gather three younger children who were playing outside. While Heidi took charge of her four-year-old brother and his friend, Genesis ran over to shield ten-month-old Michael Becerril, the son of a family friend. The infant was unharmed, but a stray bullet struck and killed Genesis.[1]

Our hearts cannot help but be moved by the image of one child shielding another. How much more are we moved to realize that our heavenly Father wants to shield us, His children? Although we aren't always able to see the ways in which He does so, the Bible tells us that God shields us from enemy fire. He protects us so that we can move forward in our Christian walk.

If you feel under fire by a barrage of personal, financial, or other attacks, take courage. Look up, into the face of your heavenly Father, who is a Shield about you!

A Shield about Us, God Covers Us with His Presence

Shields have to fit whatever or whomever they cover in order to be effective. Try putting a Honda windshield on a Chevy truck—it won't do the job! Neither will a child's raincoat shield an adult from a blowing rainstorm.

David knew this firsthand. Remember when he fought Goliath as a young lad? Saul offered his armor to David, who put it on but found it didn't fit him. He told Saul, "I cannot go with these" (1 Samuel 17:39). What shield did David take into battle? None that was visible. Rather, David took the shield of faith; he took God's presence into battle with him.

Dear friend, are you going into daily battles without God's covering? Do you try to shield your heart and mind with things other than the Lord? Do you attempt to shield your children through your own efforts and devices?

Although your efforts may be well intentioned, any shield other than the Lord will fail to protect the mind, emotions, and heart of you or your loved one. The best schools, right clothes, position, and prestige can't cover or protect you from the evil one. Only one Shield is custom-made for our souls, and that is God.

How do we carry God's presence as a shield into our days? We walk in faith, asking God to bring His Word to our minds throughout the day. We pray in faith for God to shield our families, friends, church, and nation. We rest in God who covers us with His presence. We take to heart God's words He spoke to Abraham, "Do not be afraid. . . . I am your shield, your very great reward" (Genesis 15:1 NIV).

A Shield about Us, God Protects Us from Enemy Fire

As I drove down the highway, an onslaught of bugs smashed against my windshield. It was gruesome. I'm not talking about one big bug. There were at least fifty, and they all hit at once. I was thrilled to have a windshield between my body and the open road. Otherwise, I would have been covered in yellow bugs!

Just as those bugs hit without warning, the Bible informs us that we are the target of an enemy who strikes without warning. For this reason, the apostle Paul warns us to take up "the shield of faith" in order "to extinguish all the flaming arrows of the evil one" (Ephesians 6:16).

You may be thinking, *Where? I don't see any flaming arrows!* Neither did I see the bugs coming at me until they hit my windshield in full force. In the same way, we often don't realize we're under attack until the divorce papers are served, a child is in jail, the body or mind is trapped in sin, or we have emotionally hit rock bottom. The result is a lot worse than bug guts. Flaming arrows, if not deflected, cause pain and injury.

What is the shield of faith to which Paul referred? It's the protective armor God has given us for daily battles. Paul was probably thinking of the Roman centurion who would not think of going into battle without his shield. The Roman shield, or *thureos*,[2] was a two-and-a-half by four-foot shield covered in leather that could extinguish flaming arrows. Paul compared the necessity of a Christian's taking up the shield of faith to the necessity of the Roman soldier's taking up his shield in battle.

Are you battling your sin? Are you in a battle to get your children to go to church? Is your biggest battle with your spouse or in-law? Are you engaged in political battles or fighting social injustices? Paul warns us in Ephesians 6:12 that "our struggle is not against flesh and blood, but against the rulers, against the powers, against the world forces of this darkness, against the spiritual forces of wickedness in the heavenly places."

When your temper flares, are you aware that the spiritual forces of wickedness are "high-fiving" it over you? When a loved one is experimenting with drugs, are you enraged with him or her, or do you recognize the world forces of darkness at work and stand firm in prayer and faith? When unhealthy chat rooms and pornography entice you, are you aware that the rulers and powers of darkness stand ready to ensnare you at the click of your computer mouse?

Paul warns, "Take up the full armor of God, so that you will be able to resist in the evil day, and . . . stand firm" (Ephesians 6:13). Are you resisting or giving in to your temperament and temptations? What about those for whom you pray? Faith is a shield. It won't prevent the evil one from attacking us, but it will keep him from destroying us.

A Shield about Us, God Protects Us through His Word

Just as faith is a shield, God's Word is also a shield. Psalm 119 refers often to the protective power of the Bible:

O how I love Your law!
It is my meditation all the day.
Your commandments make me wiser than my enemies. . . .

Your word is a lamp to my feet
And a light to my path. . . .
The wicked have laid a snare for me,
Yet I have not gone astray from Your precepts.
I have inherited Your testimonies forever,

For they are the joy of my heart. . . .
You are my hiding place and my shield;
I wait for Your word.

PSALM 119:97–98, 105, 110–111, 114

The psalmist grasped the truth that walking in God's ways was the wisest, safest thing he could do. Even in the throes of enemy fire and battles, he found joy in keeping God's Word. Walking in God's ways won't prevent enemy fire, but it will light your path as you battle the darkness.

For instance, if someone speaks harshly to you, you have two choices.

You can respond with a harsh word, which will stoke the enemy's fire. Or you can find protection in God's counsel: "A gentle answer turns away wrath; but a harsh word stirs up anger" (Proverbs 15:1). Is your faith shield up or down when someone speaks harshly to you?

Or in another case, if you experience a problem with a fellow Christian, you have two options: You can ignore Matthew 18:15–17 and fall prey to Satan's fiery darts. Or you can follow God's protective Word.

Perhaps you can recall a time when God's Word protected you from the Enemy's fiery darts. I remember one particular time when I was hurt and angry. I went to God with my stormy emotions, and He impressed on my heart three simple words: "Do not sin." Having just taught the life of Moses and the consequences of his striking a rock in anger, God's Word protected my heart like a shield. I knew I must not respond in anger but rather trust God to work all things for good according to His purposes.[3] As I walked through those fiery days in faith, God shielded me. Had I not had His Word to cling to, I would have grievously sinned. Putting up the shield of faith and deflecting the fiery darts with His Word protected me.

As Paul reminds us in Ephesians 6:16, the shield of faith must be *up* if it is to be effective and powerful. A top to a convertible does no good unless it is *up* when it rains. An umbrella at home is useless if we are caught outside in a storm. We must have it with us and put it up for it to be effective. A Bible at home does us no good unless we carry God's teachings in our hearts and apply them when we are hit with a fiery dart. So let me ask: Is your shield of faith in God and His Word up? When you are hit with the announcement of a pay freeze, do you burn with anger or become depressed? Or do you go to God in prayer and raise your faith shield? When you make every effort to be kind to a rude person yet she continues to deride you, do you let the searing dart burn within you? Or do you put your shield of faith up?

If your shield of faith is down, God advises you to take it and hold it up.

How can you do this? May I suggest taking "up" your Bible? Read it and take God "up" on His Word. Sometimes it helps to take something tangible in our hands. Consider taking your Bible in your hand and holding it up. Profess to God, "Lord, I believe that You are a Shield about me. I need Your protection for my heart, my children, my business, my thoughts. Shield my heart and mind from any wrong thoughts. Teach me the way in which I should go and help me walk by faith in You."

A Shield about Us, God Will Lift Our Heads

David, a warrior famous for his skills, knew the importance of a shield. When in a battle of the most grievous kind—at war with his own son Absalom—David prayed, "O Lord, how my adversaries have increased! Many are rising up against me. Many are saying of my soul, 'There is no deliverance for him in God.' But You, O Lord, are a shield about me, My glory and the One who lifts my head" (Psalm 3:1–3).

Humiliated and saddened, the hero once heralded for slaying Goliath now had to endure the shame of his son's leading a revolt against him. David discovered that the One he trusted to shield him would also lift his head.

Have you ever faced a similar circumstance? Do you know the hurt of being at war with a family member? Have you felt the searing pain of being stabbed in the back by someone close to you?

Again we are reminded of Ephesians 6:12, that we do not war with flesh and blood. Rather, we struggle against rulers, powers, world forces of darkness, spiritual forces of wickedness. Therefore, we must have our heads up so we can see the battles we face and the fiery darts coming our way.

If you're in pain today, hurting from the blow of a loved one's words or actions, put up the shield of faith. Go to God in prayer and ask Him to lift your head, to protect your mind from wrong thoughts and your heart from breaking. The Lord will be your shield. Take Him at His word.

Meditation Moment

Your heavenly Father is a Shield about you, covering you with His presence, protecting you from enemy attacks with the shield of faith, His Word, and lifting your head in the midst of battle. Look up and take courage!

KNEEL *and* PRAY

WORSHIP GOD, A SHIELD ABOUT YOU

P *Praise* God for being a Shield about you, for deflecting the flaming arrows of the evil one, for protecting you, lifting your head, and covering you with His presence through His Word. _____

_____

_____

R *Repent* if you have failed to put up the shield of faith in prayer. Confess other shields you use that in reality do not protect your loved ones or you.

_____

_____

A *Ask* God to be a Shield about you, to cover and protect you. Ask God to shield your loved ones, churches, missionaries, elected officials, and nation.

_____

_____

Y *Yield* to God. Give Him your heart and mind. Be sensitive to how He is leading you in order to shield and protect you. Practice putting up the shield of faith by praising Him! _____

_____

CHAPTER 25

LORD, YOU ARE a TOWER

WHEN I AM VULNERABLE,
I RUN TO YOU

The name of the LORD is a strong tower;
the righteous runs into it and is safe.
PROVERBS 18:10

Lord, You are a tower to whom I can run for deliverance. Forgive me for not heeding Your voice, for not taking You seriously when You warn me that I have an enemy and need Your divine protection. Guard me and protect me, Lord. I'm running to You! In Jesus's name, amen.

September 11, 2001, is a day never to be forgotten. More than two thousand innocent people died when the Twin Towers in New York City were attacked and destroyed in a flash of blazing fire before our eyes.

Just as those towers symbolized America's strength, towers have always been recognized as symbols of power. Genesis 11 tells of the people of Babel, who decided to build for themselves a tower whose top would reach into heaven, to make for themselves a name. Ever since that time mankind has continued to build towers and tried to make for itself a name. However, man-made towers will never reach to heaven; they are always vulnerable to natural disasters and enemy attack.

Only one Tower stands eternal, reaches to heaven, and will not be shaken. He is a tower of salvation for our souls, a tower of deliverance from our Enemy. He is a strong tower to whom we can run and find strength. God is a watchtower who guards our hearts and minds.

God Is a Tower of Salvation and Deliverance

In the Bible, towers were platforms from which soldiers guarded their cities against enemy attacks. As soldiers stood guard to save people's lives, so God is a tower of salvation and deliverance who watches over our souls. He saves all who enter into Him from eternal separation. He delivers all who enter into the kingdom of God.

His divine salvation and deliverance do not end with the salvation of our souls. God continues to be a tower of salvation and deliverance as we go to Him in prayer throughout our days. When we ask Him to deliver us from sin habits and attitudes, we discover, along with David, that "He is a tower of deliverance to His king, and shows lovingkindness to His anointed." Or, as the *King James Version* states, "He is the tower of salvation for his king" (2 Samuel 22:51).

Do you need to be delivered from a spiritual stronghold? Has sin imprisoned you in despair? Is your soul tormented by an enemy? Have you given up in a prison of self-pity? Are you locked in spiritual apathy? Are you a slave to your calendar or cell phone?

God is the only One who can deliver and save us and cause us to walk in victory. God is a tower of salvation and deliverance to all who call on Him to be saved, both eternally and daily.

God Is a Tower of Strength

In addition to God's being a tower of salvation and deliverance, as David recognized, He is a tower of strength. In Psalm 61:3 David praised the Lord, "For You have been a refuge for me, a tower of strength against the enemy."

The Hebrew word for "tower" in Psalm 61 is *migdal*, an elevated stage.[1] Jewish military towers were tall stone or mud brick structures, either round, semicircular, square, or rectangular in shape.[2] They were placed in strategic positions and served as places of both defense and refuge in times of attack.

How appropriate that David likens God to a military tower: elevated, strategically placed, both a defense and a refuge to whom he could go when attacked by the enemy.

Although we may not be engaged in hand-to-hand combat, the Bible alerts us to an enemy we battle and who is seen only by the destruction left in the aftermath of his presence. He is an enemy of Christ and our enemy. His strategy is cold war with cold Christians but all-out attacks on fervent Christians. God warns us and prepares for our defense by providing Himself as a tower that rises to the highest heavens and to whom we can run. He is not a tower made of brick or mud. Rather, He is a spiritual tower of strength and divine protection. We run to Him not with our bodies but in prayer.

However, just knowing that a tower exists is not enough. We need to be *in* a tower to be protected by it. Are we "in" Christ? If we're Christians, we are, for we have been born "into" the family of God. But are we "in" prayer? When Christ sees principalities waging war and directed flaming arrows toward us, undoubtedly He summons us to prayer. Do we heed His voice? Or do we go about our daily business not knowing why our fuses are lit and one problem after another assaults us?

Is Christ the Tower of Strength to whom we run? Or are we trusting in self-made or man-made towers: towers of success, towers of money, towers of pleasure, or towers of worldly achievement? Do we run to human towers that can be torn down or to the eternal Tower that reaches to the heavens?

If we are not in prayer, not only are our defenses down but we are also not *in* our defense, our Strong Tower. Whether we are battling disease, combating depression, striving to keep our families together, fighting temptation, or struggling in our work or ministry, let us pray with David, "Hear my cry, O God; Give heed to my prayer. . . . For You have been a refuge for me, *a tower of strength* against the enemy. . . . Let me take refuge in the shelter of your wings" (Psalm 61:1, 3–4).

The name of the Lord is a strong tower.[3] You are invited to run into the safety of God's arms.

GOD IS A WATCHTOWER

In addition to military towers, farmers built small watchtowers in fields and vineyards.[4] These watchtowers provided elevated positions from which they could guard and protect their fields from wild animals or thieves. The ground floor also served as living quarters for guards or fieldworkers, since ripening crops had to be guarded day and night.[5]

First Corinthians 3:9 states that we are God's field. He has sown His seed into our hearts through Christ. It is His desire to nurture into flowering maturity that which He has planted in our lives. He wants us to bear eternal fruit for His glory and be a fragrance of Christ to our neighbors. We'll find our greatest joy and satisfaction in life when we bear that which God created us to bear: His image, His fragrance, His works, His Spirit!

Is it any wonder that God, from His heavenly tower, watches over us? Is it any wonder He guards our hearts and minds in Christ Jesus?

When we are in prayer, God is able to point out to us that which threatens our walk, fruitfulness, and relationship with Him and others. Prayer is an outlook post in the vineyard of our hearts, a watchtower from which God serves as a sentinel, warning us of habits that steal our joy, of attitudes that rob us of peace, or of temperaments that hurt others.

Let us then purposefully go to our Tower each morning when we rise. Let us ask the Holy Spirit to watch over our hearts. Let us return throughout the day to see God's perspective on our thoughts and activities. Let us lie down and sleep in peace, trusting God to watch over us.

GOD IS A HIGH TOWER

Not only does the Bible reveal God to be a tower of salvation and deliverance, a watchtower, and a tower of strength, it also refers to Him as a high tower: "Blessed be the LORD my strength, which teacheth my hands to war, and my fingers to fight: My goodness, and my fortress; *my high tower*, and my deliverer; my shield, and he in whom I trust" (Psalm 144:1–2 KJV).

Consider David's words of praise on the day the Lord delivered him from Saul:

The LORD is my rock, and my fortress, and my deliverer; The God of my rock; in him will I trust: he is my shield, and the horn of my salvation, my high tower, and my refuge, my saviour; thou savest me from violence. I will call on the LORD, who is worthy to be praised: so shall I be saved from mine enemies. . . . In my distress I called upon the LORD, and cried to my God: and he did hear my voice out of his temple, and my cry did enter into his ears.

2 SAMUEL 22:2–4, 7 KJV

The Hebrew word translated as "tower" in this passage is *misgab* and means "a high place, refuge, secure height."[6] David did not find protection by hiding in a small, physical watchtower in a field. He defeated his enemies as he scaled heights and found his spiritual refuge in God, his High Tower.

God doesn't call us to sit in the lowlands but to rise to His high calling and purposes for our lives. To what height is God calling you? Is He calling you to better parent your children in the ways of the Lord or to be a more loving caregiver to a relative? Is He calling you to lead a home Bible study or to make a commitment to Christ? Is God calling you to scale new heights with Him in prayer? Has God given you a vision for what He wants to do in your home, marriage, church, business, or ministry? If so, are you aware of how important it is to continually find your refuge in God as David did?

God called and anointed David to be king of Israel years before he acquired that position. Fighting bears to protect his flock and slaying Goliath prepared David for the battles he would fight as king of Israel. The psalms, songs, prayers, and confessions in the Bible record David's struggles and victories as he scaled the heights to which God called him and as he found refuge in God, his High Tower.

Each believer has a high calling from God. However, the path in fulfilling it is often marked with hardship. In addition, as we scale the height to which God calls us, we become marks for the devil. As if that weren't enough, we battle daily to overcome our flesh by the power of the Spirit. My heart breaks when I hear of a man or woman whom God has used to affect lives for Christ but who falls into sin. Let us be mindful that the Enemy's favorite targets are those who are doing God's work. If we are to accomplish what God calls us to do, we must find our refuge in God and regularly meet Him in the high tower of prayer. Are you wisely, purposefully in prayer so that you see yourself, others, your calling, and battles from His viewpoint?

Let our testimonies be as David's, "The God of my rock; in him will I trust: he is my shield, and the horn of my salvation, my high tower, and my refuge, my saviour" (2 Samuel 22:3 KJV).

Meditation Moment

God is a tower of salvation and deliverance, a strong tower to whom you can turn, a watchtower who guards your soul, and a high tower to whom you can run.

KNEEL *and* PRAY

WORSHIP GOD, A TOWER

P *Praise* God as the Tower of Deliverance and Salvation, Strong Tower, Watchtower, and High Tower to whom you can run for protection.

_____

_____

_____

R *Repent* and confess ways you fail to turn to God for protection and deliverance, foolishly trusting in self-made or worldly towers. _____

_____

_____

_____

A *Ask* God to prompt you to run to Him as your Tower of Strength when you are weak, open to attack, and vulnerable. Ask God to watch over others as He watches over you and to prompt them to run to Him. _____

_____

_____

_____

Y *Yield* to God's protection and deliverance. Yield to His higher calling on your life, and trust Him to watch over your soul. _____

_____

_____

_____

CHAPTER 26

LORD, YOU ARE *the* ONE WHO UPHOLDS ME

WHEN MY LIFE IS FALLING APART, YOU HOLD ME UP

For I am the LORD your God, who upholds your right hand,
who says to you, "Do not fear, I will help you."
ISAIAH 41:13

Lord, You uphold me with Your righteous right hand. Thank You for holding me when I feel I may fall. Forgive me when I fail to cling to You. Uphold my children and loved ones today. Teach us to look to You and find comfort in the knowledge that You are upholding us for all eternity. In Jesus's name, amen.

Whether one lives in a Third-World country or in an affluent American suburb, pain and suffering can strike without warning. Some people experience isolated tragic events. Others live with pain for years. Does God see? Does God care? Absolutely! Just as He heard and saw the Israelites who called to Him in their bondage, God sees and hears those who call on Him today to uphold them through their suffering.

God hears every cry, including the following words written by residents at the Hill Country Youth Ranch in Ingram, Texas, a residential treatment and foster-care program for at-risk and tragedy-based children and teenagers:[1]

ALL THOSE YEARS
BY MICHELLE, AGE 14
My Daddy—he's in jail . . .
finally.

205

After what HE did to ME . . .
all those years.
FINALLY . . .
I AM starting to believe,
that maybe . . .
everything wasn't my fault.
AFTER all those tears . . .

SCARS
BY VERONICA, AGE 13

In my home
I got hit
every day
for every little thing . . .
I got hit with everything
you can think of . . .
Whatever she could reach;
I have scars.
I have scars . . .
Most of them are in my heart.

PLEASE HELP US
BY AMANDA, AGE 13

Facing my mom after all she's done
is hard . . . I don't know if I can.
Finding my mom is hard . . .
behind the drugs, behind the pain,
behind bars . . . I don't know if I can.
I wish so hard she could find her way out . . .
out of the drugs and anger . . .
out of jail . . . I don't know if she can.

206

Oh Heavenly Father, Please help us,
I know You can.

Though your own experiences may be quite different from those of these children, you can probably testify to difficult times in your life—perhaps even right now. Maybe money is going out the door faster than it's coming in. Your spouse has filed for divorce. You lost your job. You're worried about your health. You aren't married and don't want to go through life single. You need a new car. Your home is too small for your growing family. You are in an abusive relationship and don't know how to get out. You are an abuser. A loved one has died. The list of potential trials is endless.

What hope do we have in the difficult times of our lives? Is God watching from a distance, unable or unwilling to help? No, God promises that He is present to help and uphold us: "For I am the LORD your God, who upholds your right hand, who says to you, 'Do not fear, I will help you'" (Isaiah 41:13).

The word "upholds" is translated from the Hebrew word *ca`ad*, a primitive root word that means "to support, sustain, establish, strengthen, comfort."[2] God says that He will support us during the tragic times of our lives. He will sustain us and establish us. He will strengthen and comfort us.

God Upholds Us by His Righteous Right Hand

Is discouragement knocking at your door? Is temptation getting the best of you? Are you "down" physically, spiritually, or emotionally? God says, "Do not fear, for I am with you; do not anxiously look about you, for I am your God. I will strengthen you, surely I will help you, surely I will uphold you with My righteous right hand" (Isaiah 41:10).

In the Bible God's right hand symbolizes His strength. We need not fear that the One who upholds us is too weak for whatever we face. Neither should we fear that the One who upholds us will lead us astray. His right hand is the strong hand of righteousness.

I came to appreciate the Lord as the God who Upholds when I was caring for my mother in the hospital. God upheld her as she suffered with first one chronic disease and then another. He upheld her as she underwent painful procedures and spent long nights in Intensive Care. He upheld me when I was told she might not make it. He upheld me when I held her hand as she slept through the night.

Have you sat alone in a hospital room watching a loved one suffer? Perhaps you can testify, as I can, that it was God who sustained you. Have you, like someone dear to my heart, said good-bye to a loved one going to prison? If so, perhaps your testimony parallels her experience of being upheld by God. Have you clung to a dying child as he or she slipped into heaven? Have you hurt so badly you thought you would die? Who upheld you? Though we cannot see Him with our naked eye, God is an ever-present source of help who upholds us by His righteous right hand.

God Upholds Us as We Cling to Him

In Psalm 63:8 David prayed, "My soul clings to You; Your right hand upholds me." David stated unashamedly that he was clinging to God as a child clings to his mother's neck. "Cling" is translated from the Hebrew word *dabaq*, a word that means "stick, stay close, join to."[3] In other words, David stayed close to God. He stuck to Him, followed Him closely, joined himself to God. How did David cling to God? With his soul, his very life, his mind, desires, emotions, passions, his inner being.

Are you clinging to God? When you are emotionally down, spiritually discouraged, mentally challenged, or financially bankrupt, do you pray to the only One who can uphold you?

If you feel you're sliding toward disaster, maybe you should take a look at what you're clinging to. Are you clinging to your calendar with one hand and a cup of coffee with the other, leaving yourself unable to grab hold of God? Are you clinging to your investments or making a name for yourself at the expense of dropping the ball on your relationship with God? Are you sticking more closely to the things of the world than to your Christian commitment? Are you riding an emotional roller coaster or clinging to God to steady yourself? Would you miss a meal to spend time reading God's Word, or would you rather drop God's hand in order to eat, drink, work, or play?

May our testimony be as David's, who rather than saying, "My years of shepherding are seeing me through my loneliness" or "My expertise with a slingshot sees me through my battles," humbly confessed his need for God: "My soul clings to you. Your right hand upholds me."

God Upholds Us by Our Right Hand—for Eternity

Personal tragedy and holding on to the wrong hand are not the only things that cause us to teeter and feel that our world and lives are falling apart. Many things can cause us concern and keep our minds churning through the night. Sometimes our worries are personal: illness, rethinking conversations, bills, challenges with children, aging parents, or our jobs. On a larger scale we may feel our world is falling apart when we learn of terrorist attacks, national controversies, escalating evil, or the decline of the family.

Are we to lie awake at night worrying? Hardly! Our comfort and solace is found in God who upholds us as individuals and who upholds His kingdom now and for eternity. Listen to Isaiah's assuring words: "There will be no end to the increase of His government or of peace, on the throne of David and over his kingdom, to establish it and to *uphold* it with justice and righteousness from then on and forevermore. The zeal of the LORD of hosts will accomplish this" (Isaiah 9:7).

When sin or the war between good and evil gets us down, we can look up. We can praise God who is sitting on the throne and who will uphold His kingdom and us for eternity. We can remember His promise: "I am the LORD your God, who upholds your right hand, who says to you, 'Do not fear, I will help you'" (Isaiah 41:13).

The first time I studied this verse, I pondered how God could uphold my right hand with His right hand. I was reminded of how when mother became feeble, I would uphold her by wrapping my arm behind her and holding her hand as we walked side by side. What a beautiful picture God gives us: walking side by side with God, His arm around us, upholding us with His right hand!

Rather than fall into worry or teeter in sin, let us pray to God who upholds us by His strong, righteous right hand.

Meditation Moment

The Lord your God upholds you with His righteous right hand, strengthening and helping you as you cling to Him. You have no need to fear, for He will uphold you for eternity.

KNEEL *and* PRAY

WORSHIP GOD WHO UPHOLDS YOU

P *Praise* God who upholds you and His kingdom with His righteous right hand. _____

_____

R *Repent* and confess ways in which you do not call on Him or cling to Him with all your soul. _____

_____

A *Ask* God to uphold you in your present circumstances. Ask Him to uphold your church, pastor, family, marriage, relationships, and friends. Ask God to help you be an example to others of not fearing or teetering in sin but rather being upheld by God. _____

_____

Y *Yield* your heart, mind, emotions, and will to the Lord who upholds you day and night. Put your hand in His as you walk into the future.

_____

_____

CHAPTER 27

LORD, YOU ARE *the* V

WHEN I AM BARREN,
YOU TEND TO MY SOUL

"I am the true vine, and My Father is the vinedresser."
JOHN 15:1

Lord, You are the Vinedresser. I am the vine. Forgive me when I close the gate of my heart to Your presence and become entangled in the world. Forgive me when I quench the flow of Your Holy Spirit, who brings cleansing and life to my soul. Prune me of anything that is unbecoming to You. Plant the seed of Your Word in my heart so that I will bear much fruit and bring You glory. In Jesus's name, amen.

As I watered my peace lily, admiring the blooms among the dark, glossy leaves, I was surprised to discover a white web-like growth under one leaf. Apparently my plant wasn't as healthy as it appeared. I knew if I ignored the problem, the rest of the plant could become infested, so I quickly grabbed my pruning scissors. When I cut off the bug-ridden leaf, I was amazed at how beautiful and healthy one side of it looked. Only by close inspection did I discover the infestation.

As I tossed the leaf into the trash, I was reminded that God is described as the Vinedresser in both the Old and New Testaments. He lovingly inspects our hearts, checks us for overgrowths of self, prunes our souls of sin, plows the soil of our hearts so the seed of His Word can take root, and waters us with the flow of His Living Water Spirit so we can bear fruit for Him.

GOD IS THE VINEDRESSER
OF THE OLD AND NEW TESTAMENTS

he metaphor of God being a Vinedresser dates back to the beginning of creation, when God created the Garden of Eden. The Hebrew word for "vinedresser" is *korem* and means to "tend vines or vineyards."[1]

Hush! Listen to the sound of God walking through the first Garden. Hear the twigs break beneath His feet. Stop and hear the melody of the birds singing sweetly in the trees. Pause a moment to notice the lush greenery. Take a mouth-watering handful of berries to your lips. Smell the fragrant aroma of the peaches. Listen to the gurgling stream that waters the garden. Feel the gentle breeze. Now look up and see the finest work of God's hand—humanity—created in the image of God, capable of bearing fruit for God, of being a fragrant aroma to the Lord, the Vinedresser.

Travel forward from the Garden of Eden to the time of Moses. Nations have risen. Pyramids cast a shadow over God's people, who are enslaved to ruthless taskmasters in Egypt. Yet the Vinedresser has not forgotten His garden. He takes the nation of Israel, which has grown as a seedling in Egypt, and plants it in the Fertile Crescent of the Promised Land.[2]

Isaiah wrote of the Vinedresser's attentive care for Israel: "He dug [His vineyard] all around, removed its stones, and planted it with the choicest vine. And He built a tower in the middle of it and also hewed out a wine vat in it; then He expected it to produce good grapes, but it produced only worthless ones" (Isaiah 5:2).

God planted His vine, Israel, in the rich soil of Canaan, expecting it to produce good fruit. When it didn't, God sent prophets to tend to His garden and to speak against its infestation of land grabbers, drunkards, idol worshipers, those who perverted moral distinctions, those who were conceited, and the drunken judges. When they ignored the prophets, He removed His hedge and allowed enemies to plunder His vineyard. However, in the midst of it all, God safeguarded the root of the vine, promising that though the vineyard be trampled, a Branch, the Messiah, would come forth.

In the New Testament the allegory of God as the Vinedresser, Christ as the Branch, and His people as the vine is expanded to include not only Israelites but all who come to faith in Jesus. Jesus said that His Father is the Vinedresser and all who believe in Christ are "grafted" into Jesus, the True Vine.[3]

Perhaps you feel that your life has been somewhat worthless for God, that rather than bearing an abundance of luscious fruit, your life has been characterized by sour grapes. If that is the case, or if you have produced some fruit but want to produce more fruit for God, your Vinedresser is ready and attentive to your desire! As a believer, grafted into the root and branch of David, you have Christ's seed in you. You are able to grow and bear much fruit for God.[4] Ask Him!

WE CAN PRAY TO OUR VINEDRESSER WHO TENDS TO OUR SOULS

Most gardeners enjoy strolling through their gardens. With an attentive eye they can spot if a plant is healthy and productive or unhealthy. They are hands-on people. Gardeners don't mind getting dirty for the sake of their plants. They get on their knees to inspect them and to pull weeds that choke out healthy plants.

With the same attentive care, the Vinedresser nurtures us, His garden. In the New Testament, the word "vinedresser" is translated from the Greek word *georgos*, which means "a husbandman or tiller of the soil."[5] Jesus didn't just admire His vineyard from heaven; He was a true tiller of the soil. Jesus walked with His disciples. He talked to them and planted His seed in their hearts.[6] He spent time with them on His knees in prayer. He trained them to grow upward toward God. Jesus watered them with the flow of His Spirit. He nourished them with His teachings.

As Jesus was present with His disciples, so He attends to us today. He plants the seed of His Word in our hearts. He waters us with the flow of His Spirit. He daily inspects us for sin that may be infesting our lives. If He sees something "bugging" us, He convicts us to cut it off. When our Vinedresser observes dead works, overgrowths of self, or works that may be showy but produce little fruit for eternity, He prunes us. He searches our hearts for roots of bitterness or envy.

We can praise God for being our Vinedresser, ask Him to tend to our hearts, and respond by yielding much fruit!

Our Vinedresser Meets Us in the Garden of Our Hearts

In high school I attended a camp that had a prayer garden. Winding paths and benches served as places of solace and prayer.

Do you have a prayer garden? Perhaps not a literal garden but a place where you stroll with God, discuss the events of the day, and listen to His voice? Do you have a place where you turn over the leaves of your heart and mind to God, where you go to drink richly of the flow of the Spirit and be nourished by His Word?

Our spirit is the place where our Vinedresser meets with us in prayer and checks to see if we're bearing fruit for Him. It is where He watches over us and protects us from the "thief" who seeks to steal and destroy any godly fruit that is ripening in our lives.[7] It is where He uproots bitterness, anger, or self-centeredness and stimulates growth through His Spirit and the Word.

God is a caring, attentive Vinedresser. He knows that only when we're fed, watered, and pruned are we able to bear fruit.

Is there no godly fruit in your life? No manifestation of the Vinedresser's seed and Spirit? No fruit that points people to God or bears the fragrance of Christ? If that's the case, you can open the garden of your heart to the Vinedresser in prayer and keep the gate open throughout the day. You can daily receive the Word implanted so you will bear fruit for God. You can ask Him to weed out any sins that are choking His fruit from your life. When you're going through a dry or barren time, you can open your spirit to the Holy Spirit. As a soaker hose keeps soil moist, so the Holy Spirit can continually fill your heart with His presence.

Yield to your Vinedresser. Rest and grow in the Sonshine of Christ's presence. You'll begin to bear the fruit of His Spirit—love, joy, peace, patience, kindness, goodness, faithfulness, gentleness, and self-control.[8] Others will be able to smell the fragrant aroma of Christ in you and taste His sweet Spirit through your life.

Meditation Moment

God is the Vinedresser who has grafted you into Christ, who tends to your soul, and who feeds, waters, and prunes you so that you can bear the fragrant fruit of His Spirit. Meet with Him now in the garden of your heart.

Kneel and PRAY

Worship Your Vinedresser

P   *Praise* God, the Vinedresser, who has created you and grafted you into Christ Jesus, the True Vine. _____

_____

_____

R   *Repent* of any ways in which you fail to guard the garden of your heart or perhaps fail to bear fruit for your Vinedresser. Confess any seeds of bitterness that spring up or roots of worldliness that choke out the good seed of the Word Christ plants in your soul. _____

_____

_____

A   *Ask* your Vinedresser to prune you, cultivate His Word in your heart, and bear much fruit through you. Ask Him to guard you from the enemy who would steal the fruit you bear for Him. Pray for others to understand that God is their Vinedresser. Pray for the unsaved to be grafted into Christ Jesus. _____

_____

_____

Y *Yield* the garden of your heart and mind to your Vinedresser. Keep it tilled and free of sin, so that you can receive His Word implanted into your soul. Grow in the Sonshine of Christ's presence. Allow the Holy Spirit to continually flow through you so you can bear much fruit for God!

_____

_____

CHAPTER 28

LORD, YOU ARE WONDERFUL

WHEN I NEED YOUR WONDER-WORKING POWER, YOU DO THE EXTRAORDINARY

Sing to Him, sing praise to Him; speak of all His wonders.
Glory in His Holy name; let the heart of those who seek the
LORD be glad. Seek the LORD and His strength; seek His
face continually, remember His wonders which He has done.
PSALM 105:2–5

Lord, You are wonderful, performing wonders beyond my imagination. You worked wonders long ago. You work wonders today. Forgive me for forgetting what a wondrous God you are. Help me to daily look up and praise You! In Jesus's name, amen.

Hospital beds. Sterile sheets. Dimly lit hospital corridors. Loneliness. Heartache. Medicine. Chemotherapy. Hair falling out. Nausea. Pain. A doctor's solemn countenance speaking volumes before a single word declares the cancer has spread. IVs. Collapsed veins. Tears and more tears as loved ones search for comforting words.

Prayer.

"God, are you there?" "When will this end?" "I'm ready, God, for whatever Your will is. Take me. Leave me. I'm Yours."

The faint sound of a bell ringing. Hope at the end of the hall. Someone has finished her final treatment!

In a world wracked with suffering and disappointment, how do we understand and pray to the Lord who is wonderful?

217

Consider the exceptional perspective revealed in the following letter, written by a young lady who battled cancer for eight months and whose testimony gives praise to our Lord.

Dear Precious Ones,

Well, this is it. At 10:30 a.m. on Friday, January 14, 2005, I will complete my final radiation treatment. And at around 11:00 a.m. you may be lucky enough to hear the faint sound of a bell ringing. What exactly does that mean? At M. D. Anderson, all radiation patients have the honor of ringing this huge bell near the waiting room, signaling to all that you (the patient) have finished treatment. Yes, just thinking about it brings tears to my eyes. I am VERY excited! And at the moment I ring the bell, I also imagine that the angels in heaven will begin singing and God will part the clouds as rays of sunlight shine on my face. He will then look down on me and smile. We will finish the last day of this journey together.

If you can believe it, my time here in Houston began seven months ago. On June 14th I began the first round of chemotherapy, and on January 14th I will take my last round of radiation. And in between those two dates, a great miracle took place. Most of you already know, but on October 22, 2004, I was notified that I was cancer free. Knowing that, I still had to complete my final 2 rounds of chemo (out of 6) and then take 22 rounds of radiation therapy.

All of these dates and numbers may soon be forgotten, but the miracle of my healing is with me forever. It's funny that cancer, which at first we all think takes so much from our life, has actually added so much to mine. I have never felt as close to God, my family, or my friends as I do now. That just shows how great and big the body of Christ is and how powerful a person's prayer can be. From the very bottom of my heart, thank you so much for each and every prayer. Your prayers gave my family and me such a peace and helped us through the most challenging of days.

So as one journey ends, another begins. That's what the "ringing of the bell" means to me. Thank you for celebrating in this wonderful day. I couldn't have done it without you and our very faithful Father.

All my love, Rebecca[1]

Who would have thought that a young woman with cancer would one day be praising God for the wonderful day He gave her and thanking those who prayed for her?

The fact is, God is Wonderful. Although not all of us will be healed in this lifetime, all Christians will celebrate God's wonder and power when we are wholly healed and raised in His presence. In the meantime, God gives each of us the opportunity to know Him as a Wonderful God and to seek His wonder-working power, counsel, and presence in whatever situation we find ourselves.

WE CAN DEMONSTRATE
THE WONDER-WORKING POWER OF GOD

The word *wonder* is first used in conjunction with God in Exodus 4:21 when God told Moses, "When you go back to Egypt see that you perform before Pharaoh all the wonders which I have put in your power." In this passage the word "wonders" is translated from the Hebrew word *mowpheth*, which indicates "a sign, miracle, a wonder as a special display of God's power."[2]

God displayed His power in and through Moses, turning an ordinary shepherd's rod into a snake and performing other extraordinary miracles. The display of God's wonderful power was a sign, a convicting opportunity for Pharaoh to believe.

In the same way that God displayed His wonder-working power in and through Moses, our Wonderful God displays His power in and through Spirit-filled Christians. God wondrously enables the hurt to forgive, the weak to be strong, the timid to speak, the unloving to love, the stressed to find peace, the sad to be joyful, the unkind to be kind, the anxious to be patient, the faithless to be faithful, and the indulgent to exercise self-control.

These wonder-working enablements are signs to our families and friends that the Wonderful God is in us.

God expects believers to display His wondrous power, as did Moses. Are we being faithful to do so? If not, we can begin by praying to Wonderful God. He has given us His Holy Spirit so that we might live by His wonder-working power.

We Can Ask Our Extraordinary God to Work Wonders in Our Lives

In Judges 13:18, God asked Manoah, "Why do you ask my name, seeing it is wonderful?" The word translated "wonderful" in this passage is the Hebrew word *pil'iy* and means "incomprehensible, extraordinary."[3] In other words, the Lord said His name cannot possibly be expressed in words. It is indescribable. God is incomprehensible, extraordinary!

God, who is wonderful, did an extraordinary thing for Manoah and his wife: He touched her barren womb and blessed them with a son. Have you ever thought to ask God to do something wonderful in your life, something surpassing, something extraordinary that can only be attributed to Him? When we ask God in faith for that which is extraordinary, we have the opportunity to experience His wonder-working power!

How does God work wonders? Through His Holy Spirit who lives in us. When the Holy Spirit is filling us, we experience the extraordinary in both the good and sorrowful times of life. This is the object of our being vessels of God: not that we do the ordinary but that we do the extraordinary and glorify God in heaven.

This is the peculiar, the extraordinary of which Dietrich Bonhoeffer writes in *The Cost of Discipleship*: "What makes the Christian different from men is the 'peculiar,' . . . the 'extraordinary,' the 'unusual,' that which is not 'a matter of course.'"[4] As Christians our lives are to be peculiar, not in a negative sense but in a positive sense, because the extraordinary God lives in us.

We must ask ourselves if there is anything extraordinary about our lives that brings glory to God. If we're not experiencing God's wonder-working power, we must pray. We must confess ways we have grieved or quenched the Holy Spirit by our spiritual apathy, laziness, or sin. We must pray for Wonderful God to move freely in our lives, in extraordinary ways. Then others can see and believe and turn to our Wonderful God in heaven.

God does extraordinary things when we pray, believing in His name. Let us therefore praise and worship our Lord, whose name is Wonderful!

WE CAN SEEK THE COUNSEL OF OUR WONDERFUL GOD

Today an increasing number of people are going to counselors. We praise God for those whom He has called to give wise counsel. And we praise Him even more for being the one Isaiah calls Wonderful Counselor (Isaiah 9:6).

Do you need extraordinary counsel? Are you in need of counseling that goes beyond human reasoning? Job found himself in such a situation, having lost everything that was of value to him in his earthly life. As Job struggled to understand and cope with his circumstances, his friend Elihu appealed to him to consider God's wonders:

> *"Listen closely to the thunder of His voice,*
> *And the rumbling that goes out from His mouth. . . .*
> *"God thunders with His voice wondrously,*
> *Doing great things which we cannot comprehend. . . .*
>
> *"Listen to this, O Job,*
> *Stand and consider the wonders of God."*
>
> JOB 37:2, 5, 14

Then the incredible moment came when "the LORD answered Job out of the whirlwind" (Job 38:1).

To gain an appreciation of our awesome Wonderful Lord, read Job 38. His power and might are extraordinary!

When we're in need of counseling, let us go to our Wonderful Counselor.

He is but a prayer away. Let us run to Him when our hearts are heavy, our minds confused, our lives empty, or our plates full. Let us run to God when we're grieved, bitter, depressed, lonely, or joyful. He will hear and help us when we still ourselves in His presence.

His name is Wonderful Counselor.

We Can Praise Wonderful God and Speak of His Wonders to Others

Psalm 105:2–5 says, "Sing to Him, sing praise to Him; speak of all His wonders. Glory in His Holy name; let the heart of those who seek the Lord be glad. Seek the Lord and His strength; seek His face continually. Remember His wonders which He has done."

If we're not living by God's wonder-working power, it's likely we're not singing His praises, glorying in His holy name, being glad, seeking His face continually, and remembering His wonders which He has done.

One of the most helpful ways I've found to remember God's wonderful deeds is to journal my prayer requests. My earlier book, the *Prayers of My Heart* prayer journal, resulted from my asking God for a way to journal my prayers and easily keep up with His answers. Rather than record prayer requests in a long list, the Lord showed me a way to journal my prayer requests in a table format. It works wonderfully for those praying for several individuals or groups.

If you're not yet journaling your prayers, I encourage you to do so. It's an awesome way to "remember His wonderful deeds which He has done," as 1 Chronicles 16:12 tells us to do, and to praise Him for His wonders.

Let us open our hearts and minds to God's wonder-working power through prayer. Let us sing praises to Him. Let us seek His face continually. Let us remember and speak of the wonders He has done, as Rebecca did.

In speaking of God's wonders, we encourage others to seek our Wonderful Lord!

Meditation Moment

Prayerfully consider how your Wonderful God wants to work in an extraordinary wonder-working way in your life or the life of one for whom you are praying.

Kneel *and* PRAY

Worship the Wonderful Lord

P *Praise* the Lord for His wonderful counsel, deeds, and Word, for the extraordinary ways He has worked in your life. _____

_____

_____

R *Repent* and confess ways you have settled for that which is less than wonderful, for that which is less than extraordinary, on a day-to-day basis.

_____

_____

A *Ask* God to work in your life in an extraordinary way, even in the ordinary aspects of life. Follow His counsel. Ask Him to make you a bold witness of how wonderful He is._____

_____

_____

Y *Yield* to the wonder-working Holy Spirit in you. Follow His promptings. Obey His commands. Rejoice as He leads you in extraordinary ways!

_____

_____

CHAPTER 29

LORD, YOU ARE EXALTED

WHEN I SEE MYSELF IN LIGHT OF YOU,
I AM HUMBLED AT YOUR FOOTSTOOL

O magnify the LORD with me, and let us exalt His name together.
PSALM 34:3

Lord God, I praise and worship You. You are high and lifted up, exalted above the heavens. Forgive me when I do not lift Your glorious name in praise. Teach me to exalt You in every area of my life. In Christ's name, amen.

You knew her—or someone like her. She was the kind of person who controlled people through intimidation. If you didn't laugh at her jokes (even when they weren't funny), didn't do what she did (such as putting down other people), didn't wear the kind of clothes she wore (even if you didn't look good in them or couldn't afford them), you were an outcast.

There have always been those who tear down others to build themselves up. It happens with children, teens, even adults. It happens outside the church and, sadly, sometimes even within the church. If you don't like the "right" kind of music or you don't dress as "they" deem appropriate, you could be an outcast.

The problem with building ourselves up at the expense of others is that we fail to recognize that only God is worthy to be exalted. If our attitude toward Him and others is not humble and loving, we're setting ourselves up for a tumble off our high horse.

Great news is on the way, though. When we prayerfully repent of our

225

self-exaltation and recognize and praise God as the exalted Lord, we become rightly aligned not only to Him but also to others.

WE CAN JOIN MOSES IN EXALTING THE LORD THROUGH OBEDIENCE

As the adopted son of Pharaoh's daughter, Moses had everything life could offer: servants, chariots, the finest education, clothes, pyramids, power, and wealth. He was exalted because of the family into which he was adopted. However, at the time God called Moses, he was not sitting on a throne leading a nation; he was leading sheep. Then God called Moses to exalt His name in Egypt and to lead the Israelites to the Promised Land.

Jump forward to Moses's famous parting of the Red Sea and his words in which he exalted God: "I will sing to the LORD, for He is highly exalted; the horse and its rider He has hurled into the sea. The LORD is my strength and song, and He has become my salvation; this is my God, and I will praise Him; my father's God, and I will extol Him" (Exodus 15:1–2).

The word "exalt" is translated from the Hebrew word *ga'ah* and means "to be high, elevated, majestic, exalted in triumph."[1]

Moses exalted the Lord in both word and deed by doing what God commanded. In what ways do you exalt the Lord?

WE CAN JOIN NEBUCHADNEZZAR AND CONFESS OUR FAILURE IF WE DO NOT EXALT THE LORD

Unlike the humble and obedient Moses, Nebuchadnezzar was a prideful king whose self-exaltation was evident as he walked on the roof of his royal palace and reflected, "Is this not Babylon the great, which I myself have built as a royal residence by the might of my power and for the glory of my majesty?" (Daniel 4:30).

When you look around at what you have, at your family, or success, what are your first thoughts? Are you proud as you think on what you have accomplished? Or do you recognize that every blessing you have is a gift from God, that He gives and takes away? Do you recognize that the earth and all it contains is the Lord's and that we are simply His stewards?[2]

God, who knows our hearts and hears our thoughts, spoke from heaven and told Nebuchadnezzar that He was removing his power and reign. He told Nebuchadnezzar that he would be driven away to live with the beasts of the field until he recognized that "the Most High is ruler over the realm of mankind and bestows it on whomever He wishes" (Daniel 4:32).

As we discussed in a previous chapter, Nebuchadnezzar had a mighty fall. When he finally came to his senses and humbly looked up, He saw God for who He is, the Exalted King of heaven. He recognized that all he had possessed had been given him by God and that God was worthy of his praise: "Now I . . . praise, exalt and honor the King of heaven, for all His works are true and His ways just, and He is able to humble those who walk in pride" (Daniel 4:37).

God, in His love, warns us through the examples of others. Let us take to heart the truth King Nebuchadnezzar learned the hard way, "Though the LORD is exalted, yet He regards the lowly, but the haughty He knows from afar" (Psalm 138:6). If we have wondered why God seems distant to us, could the problem be our self-exaltation?

We need to ask ourselves who or what we exalt on a day-to-day basis. Daniel 5:23 offers an additional word of warning against being preoccupied with material things: "But you have exalted yourself against the Lord of heaven; . . . and you have praised the gods of silver and gold, of bronze, iron, wood and stone, which do not see, hear or understand. But the God in whose hand are your life-breath and your ways, you have not glorified." When our golf clubs, houses, jewelry, or cars take precedence over God—or we find praise for ourselves through them—we are, in effect, exalting them over the Lord of heaven.

Rather than exalting earthly things, ourselves, or others, let us take to heart that we have but one purpose: to exalt and glorify the Lord who made the heavens and earth! If we recognize that our thoughts and words do not exalt God, let us fall on our knees and repent. Let us "humble [our]selves under the mighty hand of God" that He may exalt us in His time and way (1 Peter 5:6).

We Can Join Paul and Mary in Choosing to Exalt God

She came to my house to help me with spring cleaning. I appreciated her cheerful countenance as she went about her work. However, I appreciated it even more when I discovered she was living at a shelter. She was a present-day illustration of a saint who exalts the Lord. How did she exalt the Lord? Did she wear fancy clothes and a sparkly cross around her neck? No. She wore Christ on her countenance. She exalted His name when she expressed how good God was to provide the opportunity for her to work. She exalted the Lord when she fondly dusted a cross in my entry and expressed her love for it.

How do we exalt the Lord? Do we stand on a street corner and yell Jesus's name? Do we wear placards around our necks that say, "Jesus saves"? Probably not. The way we exalt the Lord will differ from person to person, but we each are to exalt the Lord. My husband exalts the Lord in his work as a trial attorney and mediator. Most clients entering his office don't expect to see a "cross upon a rock" paperweight with the plan of salvation on a nearby card. They don't anticipate Keith's encouraging them in the Lord when the opportunity presents itself. But God uses Keith weekly as he speaks to others about Jesus.

Is our desire as Paul's, that "with all boldness, Christ will even now, as always, be exalted in my body, whether by life or by death" (Philippians 1:20)? If so, then the Exalted Lord will exalt Himself in our lives, words, and deeds. Often we look for great things we can do for God, but in reality the truest greatness is that which He does in us.

Do we want the Exalted Lord to do something great in us? Then let us open the door of our hearts to His presence as did Mary, the mother of

Jesus. Let us be willing to lose all, to be made social outcasts. Let us be willing to give up all so that we might exalt Christ. Then we can join Mary in praise and say, "My soul exalts the Lord, and my spirit has rejoiced in God my Savior. For He has had regard for the humble state of His bondslave. . . . For the Mighty One has done great things for me; and holy is His name" (Luke 1:46–49).

Most of us in this lifetime won't be as fortunate as Isaiah who "saw the Lord sitting on a throne, lofty and exalted, with the train of His robe filling the temple" (Isaiah 6:1). However, we can say as Isaiah did, "O Lord, You are my God; I will exalt You, I will give thanks to Your name" (Isaiah 25:1).

We Can Join Hannah in Exalting the Lord in Times of Both Despair and Joy

In 1 Samuel 1 we find an example of another person who exalted the Lord. However, rather than exalting God though in a state of joy, as did Mary, or in awe as did Isaiah, Hannah exalted the Lord while in a state of despair. As you may recall, Hannah was married to a man with two wives. The other wife, Peninnah, had numerous children, while Hannah was barren. In addition, Peninnah intentionally provoked Hannah. What did Hannah do? How did she exalt the Lord? Rather than kicking and screaming or returning insult for insult, she went to the Lord in prayer. As she lifted her needs to Him, whom she recognized as exalted in power, Eli the priest mistook her intense despair and weeping as her being drunk. However, Hannah quickly explained, "I am a woman oppressed in spirit; I have drunk neither wine nor strong drink, but I have poured out my soul before the Lord" (1 Samuel 1:15). What an incredible witness of exalting God, of lifting Him up, even when in despair!

In the Bible the word "soul" refers to both life in general and specifically to one's mind, emotions, and will. When Hannah poured out her soul to the Lord, she wasn't saying rote meaningless words. She was "off the chart," pouring out all that was on her heart, mind, and soul until she was empty—empty of her human effort to get pregnant, empty of any resentment she might have, empty of trying to make things right.

Have you ever emptied your heart and soul to the Lord? Guess what can fill the emptiness? The Exalted God! As long as we are full of ourselves, we cannot exalt God. However, when we prayerfully pour out our souls to the Exalted Lord and empty ourselves of our agendas, wishes, resentments, and demands, He is able to fill us.

The Bible says that Hannah "went her way and ate, and her face was no longer sad" (1 Samuel 1:18). She left her prayer time a changed woman, although not one circumstance in her life was changed. She was not pregnant. She still had to face the other contentious wife. Yet she was transformed by pouring out her soul to the Lord whom she exalted in worship.

Although we are not privy to the words Hannah prayed in the temple when she poured out her soul to the Lord, we are privy to her prayer when Samuel was born. "My heart exults in the LORD; my horn is exalted in the LORD, . . . because I rejoice in Your salvation" (1 Samuel 2:1).

Is there something in your life you're not happy about or that causes you to be resentful? Why not do as Hannah did? Empty the burdens of your soul to the Exalted Lord and wait for Him to fill you.

Meditation Moment

God alone is the Exalted Lord. Moses, Nebuchadnezzar, Mary, Paul, Isaiah, Hannah, and multitudes of others throughout eternity have worshiped and lifted up His name. Will you join the throng of those who praise Him, exalting Him by your life and words?

Kneel *and* PRAY

Worship the Exalted Lord

P *Praise* the Lord who is exalted above the heavens, above all gods, and who forgives the lowly of spirit. _____

R *Repent* and confess ways you have exalted your house, business, family, money, social status, leisure, hobby, or yourself above God. _____

A *Ask* the Lord to forgive you. Ask Him to make you a person who exalts Him in both joys and trials. _____

Y *Yield* to the Exalted Lord. Give Him your ear and heart. Humble yourself in His presence. _____

CHAPTER 30

LORD, YOU ARE YAHWEH

WHEN I CAN'T GO ON, I LOOK TO YOU— THE ONE WHO WAS, IS, AND IS TO COME

God said to Moses, "I AM WHO I AM"; and He said, "Thus
you shall say to the sons of Israel, 'I AM has sent me to you.'"
God, furthermore, said to Moses . . . , "This is My name forever,
and this is My memorial-name to all generations."
EXODUS 3:14–15

Lord Jehovah, Yahweh, I praise Your holy name. You are the dynamic, self-existent Lord, who was, who is, and who is to come. Forgive me for not being more mindful of Your awesome grandeur. May my life be an offering to You, and may I live more faithfully in Your presence. In Christ's name I pray, amen.

God has a way of catching up with people in the most unexpected places, in the most unexpected ways. Who would think that God would care about a runaway convict and murderer? Yet God did and still does. Centuries ago God found Moses, a murderer and fugitive, in the desert. He spoke to him through a burning bush. More recently, God caught up to Brian Nichols, a fugitive murder suspect, and talked to him through the woman he held hostage as she read to him from Rick Warren's book *The Purpose-Driven Life.*

Whether through a book or a bush or some other means, Yahweh will find a way to get our attention and reveal Himself to us! Why? Because He cares for each of us.

YAHWEH IS THE SELF-EXISTENT LORD

Although we are not privy to the words Yahweh spoke to Brian Nichols's heart, Exodus 3 tells us Yahweh's words to Moses when He called him to lead the Israelites out of bondage: "Do not come near here; remove your sandals from your feet, for the place on which you are standing is holy ground" (v. 5). As an adopted heir of the Egyptian throne turned fugitive and shepherd, Moses's mind must have filled with guilt-ridden flashbacks of when he committed murder. Although Moses had buried the one he murdered, he had not been able to bury his deed. One can only wonder what fear gripped his heart as he faced Holy God!

"I am the God of your father," Yahweh continued (v. 6).

You knew my father? Moses must have wondered, as his ears, already aflame, burned intensely and the Lord's words seared his heart.

"I have surely seen the affliction of my people. . . . So I have come down to deliver them from the power of the Egyptians. . . . Come now, and I will send you to Pharaoh, so that you may bring My people, the sons of Israel, out of Egypt" (vv. 7–8, 10).

It made perfectly good sense. Joseph, an Israelite Egyptian prince, had been responsible for bringing the nation into Egypt. Now Moses, *another* Israelite Egyptian prince, would lead the nation out.

As his mind filled with the names of the Egyptian gods—Re, the Sun god; Hapi, the spirit of the Nile; Osiris, the giver of life—Moses could not help but ask God His name: "Behold, I am going to the sons of Israel. . . . Now they may say to me, 'What is His name?' What shall I say to them?" (v. 13).

God answered, "I AM WHO I AM. . . . Thus you shall say to the sons of Israel, 'I AM has sent me to you'" (v. 14).

God's awesome revelation to Moses was that He was not *a* god. He was *the* God, Yahweh.

Yahweh, or Jehovah, is the Hebrew name for God that emphasizes His dynamic and active self-existence. Yahweh is also the covenant name of

God, the name He used in relation to His redemptive promise to Israel. In verse 15, Yahweh told Moses, "Thus you shall say to the sons of Israel, 'The LORD, the God of your fathers, the God of Abraham, the God of Isaac, and the God of Jacob, has sent me to you.' This is My name forever, and this is My memorial-name to all generations."

When we call on Yahweh to save us, we join the eternal throng of those who trust in the self-existent God who was, who is, and who is to come; who has promised to redeem our lives from the pit and remove our sin as far as the east is from the west.[1]

YAHWEH IS INCOMPREHENSIBLE YET INVITES US TO KNOW HIM

Yăhovah, or Jehovah, is "the proper name of the one true God."[2] So distinguished is His name that rabbinical writings refer to Yahweh as "The Great and Terrible Name," "The Unutterable Name," "The Holy Name," and "The Name of Four Letters" (because from the Hebrew it is rendered YHVH). Recently I was researching a Jewish Web site and found blank spaces in the text. I assumed there had been an error, until I realized that every blank stood for the unwritten, unutterable name, Yahweh.

Could it be that due to our familiarity with the Lord, we have become irreverent and unappreciative of God's divine majesty and name? If we were told we could never again approach Yahweh's throne or call out to Him, would we rush humbly into His presence and drink richly of His majesty for one last time? Herbert Lockyer wrote of Yahweh's incomprehensible majesty:

He possesses essential life and permanent existence. No man is able to receive the whole revelation of His majesty at once. Only one part at a time can be comprehended yet such is sufficient to give great joy and satisfaction. This is why it was the special purpose of the Great High God, who is One, to reveal Himself to saints of old in the development of their spiritual life in different names and titles of His nature and purpose.[3]

235

The vastness of God is hard to conceive. Yet in the divine revelation of God's wholeness and individuality, we are blessed. If we truly love the Lord, Yahweh, and want to be transformed into the glory of His likeness, then let us purpose in our hearts to increasingly know Him.

YAHWEH IS *Jehovah-Jireh*, THE LORD WILL PROVIDE

Genesis 22 recounts the story of Yahweh's calling on Abraham to do something beyond his wildest thoughts: to sacrifice his only son, Isaac, through whom God's covenant promise was to be fulfilled. By human logic, what Yahweh required did not make sense. Abraham's absolute resolve and trust in Yahweh, however, led him to know God as *Jehovah-Jireh*, The Lord Will Provide:

> *The angel of the LORD called to him from heaven and said, "Abraham, Abraham!" And he said, "Here I am." He said, "Do not stretch out your hand against the lad, and do nothing to him; for now I know that you fear God, since you have not withheld your son, your only son, from Me." Then Abraham raised his eyes and looked, and behold, behind him a ram caught in the thicket by his horns; and Abraham went and took the ram and offered him up for a burnt offering in the place of his son. Abraham called the name of that place The LORD Will Provide, as it is said to this day, "In the mount of the LORD it will be provided."*
>
> GENESIS 22:11–14

Not only did Abraham experience the magnificent faithfulness of Yahweh; imagine what it must have been like for Isaac. As he was untied and watched the ram be sacrificed in his place, certainly his mind was seared with gratefulness, having seen firsthand The Lord Will Provide.

Are we experiencing Yahweh's daily provisions as we walk by faith into realms of obedience beyond our comfort zone? Are our children receiving the blessing of observing Yahweh provide in incredible ways?

When we refuse to go through difficult trials and tests, we—and others—miss the blessing of seeing Yahweh provide. Abraham thought he was a lone man in a lone wilderness doing a lone act. But he wasn't. We are still being blessed by his faith in Jehovah-Jireh. Neither are your acts of obedience or lack of obedience isolated incidents. When Yahweh calls on you to do something difficult, walk by faith. You never know who is watching or what provision or message Yahweh is sending through your obedience.

YAHWEH IS *Jehovah-Nissi*, THE LORD OUR BANNER

Moses built an altar and named it The LORD is My Banner.

EXODUS 17:15

Banners were used in ancient times to let soldiers know where their divisions were and, if the battle was going against them, as rallying points around which they would gather to regroup for another attack. If the person carrying the banner fell to the ground and the banner was not retrieved by another soldier and lifted up, it could cause great confusion among the troops and even cause them to lose the battle.[4]

In the battle the Israelites fought against Amalek, Moses stood on top of a hill and raised the staff of God for the Israelites to see. As long as Moses's hand was raised, Israel prevailed. However, when Moses got tired and let his hand down, Amalek prevailed. Therefore, Aaron and Hur found a stone on which Moses could sit. Then they stood with him, one on each side, and supported his hands. Israel won the battle, and Moses built an altar to the Lord, called *Jehovah-Nissi*, The Lord Our Banner.

What about you? Have you discovered that Yahweh is a rallying point and how important it is for you to keep His name lifted high? When a relative calls with a problem, do you lift God's name in prayer? Do you share prayer needs with a spouse or friend, rally under God's name, and fight in prayer? When your friend calls and shares, "We're thinking about getting a divorce. It's hopeless," do you rally under Jehovah-Nissi? Do you fight with your friend for their marriage under the banner of Yahweh, with your eyes fixed on Him? When temptations knock on your door, do you turn your eyes heavenward and fight for purity under The Lord Your Banner?

Yahweh, the self-existent God, is Jehovah-Nissi. Lift His name on high and rally under Him!

Yahweh Is *Jehovah-Raphi*, The Lord, The Physician

Bless the LORD, O my soul,
And all that is within me, bless His holy name.
Bless the LORD, O my soul,
And forget none of His benefits;
Who pardons all your iniquities,
Who heals all your diseases;
Who redeems your life from the pit,
Who crowns you with lovingkindness and compassion.

Psalm 103:1–4

Perhaps there is not a better definition of what it means to praise God than David's words, "Bless the LORD, O my soul, and all that is within me." Praise is not the act of moving our mouths in rhythm with music. It is worshiping God with all our soul, with everything that is in us. How do we obtain such focused concentration? David suggests blessing His holy name and remembering all Yahweh has done for us, including healing our diseases.

What does the divine revelation of Jehovah-Raphi mean to us? It means that when we have a sin-sick friend, we can call on Yahweh to heal that friend. It means that when a loved one or fellow church member is sick, we can go to the Great Physician in prayer. We can pray for God to give the attending physician His wisdom and skill. We can rally under Him and look up to Him for healing. We can take confidence that if our loved one is not healed in this lifetime, he or she will be healed by Jehovah-Raphi, the Great Physician, in the life to come.

YAHWEH IS *Jehovah-Rohi*, THE LORD MY SHEPHERD

The LORD is my Shepherd, I shall not want.

PSALM 23:1

Of all the ways we know Yahweh, perhaps *Jehovah-Rohi*, the Lord our Shepherd, is one of the most endearing. We say the Twenty-Third Psalm at church services, funerals, and at home. We find encouragement and hope, knowing that God shepherds our souls.

Whether we're in the throes of making major decisions at work, on the mission field sharing Christ, or at home tackling a busy day, Yahweh is a Shepherd who wants to lead, protect, and guide us. If you're at your wit's end with your children, you can kneel at Yahweh's footstool and ask Him to shepherd you in how to best discipline and encourage them. When you face a tough assignment, you can invite Jehovah-Rohi to shepherd you on the right path. When your energy is depleted or you've strayed off course, you can pray for Jehovah-Rohi to restore your soul and guide you in the path of righteousness. When you've gone over the hill financially, you can pray for Jehovah-Rohi to shepherd you in being a good steward of your finances.

You can trust Jehovah-Rohi to provide all you need, including the calm of His presence even in the face of enemies. At the end of your life, Jehovah-Rohi will be there. He will take your hand and shepherd you into eternity with Him forever.

YAHWEH IS *Jehovah-Shammah*, THE LORD IS THERE

Isaiah 63:7–9 is a beautiful passage praising *Jehovah-Shammah* for His lovingkindness, compassion, and presence with Israel. Verse 9 declares: "In all their affliction He was afflicted, And the angel of His presence saved them; In His love and in His mercy He redeemed them, And He lifted and carried them all the days of old."

The divine title Jehovah-Shammah reminds us of the Lord's presence and glory with Israel when He led them to the Promised Land. Jehovah-Shammah reminds us of Yahweh's presence with Jonah when he called to God from the belly of the great fish. Jehovah-Shammah was with Daniel in the lions' den and with Shadrach, Meshach, and Abednego in the fiery furnace.

Psalm 139 has been one of my favorite psalms since I was a teenager. Verses 7 through 12 comfort us that no matter where we are or what we face, Jehovah-Shammah is there.

Where can I go from Your Spirit?
Or where can I flee from Your presence?
If I ascend to heaven, You are there;
If I make my bed in Sheol, behold, You are there.
If I take the wings of the dawn,
If I dwell in the remotest part of the sea,
Even there Your hand will lead me,
And Your right hand will lay hold of me.

Whatever you're going through, Yahweh, Jehovah-Shammah, wants you to know He is there with you. He is with you in ICU. He is with you in the airplane. He is with you in your lonely house. He is there with you at work. Are you aware of His divine presence?

Yahweh is all that we need and more than we will ever be able to comprehend. In addition to the above revelations of His divine character, He reveals Himself as *Jehovah-Tsidkenu*, The Lord Our Righteousness; *Jehovah-M'Kaddesh*, The Lord Doth Sanctify; *Jehovah-Eloheka*, The Lord Your God; and *Jehovah-Hoseenu*, The Lord Our Maker.

Let us daily pray that He will transform us into believers who reflect the majesty of His divine character.

Meditation Moment

Yahweh is the self-existent God who reveals Himself as your Maker; the Lord of Hosts; the Majestic, Omnipotent God; your Shepherd, Healer, Provider, and Banner. Bow at His footstool!

Kneel *and* PRAY

Worship Yahweh, the Lord Jehovah

P *Praise* Yahweh, who was, who is, and who is to come. Worship Him for the fullness of His divinity and His profound love for you._____

_____

R *Repent* and confess ways you forget that Yahweh is there for you and you do not live in the glory of His divine attributes._____

_____

_____

A *Ask* Yahweh to help you live at all times and in all circumstances in relation to His divine nature as you reflect back on all He is. _____

_____

_____

Y *Yield* to the Lord Jehovah. Humble yourself in His presence. Discover the fullness of Yahweh's presence as you give Him your hand and walk in His power and glory. _____

_____

CHAPTER 31

Lord, You Are Zealous

When I Am Complacent,
You Remain Passionate

There will be no end to the increase of His government or of peace,
on the throne of David and over his kingdom, to establish it and
to uphold it with justice and righteousness from then on and
forevermore. The zeal of the LORD of hosts will accomplish this.
ISAIAH 9:7

Lord, You are a Zealous God who accomplishes justice, righteousness, and peace.
I praise You for Your zeal. Forgive my complacency about spiritual things, for not
more zealously joining You in Your work. Infuse me with Your zeal. Work through
me to accomplish Your purposes. I love You, Lord! In Jesus's name, amen.

Each year an International Snow and Ice Festival is held in Harbin, China.
Teams converge from all over the world to compete. With skill and zeal they
transform massive blocks of ice into beautiful sculptures. Visitors to the
show can walk on an ice-sculpted mock "Great Wall" or tour an entire ship
constructed of ice. After sunset, neon lights set within the sculptures make
them glow against the black sky.

If sculptors, envisioning the potential in common blocks of ice, zealously
work in freezing temperatures to transform blocks of ice into lighted works
of form and beauty, is it any wonder that God, who created us in His image,
works zealously to transform us into Christians who reflect His glory?

Ever since Adam, humans have been born with a sin nature, but God
has not left us to die in our sin. With passion in His eyes and fire in His

soul, He sent Jesus to earth to seek and to save us![1] God not only zealously "rescued us from the domain of darkness," He also zealously "transferred us to the kingdom of His beloved Son, in whom we have redemption, the forgiveness of sins" (Colossians 1:13–14).

Having rescued and transferred us to His kingdom, our glorious heavenly Father is both jealous and zealous for us. The Hebrew word for "zeal" is *qin'ah* and means "ardour, jealousy."[2] God jealously desires to carve away any lingering habits that reflect the kingdom of darkness from which He rescued us. He who created us zealously wants the light of His Spirit to shine brightly within our hearts. He wants our minds illumined with His wisdom. God, who sees what we can become, wants to take our frozen hearts and light them with His glory. He wants to take our icy emotions and make them burn with His passion. He wants to take our hardened spirits and sculpt us into believers aglow with His Spirit. God wants to form our lives into works of beauty that glorify Him.

What might God want to make out of your life? Don't allow your imagination to be limited by your view of yourself. Rather, imagine your life in light of God's divine zeal and the attributes that we've studied. Pray to God to sculpt you into a person who reflects His divine nature.

Pray to Be an Instrument of God's Zeal and a Light to Those in Darkness

The prophet Isaiah, during a dark time in the life of Israel, revealed a promise of coming hope: "The people who walk in darkness will see a great light" (Isaiah 9:2). He said their yoke of bondage would be broken, and he spoke of a day when there would be gladness and rejoicing.

How was all this to come about? Was the nation to "muster up" gladness or throw off oppression in their own strength? Hardly. Isaiah 9:7 states, "The zeal of the Lord of hosts will accomplish this."

What would the zeal of the Lord accomplish? He would send a Messiah. The source of Israel's hope and joy would be a child given to them by the Lord. The child would be called "Wonderful Counselor, Mighty God, Eternal Father, Prince of Peace" (Isaiah 9:6). This must have been incredibly good news to people living in darkness, under a heavy yoke of bondage.

Today people are walking in darkness, just as in Isaiah's day. People still need to hear the good news of Jesus Christ. Jesus has commissioned us to be His witnesses.[3] What are you doing to join God's zeal and to take the light of salvation to people?

PRAY TO THE LORD TO ZEALOUSLY WORK IN AND THROUGH YOU

The word "zeal" is first used in relation to God when He promised the nation of Judah that He would miraculously provide for them. Second Kings 19:31 states, "The zeal of the LORD will perform this." As He promised to revive their crops, He also promised to revive the nation through a remnant of people whom He would make fruitful and prosperous.

God's zeal is still intact. He desires to revive our nation. He can do so if a remnant of people will believe and join Him in His zeal.

Would you pray and ask God, who zealously worked on behalf of Judah, to work miraculously in you? Would you begin to agree with God and zealously pray: "Not by might, nor by power, but by Your Spirit" (Zechariah 4:6)?

PRAY TO LIVE IN READINESS FOR THE ZEALOUS LORD'S RETURN

Was the coming of the Messiah the final fulfillment of God's zeal? No. God showed Isaiah not only Christ's first coming, which is history to us, but also His second coming, which is future to us. What will happen when the Lord returns to earth? Isaiah 42:13 states: "The LORD will go forth like a warrior, He will arouse His zeal like a man of war. He will utter a shout, yes, He will raise a war cry. He will prevail against His enemies."

When will this take place? At the battle of Armageddon.[4]

The picture of the Lord returning to earth to do battle is an awesome sight. He wears a breastplate of righteousness. No enemy fire can pierce His holiness! He dons a helmet of salvation. Nothing is on His mind but the salvation and vindication of His saints! He is clothed in a mantle of zeal, a robe worn by men of rank. His spirit is aflame with fervor. Wrapped in zeal, He is in pursuit of His enemies.

God is zealous! He will bring salvation to the righteous. He will execute vengeance on the unrighteous.

Often we tend to think of the Lord in the context of His tenderly inviting little children into His arms. However, we are remiss if we overlook His role as a zealous God who will pour forth wrath and execute justice. Both the Old and New Testaments portray the Lord as being full of fervor, zealous to have people sanctify their hearts and bodies for His presence. Consider the similarities regarding the Lord's zeal as described in Ezekiel 38:18–23 and in John 2:13–17.

Ezekiel declares God's word:

"It will come about on that day, when Gog comes against the land of Israel, . . . that My fury will mount up in My anger. In My zeal and in My blazing wrath I declare that on that day there will surely be a great earthquake in the land of Israel. . . . All the men who are on the face of the earth will shake at My presence; the mountains also will be thrown down, the steep pathways will collapse and every wall will fall to the ground. . . . With pestilence and with blood I will enter into judgment with him; and I will rain on him and on his troops, and on the many people who are with him, a torrential rain, with hailstones, fire and brimstone. I will magnify Myself, sanctify Myself, and make Myself known in the sight of many nations; and they will know that I am the LORD."

Personally, I don't want to be around when that happens. I want to be in heaven praising God for redeeming me by the blood of the Lamb. I don't want to be in the company of scoffers who have renounced Christ. Where do you want to be when the Lord executes vengeance against His enemies?

Now consider the Lord's zeal in the New Testament:

The Passover of the Jews was near, and Jesus went up to Jerusalem. And He found in the temple those who were selling oxen and sheep and doves, and the money changers seated at their tables. And He made a scourge of cords, and drove them all out of the temple, with the sheep and the oxen; and He poured out the coins of the money changers and overturned their tables; and to those who were selling the doves He said, "Take these things away; stop making My Father's house a place of business." His disciples remembered that it was written, "Zeal for your house will consume Me."

JOHN 2:13–17

Would you have wanted to be taking money when Jesus made a whip and came toward your table? Had there been a *Jerusalem Post*, the headlines might have read, "Man Goes Berserk in Temple." Think about Jesus's zeal. He made a scourge, a whip. He overturned tables. He single-handedly drove out all the sheep and oxen. The Greek word for "zeal" is *zelos* and means "excitement of mind, fervour of spirit, pursuing."[5] Jesus was serious about cleansing His Father's house and making it a house of prayer. Jesus is serious about cleansing your body, which is His temple, and making it a house of prayer, where you and He meet![6]

If the Zealous Lord were to visit your heart today, what would He overturn? An attitude? What would He drive out? Would it be jealousy or envy, perhaps self-centeredness? Would He make a scourge and drive out your spiritual apathy and replace it with His passion for the lost? What business or busyness would Jesus drive out that is contrary to His presence and affects your communion with Him?

In Revelation 3:19, God says, "As many as I love, I rebuke and chasten: be zealous therefore, and repent." God is zealous. Therefore let us be zealous to repent of anything that hinders us from being people of prayer, aglow with His Spirit.

Meditation Moment

In God's zeal for you, He has rescued you from the domain of darkness and transferred you to the kingdom of His beloved Son. He remains both jealous for you and zealous for you. Are you joining Him in His zeal for others? Are you a house of prayer aglow with the light of His presence?

Kneel *and* PRAY

Worship the Zealous Lord

P *Praise* God for His zeal, for rescuing you from the kingdom of darkness and transferring you to the kingdom of His beloved Son, in whom you have redemption, the forgiveness of sins. _____

_____

_____

R *Repent* and confess any indifference or complacency you have in regard to the things for which God is zealous, including your personal purity, your heart's being a place of prayer, and your energies' being spent on behalf of those who still need to be transferred to His kingdom. _____

_____

_____

A *Ask* God to fill you with His Spirit and infuse you with His zeal. Pray for Him to use you as a light for those still in the domain of darkness. Pray that they will respond to the Zealous Lord and thereby escape the judgment of those who refuse His love. _____

_____

_____

Y *Yield* to the Zealous Lord's promptings. Where He sends you, go. What He prompts you to say, speak. Learn to listen to and love His voice as He zealously conforms you to His image and prepares you for the glories of heaven! _____

_____

ADDITIONAL RESOURCES

GROUP LEADER GUIDE

Thank you for your willingness to lead a discussion group.
I pray you will be blessed as you give your time to lead others.

HOW TO GET STARTED

I suggest that you make your first group meeting an introductory session. After opening in prayer, welcome the group by introducing yourself. Then ask members to introduce themselves and tell how they happened to come to the study. To make the most of your time together in the weeks ahead, you'll want to outline how your time together will be spent:

- Spend a few minutes reviewing "Ways to Use This Book," in the Introduction. Encourage members to use it for their individual spiritual development as well as in preparing for the group discussions.

- Be sure to clarify whether you will be covering more than one chapter or attribute in each session. Prepare the weekly schedule ahead of time, and hand it out so group members will know what's being covered if they must miss a meeting. Encourage regular attendance and emphasize the blessing of getting to know one another through Bible study.

- Review the format for "Delving-Deeper Study Questions" and the importance of preparing for each group session by completing the reading ahead of time. Point out that the first three questions in the A to Z chapters are designed to allow for discussion of how God is speaking to them through the Scriptures. Encourage them to note the verses or page numbers of points they find stimulating as they're reading, so they can easily refer back to them for discussion. Also encourage attendees to bring their Bibles so they can use them when referring to scriptures. The last question for each lesson, labeled *For deeper reflection*, prompts the members to read and comment on a verse about the particular attribute being discussed. Your group's desires and the time limits will dictate whether or not you discuss that question or, if you prefer, answer it in the place of another question.

- Be sure to allow time for group members to raise any questions they have.

- Close in prayer, asking God to bless your group as you pray with purpose and live with passion.

How to Keep Your Meetings on Track

What follows is a general format you may want to follow for both the discussion and the prayer time.

Welcome and Open in Prayer (2–5 minutes)

Welcome the group and open with a brief prayer. Model praying according to God's divine nature by incorporating the attributes of God that you have studied each week. For instance, if your group is reading five chapters a week, you might PRAY according to the following example:

Praise: Lord, You are Almighty, Beloved Son, Comforter, the Door to heaven, Eternal! We praise and worship Your holy name!

Repent: Forgive us for not turning to You in our weakness, for not rejoicing in Your love, for not resting in Your comfort, for not coming to You more often through the eternal door You have opened in prayer.

Ask: Help us look to You in our weakness, rest in Your love, be comforted by Your Spirit, come to You through the open door of prayer, and seek Your eternal will.

Yield: We yield our hearts and minds to You.

Lead the Discussion (20–40 minutes)

Begin the discussion by noting which of God's divine attributes is the topic of this week's study and reading the verse that appears at the start of the chapter. Then lead the group through the "Delving-Deeper Study Questions" that begin on page 255. The opening questions of each lesson are designed with a consistent format to encourage readers to continually apply what they learn to their own lives. The statements selected from the chapters are intended to generate meaningful discussion within the group, as well as to help members pause and absorb what they're reading rather than simply rushing through. The *For deeper reflection* question directs your group to turn to God's Word and dig out further insights. If necessary, remind the group to underline or star meaningful points as they read the chapters so they'll be prepared to participate in the discussion.

Lead Group in Prayer Using the PRAY Format (5–10 minutes)

Using the PRAY format for group prayer is an effective way to ensure that everyone has an opportunity to participate. Explain that you will lead the group through each of the elements of PRAY. Encourage members to join in with a word or sentence as you transition through each of the PRAY elements. Below are examples that demonstrate how the group might PRAY according to God's divine names. However, be flexible and allow the Holy Spirit to lead.

First, lead the group in a time of Praise. Example:
Lord, You are Almighty. (Leader)
The Beloved Son. (Group member)
Lord, You are the Comforter. (Group member)
The Door of Life. (Group member)
Eternal. (Group member)

Note: As you progress through the chapters, add to the prior weeks' attributes of God in your time of praise. Begin with A and go through the current week. By the end of the study, your group will have memorized and be praising God for His twenty-six A to Z divine attributes. Your group's praise will be a sweet aroma to the Lord. Again, allow the prayer time to be spontaneous, led by the Spirit.

Second, lead the group in a time of Repentance. Example:
Almighty: Forgive me for not turning to You in my weakness. (Leader)
Beloved Son: Forgive me for not loving others as You love me. (Group member)

The COMFORTER: Forgive me for not turning to You for comfort. (Group member)

The DOOR: Forgive me for not pointing others to You, the Door. (Group member)

ETERNAL: Forgive me for not keeping an eternal perspective and getting so caught up in the world. (Group member)

Third, lead the group in a time of ASKING. Example:

ALMIGHTY: Give me Your strength to meet each day's demands. (Leader)

BELOVED Son: Help me to love as You love. (Group member)

The COMFORTER: Help me turn to You for comfort rather than to other things. (Group member)

The DOOR: Use me today to point someone to You. (Group member)

ETERNAL: Help me keep my eyes on what's important for eternity and not get caught up in the unimportant things of this world. (Group member)

Finally, lead the group in a time of YIELDING.

Note: Your group may want to offer individual prayers or you may want to wrap up the time with a prayer for the group: "Lord, help us yield to You in all we do this week according to Your divine name. We yield our hearts to Your voice and our lives to Your promptings."

Delving-Deeper Study Questions

Chapter 1: Stop, Drop, and PRAY

1. What verse or point particularly stimulated your thoughts regarding stopping, dropping to your knees, and praying?

2. How could the technique of Stop, Drop, and PRAY help you in the midst of daily struggles and decisions?

3. What insight or application can you draw from these statements from chapter 1:

   a. Perhaps we lack passion for the things of God because we haven't yet captured the vision that Christ's abundant life is a promised reality.

   b. God would not give us the promise of a transformed life if it weren't possible.

   c. As we consider the needs of others and ourselves and then stop, drop, and PRAY, we discover that God is gloriously sufficient for every situation.

4. *For deeper reflection*: Read Philippians 2:13. How do you think God desires to work in you?

Chapter 2: Praise God

1. What verse or point particularly stimulated your thoughts regarding praising God?

2. How can praising God in the midst of daily struggles, decisions, and opportunities transform your countenance?

3. What insight or application can you draw from these statements from chapter 2:

   a. Praise does not mean pretending to be happy about an awful situation.

Rather, it means looking up at God in the midst of every situation and worshiping Him who sits enthroned on high, above the world, sovereign.

b. Praise is the spirit dancing in delight with the Lord. Praise is the soul choosing to boast in the Lord. Praise is a choice. Praise is a command.

c. I want to be like the leper who turned back! What about you?

4. *For deeper reflection*: Read Psalm 103:1–4. How might praising God, A to Z, effect a change in your countenance and even your life?

CHAPTER 3: REPENT *and* CONFESS SINS

1. What verse or point particularly stimulated your thoughts regarding repenting and confessing?

2. How does repenting affect your relationship with God in a positive way?

3. What insight or application can you draw from these statements from chapter 3:

a. Although "arrow prayers"—brief sentence prayers throughout the day—can be a valuable way of communing with God, there is something to be said for a set time to meet with God each day.

b. Sin creates tension between God and us, as well as between others and us.

c. Unconfessed sin is a joy breaker.

4. *For deeper reflection*: Read 2 Corinthians 7:10. Describe a time when you experienced God's cleansing and forgiveness through truly repenting—not just being sorry.

CHAPTER 4: ASK

1. What verse or point particularly stimulated your thoughts about asking God for your needs?

2. How does being able to ask God for your needs and the needs of others encourage you?

3. What insight or application can you draw from these statements from chapter 4:

a. Our greatest worries are not too great for God, and our smallest concerns are His.

b. Do you have a boatload of problems? Tie them to the end of your fishing line and cast them heavenward.

c. Asking God for our needs and interceding for others is an intelligent exercise of the mind expressed through the spirit to God.

4. *For deeper reflection*: Read Matthew 7:9–11 or Luke 11:11–13. Describe a time when God answered your prayers by giving you something good.

CHAPTER 5: YIELD—GIVE HIM YOUR HAND!

1. What verse or point particularly stimulated your thoughts regarding yielding to God?

2. How can you better yield to God in the midst of daily struggles, decisions, and opportunities?

3. What insight or application can you draw from these statements from chapter 5:

a. Although we may not often think of listening as a part of prayer, it is, in fact, a vital organ of our prayer life. In order to hear God speak, we must wait on Him.

b. An intimate relationship with Him involves tuning our hearts in the morning to listen to His voice "all the day."

c. Could it be that our prayers are often stagnant and our lives less than passionate because we don't take time to put up our spiritual antennae and listen to God's voice?

4. *For deeper reflection*: Read John 16:7. To what degree do you let the Holy Spirit, whom Jesus calls the Helper, help you? In what ways might you be more sensitive to His voice?

CHAPTER 6: LORD, YOU ARE ALMIGHTY

As Abraham walked with the Almighty, we are invited to walk in the shadow of His powerful hand.

1. What verse or point particularly stimulated your thoughts regarding Almighty God?

2. From what you have learned about the Almighty, how can you PRAY for yourself and others in the midst of daily struggles, decisions, and opportunities?

3. How does praying to the Almighty encourage you?

4. What insight or application can you draw from these statements from chapter 6:

    a. Mighty promises require mighty power; not fleshly, human power.

    b. The Almighty's promises are for us, yet they are not produced by us but in us through the Holy Spirit as we seek His power in prayer.

    c. Rather than being an impersonal God, the Almighty relates to us as a loving father who influences us for our good and who allows us to be tested so that we might discover His strength.

5. *For deeper reflection*: Read Genesis 22:1–3. When God called Abraham to do the most difficult thing imaginable—to sacrifice Isaac—Abraham did not rebel. Instead, he bowed his will at the altar of sacrifice. In what way has the Almighty called you to bow your will to Him? How is the Almighty divinely influencing your life?

Chapter 7: Lord, You Are *the* Beloved Son

God the Father and the Beloved Son love you.

1. What verse or point particularly stimulated your thoughts regarding the Beloved Son?

2. From what you have learned about God's love for you, how can you PRAY for yourself and others in the midst of daily struggles, decisions, and opportunities?

3. How does praying in relation to the Beloved Son's love encourage you?

4. What insight or application can you draw from these statements from chapter 7:

    a. Consider the care with which the Father formed His Beloved Son's tiny back, knowing that it would one day carry the weight of our sins at Golgotha.

    b. Where was His Father when Jesus endured scourging, almost to the point of death? Where was His Father when Jesus stumbled and fell under the weight of the cross? . . . The Father's love-filled eyes were looking at you and at me.

    c. Knowing that the Father and Beloved Son love us should cause us to pray and live differently than if we didn't have such assurance.

5. *For deeper reflection*: Read 1 John 4:7–13. How does this passage challenge you?

CHAPTER 8: LORD, YOU ARE *the* COMFORTER

The Comforter calls you to His side to encourage and teach you.

1. What verse or point particularly stimulated your thoughts regarding the Comforter?

2. From what you have learned about the Comforter, how can you PRAY for yourself and others in the midst of daily struggles, decisions, and opportunities?

3. How does praying to the Comforter encourage you?

4. What insight or application can you draw from these statements from chapter 8:

    a. The closer we stay to God in prayer and Bible study, the more fully we experience the warmth of His abiding presence.

    b. Just as curling up under a comforter and taking a nap revives us, resting in the comfort of God's Word revives us.

    c. God, our Comforter, doesn't leave us alone in our weaknesses. Rather, He invites us to His throne room where He comforts us with His presence, where the Holy Spirit helps us and even intercedes for us, according to the will of God.

5. *For deeper reflection*: Read 2 Corinthians 1:4. Explain how you have personally experienced God's comfort and how God has then used you to comfort others.

CHAPTER 9: LORD, YOU ARE *the* DOOR

Jesus is the Door to eternal and abundant life.

1. What verse or point particularly stimulated your thoughts regarding Jesus, the Door?

2. From what you have learned about Jesus's being the Door, how can you PRAY for yourself and others in the midst of daily struggles, decisions, and opportunities?

3. How does praying in relation to Jesus as the Door encourage you?

4. What insight or application can you draw from these statements from chapter 9:

    a. God doesn't lock us out of His presence. He loves us and opens the door to His presence through Jesus Christ.

    b. All nationalities and people are welcomed in heaven, but all must enter through the same Door: Jesus. He is a sure door—the only Door—that opens to the prize of God Himself!

    c. Keep the door of your heart open to God, as He keeps the door of His presence open to you.

5. *For deeper reflection*: Read John 10:9. What blessings have you experienced as a result of entering into eternal life through Christ, the Door?

Chapter 10: Lord, You Are Eternal

Eternal God invites you to dwell in Him and to pray ceaselessly.

1. What verse or point particularly stimulated your thoughts regarding Eternal God?

2. From what you have learned about Eternal God, how can you PRAY for yourself and others in the midst of daily struggles, decisions, and opportunities?

3. How does praying to the Eternal God encourage you?

4. What insight or application can you draw from these statements from chapter 10:

    a. The Eternal Lord does not explain Himself or our relationship to Him as a water spigot to be turned on and off, but as a wellspring of life, of living water flowing in and through us.

    b. Rather than living for that which will pass away, we are to passionately live by His power and Spirit for that which will last for eternity.

    c. Leave the faucet of prayer open.

5. *For deeper reflection*: Read Paul's words in 1 Timothy 1:15–17. How can you give honor and glory to the Eternal God?

Chapter 11: Lord, You Are Faithful

God is faithful in His love, compassion, and forgiveness.

1. What verse or point particularly stimulated your thoughts regarding Faithful God?

2. From what you have learned about Faithful God, how can you PRAY for your-self and others in the midst of daily struggles, decisions, and opportunities?

3. How does praying in relation to Faithful God encourage you?

4. What insight or application can you draw from these statements from chapter 11:

   a. God is Faithful and True. That is His name.

   b. Although people may break promises to us and we may fail to live up to our words, God is faithful to keep His covenant of salvation.

   c. As a fountain of living waters, God erupts not in anger but in mercy every time we ask for forgiveness, without fail.

5. *For deeper reflection*: Read Isaiah 25:1. How can you testify to the Lord's faithfulness, as Isaiah did?

CHAPTER 12: LORD, YOU ARE *the* GUARDIAN *of* MY SOUL

God, the Guardian of your soul, encircles and protects you in His love.

1. What verse or point particularly stimulated your thoughts regarding the Guardian of your soul?

2. From what you have learned about the Guardian of your soul, how can you PRAY for yourself and others in the midst of daily struggles, decisions, and opportunities?

3. How does praying in relation to the Guardian of your soul encourage you?

4. What insight or application can you draw from these statements from chapter 12:

   a. God, as our faithful Guardian, offers protection from our sins, encircles and protects us, goes behind and before us, and guards our hearts and minds.

   b. God is a mighty warrior on our behalf, guarding and protecting us as the pupil of His eye.

   c. God is a rear guard, but guess whose rear He is guarding? God is guard-ing the rear of the one who is following Him!

5. *For deeper reflection*: Read Deuteronomy 32:10. Describe ways in which God has guarded you and encircled you with His love.

Chapter 13: Lord, You Are Holy

God is holy and has set Christians apart to enjoy and reflect His holiness.

1. What verse or point particularly stimulated your thoughts regarding Holy God?

2. From what you have learned about Holy God, how can you PRAY for yourself and others in the midst of daily struggles, decisions, and opportunities?

3. How does praying in relation to Holy God encourage you?

4. What insight or application can you draw from these statements from chapter 13:

    a. That which is common—you, me, our thoughts, words, deeds, ministries, businesses, leisure, and relationships—is transformed from common to holy by the presence of Holy God.

    b. We have the privilege of being used by God for His holy purposes.

    c. What does Holy God want you to realize is not yours but His? Your tongue? Your mind? Your home? Perhaps your children? Might it be your finances or time?

5. *For deeper reflection*: Read Isaiah 6:1–8. What response does contemplating God's holiness evoke in you? In what ways have you responded to Holy God's question, "Whom shall I send, and who will go for Us?" How are you serving Holy God in your generation?

Chapter 14: Lord, You Are Immanuel

The Lord, Immanuel, is an ever-present help in time of need.

1. What verse or point particularly stimulated your thoughts regarding Immanuel?

2. From what you have learned about Immanuel, how can you PRAY for yourself and others in the midst of daily struggles, decisions, and opportunities?

3. How does praying to Immanuel encourage you?

4. What insight or application can you draw from these statements from chapter 14:

    a. We can look to Immanuel, God with us, in any situation and experience the blessing of His presence.

b. The God who created us planned that we live in a dynamic, interactive relationship with Him.

c. Jesus paints a portrait of the Holy Spirit smack dab in the middle of our souls! Could we ask for the Lord Immanuel to be any more present?

5. *For deeper reflection*: Read Matthew 28:20. Tell how you have experienced Immanuel's presence with you.

CHAPTER 15: LORD, YOU ARE JUST

God is just in all His ways.

1. What verse or point particularly stimulated your thoughts regarding our Just God?

2. From what you have learned about God, who is Just, how can you PRAY for yourself and others in the midst of daily struggles, decisions, and opportunities?

3. How does praying to our Just God encourage you?

4. What insight or application can you draw from these statements from chapter 15:

a. Some people think that God is sitting back, not paying attention when injustice is done in our courts, in our homes, businesses, and relationships. However, God neither slumbers nor sleeps.

b. Have we, like Nebuchadnezzar, forgotten that the sovereign Lord has entrusted to us all that we possess and it is to be used for His glory?

c. We, who were rebellious toward God and unable to keep His righteous law, were doomed in our sin. He would have been just had He abandoned our souls to hell. But God, being rich in mercy, went beyond being reasonably just to being aboundingly just.

5. *For deeper reflection*: Read Zechariah 9:9. How does the fact that God is Just, that He came once and is coming again, affect your relationship to Him and others?

CHAPTER 16: LORD, YOU ARE *the* KING *of* KINGS

God is the King of kings, the King above all gods, the King of glory, the King who rescued you from the domain of darkness and transferred you to His kingdom of light.

1. What verse or point particularly stimulated your thoughts regarding the King of kings?

2. From what you have learned about the King of kings, how can you PRAY for yourself and others in the midst of daily struggles, decisions, and opportunities?

3. How does praying to the King of kings encourage you?

4. What insight or application can you draw from these statements from chapter 16:

   a. We can pray great big prayers because we have a great big King, who is large in magnitude, whose extent is all-reaching.

   b. Our gods are the things to which we give ourselves, the things that control us and have power over us.

   c. While I used to rebel at the thought of being anyone's servant, I have come to understand that we all serve someone or something, even if it is ourselves.

5. *For deeper reflection*: Read Psalm 95:2–6. How do these verses inspire you to live in light of your King?

CHAPTER 17: LORD, YOU ARE LIGHT

God is the Father of Lights. Christ is the Light of the world. God invites us to walk in His light and let our light shine before people.

1. What verse or point particularly stimulated your thoughts regarding the Light of the world?

2. From what you have learned of Jesus as the Light of the world, how can you PRAY for yourself and others in the midst of daily struggles, decisions, and opportunities?

3. How does praying to Jesus as the Light of the world encourage you?

4. What insight or application can you draw from these statements from chapter 17:

   a. There is little need for God to generate spiritual light and power in the one who doesn't intend to use it but instead walks in the flesh.

   b. If you are a Christian, regularly spending time in God's presence is the means by which He will illumine you.

    c. Our lives have greater meaning and purpose when we understand that God has made us to be His lights on earth.

5. *For deeper reflection*: Read Matthew 5:14–16. Consider the people you know who are sources of Christ's light; in what ways does His light shine through them? In what way or place might the Light of the world be calling you to shed His light?

Chapter 18: Lord, You Are Majestic

God is Majestic in holiness, power, and wonders.

1. What verse or point particularly stimulated your thoughts regarding Majestic God?

2. From what you have learned about Majestic God, how can you PRAY for yourself and others in the midst of daily struggles, decisions, and opportunities?

3. How does praying to the Majestic Lord encourage you?

4. What insight or application can you draw from these statements from chapter 18:

    a. God is majestic in holiness and able to work wonders in our homes, lives, relationships, and areas of service.

    b. One voice that is like no other and to which we can learn to be attuned is the Lord's voice.

    c. We can pray for the filling of the Holy Spirit to gurgle and flow through us.

5. *For deeper reflection*: Read Psalm 8:1, 3–9. How does going outside to look up at the stars and praise God, as David does, inspire and encourage you?

Chapter 19: Lord, You Are *the* God *of* New Life

The God of New Life gives us new spirits and new hearts by which we become new creations.

1. What verse or point particularly stimulated your thoughts regarding Christ, the God of New Life?

2. From what you have learned about the God of New Life, how can you

PRAY for yourself and others in the midst of daily struggles, decisions, and opportunities?

3. How does praying to the God of New Life encourage you?

4. What insight or application can you draw from these statements from chapter 19:

   a. A new heart and new spirit create new energy, new desires, new tastes, and new hope.

   b. We serve the body of Christ not because we have to but because He has gifted us to do so and it is where we find our greatest joy.

   c. If we wait until heaven to put on our new self, we'll miss the joy of the Spirit-filled life today.

5. *For deeper reflection*: Read Ephesians 4:20–24. What difference does it make in your life when you lay aside the old self and put on the new self?

Chapter 20: Lord, You Are *the* Overcomer

God is the Overcomer who has triumphed over the world, darkness, evil, sin, and tribulation.

1. What verse or point particularly stimulated your thoughts regarding the Overcomer?

2. From what you have learned about the Overcomer, how can you PRAY for yourself and others in the midst of daily struggles, decisions, and opportunities?

3. How does praying to the Overcomer encourage you?

4. What insight or application can you draw from these statements from chapter 20:

   a. Where do problems, temptations, and enemies come from? Whether they originate with others or with us, Jesus puts them under the umbrella of the "world." And He tells us He has overcome the world.

   b. The God to whom we pray makes black-and-white statements in a "gray" world that resists absolutes.

   c. Living in the world but not being *of* it—holding different values and serving a different Master—affects our relationship with the world.

5. *For deeper reflection*: Read John 16:33. Share your testimony of how, through Christ, you have overcome a difficult situation or sin.

CHAPTER 21: LORD, YOU ARE *the* POTTER

God is the master Potter who molds our lives to be vessels of honor, serving His purposes.

1. What verse or point particularly stimulated your thoughts regarding the Potter?

2. From what you have learned about the Potter, how can you PRAY for yourself and others in the midst of daily struggles, decisions, and opportunities?

3. How does praying to the Potter encourage you?

4. What insight or application can you draw from these statements from chapter 21:

   a. We are not our own. We have been created by God, for God.

   b. Clay is only valuable in the potter's hand when it is pliable to the potter's touch.

   c. We are hypocrites if we say, "Lord, You are my Potter," but we are always climbing off the Potter's wheel!

5. *For deeper reflection*: Read 2 Corinthians 4:7–10. What does it mean to you that you carry in your body (earthen vessel) the glorious treasure and power of the gospel of Christ? How can you testify to not being destroyed, although you have been afflicted?

CHAPTER 22: LORD, YOU ARE *the* QUICKENING SPIRIT

God is the Quickening Spirit who prompts us to obey and do His will.

1. What verse or point particularly stimulated your thoughts regarding the Quickening Spirit?

2. From what you have learned about the Quickening Spirit, how can you PRAY for yourself and others in the midst of daily struggles, decisions, and opportunities?

3. How does praying to the Quickening Spirit encourage you?

4. What insight or application can you draw from these statements from chapter 22:

    a. If our walk with God is dull, boring, or inactive, if He is not using us to impact others for His kingdom, we need to consider why.

    b. We must not ignore the importance of quieting our hearts before God, waiting on Him, listening for His urgings and promptings, and then obeying when He quickens us to act.

    c. How can we pray in relation to the Quickening Spirit? We can pray that God's Spirit will quicken us through the Bible to know and do His will.

5. *For deeper reflection*: Read Acts 8:29–30. Describe an occasion when the Quickening Spirit prompted you. What was the result? Which better describes your past response to the Quickening Spirit: a heel dragger or a runner for God? What is your prayer regarding your future response to the Quickening Spirit?

Chapter 23: Lord, You Are Righteous

The Lord, who is Righteous, takes away our sin, gives us His righteousness, and holds us tightly when our feet slip.

1. What verse or point particularly stimulated your thoughts regarding the Righteous God?

2. From what you have learned about Righteous God, how can you PRAY for yourself and others in the midst of daily struggles, decisions, and opportunities?

3. How does praying to Righteous God encourage you?

4. What insight or application can you draw from these statements from chapter 23:

    a. We can almost hear our Savior whisper, "Take My identity and righteousness. I'll take your sin and punishment."

    b. Can you remember a time when you were living in sin but the Lord your Righteousness kept nudging you to stop and turn back to Him? . . . The Lord holds on to us because He has a plan for our lives.

    c. When we feel drained, dry, or empty—for whatever reason—our souls crave a fresh drink of the Holy Spirit, whether we realize it or not.

5. *For deeper reflection*: Read Jeremiah 20:12. In what ways are you learning to depend on God's righteousness in areas where you have previously failed His tests?

Chapter 24: Lord, You Are a Shield about Me

God is a Shield, who covers us with His presence, protects us from enemy attacks, and lifts our heads in the midst of battle.

1. What verse or point particularly stimulated your thoughts regarding the Lord's being a Shield about you?

2. From what you have learned about our Shield, how can you PRAY for yourself and others in the midst of daily struggles, decisions, and opportunities?

3. How does praying in relation to the Lord as your Shield encourage you?

4. What insight or application can you draw from these statements from chapter 24:

   a. Although your efforts may be well intentioned, any shield other than the Lord will fail to protect the mind, emotions, and heart of you or your loved ones.

   b. Faith is a shield. It won't prevent the evil one from attacking us, but it will keep him from destroying us.

   c. If your shield of faith is down, God advises you to take it and hold it up. How can you hold it up? May I suggest taking "up" your Bible? Read it and take God "up" on His Word.

5. *For deeper reflection*: Read Ephesians 6:16. How has God shielded you from the evil one?

Chapter 25: Lord, You Are a Tower

God is a tower of salvation and deliverance, a Strong Tower to whom we can turn, a Watchtower who guards our souls, and a High Tower to whom we can run.

1. What verse or point particularly stimulated your thoughts regarding the Lord as a Tower?

2. From what you have learned about our Tower, how can you PRAY for yourself

and others in the midst of daily struggles, decisions, and opportunities?

3. How does praying to God as your Tower encourage you?

4. What insight or application can you draw from these statements from chapter 25:

   a. His [Satan's] strategy is cold war with cold Christians but all-out attacks on fervent Christians.

   b. Just knowing that a tower exists is not enough. We need to be *in* a tower to be protected by it.

   c. Are we trusting in self-made or man-made towers: towers of success, towers of money, towers of pleasure, or towers of worldly achievement?

5. *For deeper reflection*: Read Proverbs 18:10. How have you discovered God's name to be a strong Tower to which you can run? How does praising God's name, A to Z, affect your life?

Chapter 26: Lord, You Are *the* One Who Upholds Me

The Lord upholds us with His righteous right hand.

1. What verse or point particularly stimulated your thoughts regarding God Who Upholds?

2. From what you have learned about God Who Upholds, how can you PRAY for yourself and others in the midst of daily struggles, decisions, and opportunities?

3. How does praying to God as the One Who Upholds encourage you?

4. What insight or application can you draw from these statements from chapter 26:

   a. Are you clinging to God? When you are emotionally down, spiritually discouraged, mentally challenged, or financially bankrupt, do you pray to the only One who can uphold you?

   b. When sin or the war between good and evil gets us down, we can look up. We can praise God who is sitting on the throne and who will uphold His kingdom and us for eternity.

   c. What a beautiful picture God gives us: walking side by side with God, His arm around us, upholding us with His right hand!

5. *For deeper reflection*: Read Psalm 63:8. How have you experienced God upholding you?

Chapter 27: Lord, You Are *the* Vinedresser

God is the Vinedresser who has grafted us into Christ, who tends to our souls, and who feeds, waters, and prunes us so that we can bear the fragrant fruit of His Spirit.

1. What verse or point particularly stimulated your thoughts regarding the Vinedresser?

2. From what you have learned about the Vinedresser, how can you PRAY for yourself and others in the midst of daily struggles, decisions, and opportunities?

3. How does praying to the Vinedresser encourage you?

4. What insight or application can you draw from these statements from chapter 27:

   a. As a believer, grafted into the root and branch of David, you have Christ's seed in you. You are able to grow and bear much fruit for God.

   b. Do you have a prayer garden?

   c. Our spirit is the place where our Vinedresser meets with us in prayer and checks to see if we're bearing fruit for Him.

5. *For deeper reflection*: Read John 15:4. In what ways are you taking seriously the Vinedresser's instruction to abide in Him and bear much fruit?

Chapter 28: Lord, You Are Wonderful

Wonderful God wants to work in extraordinary wonder-working ways in our lives and in the lives of those for whom we pray.

1. What verse or point particularly stimulated your thoughts regarding Wonderful God?

2. From what you have learned about our wonderful God, how can you PRAY for yourself and others in the midst of daily struggles, decisions, and opportunities?

3. How does praying to Wonderful God encourage you?

4. What insight or application can you draw from these statements from chapter 28:

   a. When we ask God in faith for that which is extraordinary, we have the opportunity to experience His wonder-working power!

b. This is the object of our being vessels of God: not that we do the ordinary but that we do the extraordinary and glorify God in heaven.

c. In speaking of God's wonders, we encourage others to seek our Wonderful Lord!

5. *For deeper reflection*: Read Psalm 105:2–3. List all God's wonders you can think of, from the rising of the sun to how Wonderful God is working in your life. What effect does it have when you speak of God's wonders?

CHAPTER 29: LORD, YOU ARE eXALTED

The Lord is exalted above the heavens, above all gods, and above all kingdoms.

1. What verse or point particularly stimulated your thoughts regarding the exalted God?

2. From what you have learned about the exalted God, how can you PRAY for yourself and others in the midst of daily struggles, decisions, and opportunities?

3. How does praying to the exalted God encourage you?

4. What insight or application can you draw from these statements from chapter 29:

a. We need to ask ourselves who or what we exalt on a day-to-day basis.

b. Often we look for great things we can do for God, but in reality the truest greatness is that which He does in us.

c. As long as we are full of ourselves, we cannot exalt God.

5. *For deeper reflection*: Read Daniel 4:37. Perhaps you, like Nebuchadnezzar, have had a mighty fall but now desire to exalt God in your life. Give praise to the Exalted Lord by describing how far He has brought you in your Christian walk.

CHAPTER 30: LORD, YOU ARE YAHWEH

Yahweh is the self-existent God who reveals Himself as our Maker; the Lord of Hosts; the Majestic, Omnipotent God; our Shepherd, Healer, Provider, and Banner.

1. What verse or point particularly stimulated your thoughts regarding Yahweh?

2. From what you have learned about Yahweh, how can you PRAY for yourself and others in the midst of daily struggles, decisions, and opportunities?

3. How does praying to Yahweh encourage you?

4. What insight or application can you draw from these statements from chapter 30:

   a. Yahweh, or Jehovah, is the Hebrew name for God that emphasizes His dynamic and active self-existence.

   b. When Yahweh calls on you to do something difficult, walk by faith. You never know who is watching or what provision or message Yahweh is sending through your obedience.

   c. Praise is not the act of moving our mouths in rhythm with music. It is worshiping God with all our souls, with everything that is in us.

5. *For deeper reflection*: Read aloud the verse that describes the name of Yahweh you find most meaningful.

CHAPTER 31: LORD, YOU ARE ZEALOUS

God is both jealous for us and zealous for us.

1. What verse or point particularly stimulated your thoughts regarding Zealous God?

2. From what you have learned about our Zealous God, how can you PRAY for yourself and others in the midst of daily struggles, decisions, and opportunities?

3. How does praying to the Zealous God encourage you?

4. What insight or application can you draw from these statements from chapter 31:

   a. God, who sees what we can become, wants to take our frozen hearts and light them with His glory. He wants to take our icy emotions and make them burn with His passion. He wants to take our hardened spirits and sculpt us into believers aglow with His Spirit.

   b. Jesus has commissioned us to be His witnesses. What are you doing to join God's zeal and to take the light of salvation to people?

   c. If the Zealous Lord were to visit your heart today, what would He over-turn? . . . What would He drive out?

5. *For deeper reflection:* Read Revelation 3:19. How has the Zealous Lord shown His love for you by calling you to repentance? How does recognizing the power of His name enable you to pray with purpose and live with passion?

Sample Prayer

Lord, You Are Almighty

Worship the Almighty God.

P *Praise* the Almighty, most powerful God, who produces fruit in barrenness, provides shelter and shade, judges and reigns in righteousness, and as a loving Father influences you for His divine purposes.

> *Lord, You are the Almighty God, awesome in wonders, mighty in deeds! I worship, adore, and praise You for Your mighty hand that raised Jesus from the dead and gives me strength for each day.*

R *Repent* of any ways in which you seek to live in your own strength rather than relying on the Almighty. Confess if your heart is hardened and you don't give your ear to the Almighty's voice and influence.

> *Almighty God, I confess that too often I do not look to You for strength. I do not walk in the power of Your might. Forgive me.*

A *Ask* the Almighty to fill you with His Spirit so that you might live by His divine power and influence. Pray for others to come under the Almighty's divine influence and for the unsaved to turn to the Almighty for the forgiveness of their sins.

> *Lord, fill me with Your Spirit. Help me walk in the strength of Your might today. Prompt the unsaved to look to You, the Almighty God!*

Y *Yield* to the Almighty who wants to influence your heart and life so that you might know His joy. Pray to be increasingly sensitive to His sway. Purposefully listen to His voice in the quiet of prayer.

> *Lord, You are Almighty. I yield my thoughts, words, and heart to You. Empower me to live in a way that pleases You. In Jesus's name, amen.*

At-a-Glance A–Z Reference Chart

Lord, You Are...	Praise	Repent	Ask	Yield
Almighty	Lord, You are almighty, strong, and powerful.	Forgive me for walking in weakness.	Fill me with Your power.	I give You my hand and heart.
Beloved Son	You are the Beloved Son. Your love is as high as the heavens.	Forgive me for not responding to You in greater love.	Fill me with Your love.	Show me how to love others in Your name.
The Comforter	I praise You, the Comforter. Your Spirit blankets me with Your presence!	Forgive me for shoving You aside.	Help me be sensitive to Your ever-present encouragement.	Take my hand and lead me. Tune my ear to You.
The Door	You are the Door. You open the way to heaven and abundant life.	Forgive me for not living in the halls of Your abundance.	Teach me to come to You for all things, in all situations.	Lead me to greater intimacy with You.
Eternal	I praise You, Eternal Lord, who was, who is, and who is to come.	Forgive me for not living in light of eternity!	Train me to set my mind on eternity and You.	Prompt me to speak to others of eternity.
Faithful	Lord, You are faithful in Your love, forgiveness, and protection of me.	Forgive me for being unfaithful to You, for walking in my flesh.	Tune my heart to be ever faithful to You.	Teach me to faithfully follow Your voice.

LORD, YOU ARE . . .	PRAISE	REPENT	ASK	YIELD
GUARDIAN OF MY SOUL	Lord, You are the Guardian of my soul. You guard my going out and coming in.	Forgive me when I stray from Your presence.	Encircle me with Your love and protection today!	Train me to walk in Your ways.
HOLY	Lord, You are holy. There is none like You!	Forgive me for being unholy, for . . .	Fill me with Your Holy Spirit.	Lead me in Your holy ways.
IMMANUEL	I praise You, Immanuel, the ever-present One!	Forgive me when I forget You are present within me and I sin.	Help me be aware of You and share Your love with others.	I give You my heart and hand. Lead me by Your Spirit!
JUST	Lord, I praise You. You are just in all Your ways!	Forgive my anger and my desire to take vengeance.	Teach me to forgive and trust vengeance to You.	Teach me to be sensitive to Your justice and ways.
KING OF KINGS	Lord, You are King of kings, the King above all kings.	Forgive me for rebelling against Your reign in my life.	Please sit on the throne of my heart.	Help me yield to the touch of Your voice, my King!
LIGHT	Lord, You are Light. In You there is no darkness!	Forgive me when I do not walk in Your light.	Enlighten my mind to understand Your ways and truths.	Teach me to walk in Your light.
MAJESTIC	Lord, You are majestic. Your wonders abound!	Forgive me for looking at the drab.	Teach me to look up and see You, to marvel in Your wonders.	Help me be sensitive to You and Your majestic ways.

Lord, You Are . . .	Praise	Repent	Ask	Yield
New Life	Lord, You are the source of new life. You give new beginnings and new starts.	Forgive me when I walk in my old ways.	Fill me with Your Spirit so that I walk in newness of life.	Prompt me to walk in newness of life by Your Spirit.
the Overcomer	Lord, You are the Overcomer, who overcomes all by the power of Your life.	Forgive me for sinning rather than overcoming in You.	Help me overcome _____ in Your strength.	I yield my heart and will to You.
the Potter	Lord, You are the Potter. You mold and form me to do Your will.	Forgive me for not being soft and pliable in Your hands.	Mold me and make me a person who brings glory to You.	Teach me to respond to Your touch as You mold me.
the Quickening Spirit	I praise You, the Quickening Spirit. You quicken and enliven me to do Your will.	Forgive me when I ignore You or am dull to Your quickening.	Train me to be sensitive to Your quickening touch.	Help me be obedient to Your quickening Spirit.
Righteous	Lord, there is none righteous but You! I praise Your holy name.	Forgive me for my sin of _____.	Help me hate sin and love righteousness.	I yield my body to You. Fill me with Your righteousness.
a Shield	Lord, You are a shield about me!	Forgive me when I put You down.	Shield my mind and heart in Christ Jesus as I follow Your Word.	Train me to lift You up when sin and doubt assail me.
a Tower	Lord, You are a strong tower to whom I can run!	Forgive me when I stay in sin rather than run to You.	Protect me from evil. Teach me to run to You with my thoughts.	I give You my heart to protect, my mind to tower above.

LORD, YOU ARE . . .	PRAISE	REPENT	ASK	YIELD
ONE WHO UPHOLDS	Lord, You uphold Your kingdom and me with Your righteous right hand.	Forgive me when I don't trust in and cling to You.	Uphold me today as I face _____.	Help me walk ever sensitive to Your upholding hand.
THE VINEDRESSER	I praise You, God. You are a caring and attentive vinedresser.	Forgive me when I refuse Your pruning and do not bear fruit.	Prune my sin! Grow in my heart so I bear much fruit for You!	I open the gate of my heart to You. Flow in me!
WONDERFUL	Lord, You are wonderful and do works of wonder!	Forgive me for not being mindful of Your wonders.	Train me to set my mind on Your wonders.	Lead me to walk in Your wonders by Your Spirit.
eXALTED	Lord, You alone are exalted, high, and lifted up! I praise Your name!	Forgive me for not praising and exalting You more in my life!	Receive my praise, O Lord. You alone are worthy to be praised!	I yield to Your exalted ways instead of mine.
YAHWEH	Lord, You are Yahweh, Jehovah Lord God, the self-existent I AM!	Forgive me when I live for myself rather than for You, Lord!	Help me be mindful of the privilege of existing for You.	Lead me in ways so that my existence can bring glory to You.
ZEALOUS	Lord, You are Zealous! Your zeal reaches from the heavens to my heart.	Forgive me for hardening my heart against Your zeal.	Zealously work in my life so that I am a faithful servant.	Take and zealously lead me—body, mind, soul, and spirit!

✦ NOTES ✦

INTRODUCTION

1. Deuteronomy 4:24; Hebrews 12:29.
2. Genesis 15:17.
3. Exodus 3:2.
4. Exodus 13:21–22
5. 1 Kings 18:28.
6. Luke 24:32.
7. Acts 2:3.
8. Acts 1:4–5, 14, 16.
9. Debbie Williams, *Prayers of My Heart* (West Monroe, La.: Howard Publishing, 2004).

CHAPTER 1: STOP, DROP, *and* PRAY

1. Psalm 44:21; Hebrews 4:13.
2. 1 Corinthians 10:13.
3. Matthew 26:39, 42–43.

CHAPTER 2: PRAISE GOD

1. James Strong, *The Exhaustive Concordance of the Bible: Showing Every Word of the Text of the Common English Version of the Canonical Books, and Every Occurrence of Each Word in Regular Order,* electronic ed. (Ontario: Woodside Bible Fellowship, 1996), H1984.
2. Strong, *Exhaustive Concordance,* G134.
3. Gary Hill, ed., *The Discovery Bible, New American Standard New Testament Reference Edition* (Chicago: Moody Press, 1987), xv, 509, and Key to Discovery Symbols (inside back cover).
4. Strong, *Exhaustive Concordance,* G5214.
5. Strong, *Exhaustive Concordance,* G1392.
6. Matthew 6:9.
7. Matthew 14:19.
8. John 11:41.
9. Matthew 26:30.

CHAPTER 3: REPENT *and* CONFESS SINS

1. 2 Corinthians 2:14–15.
2. Matthew 5:21–22, 27–28.

3. See also Psalm 66:18, Proverbs 15:29, and Micah 3:4.
4. Strong, *Exhaustive Concordance*, G3670.
5. Galatians 5:16.
6. 2 Corinthians 5:21.
7. 2 Corinthians 5:19.
8. John 17:23.

CHAPTER 4: ASK

1. Famous Quotes Web site, http://home.att.net/~quotations/christian.html.
2. Copyright © 2005 Debbie Williams.
3. Famous Quotes Web site, http://home.att.net/~quotations/christian.html.

CHAPTER 5: YIELD

1. Strong, *Exhaustive Concordance*, H5414.
2. Strong, *Exhaustive Concordance*, H3027.
3. Matthew Henry, *Matthew Henry's Commentary on the Whole Bible: Complete and Unabridged in One Volume* (Peabody, Mass: Hendrickson, 1991), 2 Chronicles 30 [1].

CHAPTER 6: LORD, YOU ARE ALMIGHTY

1. Strong, *Exhaustive Concordance*, H8549.
2. John F. Walvoord, Roy B. Zuck, and Dallas Theological Seminary, *The Bible Knowledge Commentary: An Exposition of the Scriptures,* electronic ed. (Wheaton, Ill: Victor Books, 1983–c1985).
3. Strong, *Exhaustive Concordance*, G3841.
4. Ephesians 3:16, 20.
5. Genesis 15:5.
6. 2 Corinthians 4:7; Colossians 1:10–11.
7. Zechariah 4:6.
8. 2 Corinthians 12:9.
9. Romans 4:21; Philippians 4:19.
10. Romans 4:19–20.
11. Strong, *Exhaustive Concordance*, H3427.
12. Genesis 17:1.
13. John 15:4.
14. Strong, *Exhaustive Concordance*, G3841.
15. Matthew 26:39.
16. Mark 1:35.
17. Luke 6:12–13.
18. Matthew 26:40–42.
19. Ephesians 6:12, 18.

Chapter 7: Lord, You Are *the* Beloved Son

1. Strong, *Exhaustive Concordance*, G27.
2. Hebrews 4:16.
3. 1 John 4:11.
4. Galatians 5:22.
5. Galatians 3:26; 4:4–7.

Chapter 8: Lord, You Are *the* Comforter

1. Strong, *Exhaustive Concordance*, G3870.
2. Genesis 8:21.
3. James 4:8.

Chapter 9: Lord, You Are *the* Door

1. Strong, *Exhaustive Concordance*, G2374.
2. Exodus 12.

Chapter 10: Lord, You Are Eternal

1. Acts 26:9–20.
2. Deuteronomy 33:27.
3. Strong, *Exhaustive Concordance*, H5703.
4. Strong, *Exhaustive Concordance*, G166.
5. Romans 1:20; 1 Peter 5:10.
6. Deuteronomy 33:27.
7. John 7:37–38.
8. Ephesians 3:11–12.
9. 2 Thessalonians 2:16.
10. John 4:36.
11. 1 Corinthians 3:14.
12. Matthew 7:7–8.
13. Brother Lawrence of the Resurrection, *The Practice of the Presence of God*, trans. Mary David (Westminster, Md.: Newman Book Shop, 1947), 82–85.
14. Mark 9:47–49.
15. Matthew 25:46.
16. John 3:16.
17. John F. Walvoord, Roy B. Zuck, and Dallas Theological Seminary, *The Bible Knowledge Commentary: An Exposition of the Scriptures,* electronic ed. (Wheaton, Ill.: Victor Books, 1983–c1985).
18. 1 Corinthians 3:10–14.

Chapter 11: Lord, You Are Faithful

1. Mark Kelly, "Serving God in dark places is a privilege, shooting survivor tells new missionaries," *The Baptist Standard*, August 9, 2004.

2. Strong, *Exhaustive Concordance*, H530.
3. Strong, *Exhaustive Concordance*, G4103.
4. 1 Kings 18:27–29.

CHAPTER 12: LORD, YOU ARE *the* GUARDIAN *of* MY SOUL

1. Beth Levine, "Animal Instincts," *Good Housekeeping*, December 2004, 100–102.
2. Strong, *Exhaustive Concordance*, G1985.
3. Strong, *Exhaustive Concordance*, H5431.
4. Strong, *Exhaustive Concordance*, G5432.
5. Colossians 3:2.

CHAPTER 13: LORD, YOU ARE HOLY

1. Strong, *Exhaustive Concordance*, H6942.
2. Strong, *Exhaustive Concordance*, G37.
3. 2 Peter 3:9.
4. Romans 10:13.
5. Galatians 5:22–23

CHAPTER 14: LORD, YOU ARE IMMANUEL

1. Strong, *Exhaustive Concordance*, H6005.
2. Matthew 1:23.
3. Genesis 12:1–30.
4. Exodus 3:5–12.
5. Exodus 3:10, 12, 17, 20–21.
6. Genesis 17:2, 6–8, 16.
7. Joshua 1:1–3, 7–9.
8. Exodus 33:11.
9. Genesis 3:8–9.
10. Genesis 6:8; 7:1.
11. 1 Samuel 12:14–25.
12. 1 Samuel 17:37–50.
13. Daniel 6:16–23.
14. Matthew 14:25–31.
15. John 8:1–11.
16. Luke 7:12–15; 8:41–42; 49–56; John 11:14–45.
17. John 14:15–17.
18. Acts 1:4–5.
19. Strong, *Exhaustive Concordance*, G907.
20. Acts 2.
21. John 14:26.
    John 15:4–5.

23. John 15:11.
24. John 15:12.
25. Acts 1:8.

Chapter 15: Lord, You Are Just

1. Strong, *Exhaustive Concordance*, H6662.
2. Psalm 121:4.
3. Strong, *Exhaustive Concordance*, G1342.

Chapter 16: Lord, You Are the King of Kings

1. Copyright © 2005 by Debbie Taylor Williams.
2. Strong, *Exhaustive Concordance*, G935.
3. Strong, *Exhaustive Concordance*, H3519.
4. Strong, *Exhaustive Concordance*, H1419.
5. Strong, *Exhaustive Concordance*, H5921.
6. Romans 12:6–8; 1 Corinthians 12:1–11; Ephesians 4:7–13.

Chapter 17: Lord, You Are Light

1. Major Power Outage Hits New York, other large cities, August 14, 2003, CNN.com./u.s., http://www.cnn.com/2003/US/08/14/power.outage/.
2. Strong, *Exhaustive Concordance*, G5457.
3. Ephesians 1:18–19.
4. Strong, *Exhaustive Concordance*, G4570.

Chapter 18: Lord, You Are Majestic

1. Strong, *Exhaustive Concordance*, H117.

Chapter 19: Lord, You Are the God of New Life

1. Strong, *Exhaustive Concordance*, G2537.
2. Hebrews 10:19–20, 22.
3. John 15.
4. Revelation 2:17.
5. Revelation 5:9.

Chapter 20: Lord, You Are the Overcomer

1. Strong, *Exhaustive Concordance*, G2889.
2. Strong, *Exhaustive Concordance*, G3528.
3. Acts 7:57–60.
4. John 15:14; James 4:4.
5. Strong, *Exhaustive Concordance*, G2347.
6. Romans 8:28.

CHAPTER 21: LORD, YOU ARE *the* POTTER

1. Jeremiah 19:15.
2. Jeremiah 20:1–2.
3. Jeremiah 20:14–18.
4. Jeremiah 20:8–9.
5. Strong, *Exhaustive Concordance*, H3335.
6. 2 Corinthians 4:8–10.
7. 2 Corinthians 4:7.

CHAPTER 22: LORD, YOU ARE *the* QUICKENING SPIRIT

1. Romans 12:1–2.
2. 1 Thessalonians 5:19; Ephesians 4:30.
3. Strong, *Exhaustive Concordance*, H2421.
4. Matthew 25:21.
5. Ephesians 1:18.

CHAPTER 23: LORD, YOU ARE RIGHTEOUS

1. Strong, *Exhaustive Concordance*, H6662.
2. John 7:38–39.
3. Strong, *Exhaustive Concordance*, H2421.

CHAPTER 24: LORD, YOU ARE *a* SHIELD *about* ME

1. Jan Moller, "Slain NLV Girl Shielded Infant from Gunfire," *Las Vegas Review-Journal,* September 9, 2002, http://www.reviewjournal.com/lvrj_home/2002/Sep-09-Mon-2002/news/19590052.html.
2. Strong, *Exhaustive Concordance*, G2375.
3. Romans 8:28.

CHAPTER 25: LORD, YOU ARE *a* TOWER

1. Strong, *Exhaustive Concordance*, H4026.
2. Paul J. Achtemeier, gen. ed., *Harper's Bible Dictionary*, 1st ed., includes index (San Francisco: Harper & Row, 1985).
3. Proverbs 18:10.
4. Isaiah 5:2; Matthew 21:33.
5. Achtemeier, *Harper's Bible Dictionary*.
6. Strong, *Exhaustive Concordance*, H4869.

CHAPTER 26: LORD, YOU ARE *the* ONE WHO UPHOLDS ME

1. "Poetry by Children Who Have Suffered Abuse and Loss," Hill Country Youth Ranch Web site, http://www.youth-ranch.org/poetry.htm.
2. Strong, *Exhaustive Concordance*, H5582.

3. Strong, *Exhaustive Concordance*, H1692.

Chapter 27: Lord, You Are *the* Vinedresser

1. Strong, *Exhaustive Concordance*, H3755.
2. Psalm 80:8.
3. John 15:4–5.
4. John 15:1–8.
5. Strong, *Exhaustive Concordance*, G1092.
6. Luke 8:11–15.
7. John 10:10.
8. Galatians 5:22–23.

Chapter 28: Lord, You Are Wonderful

1. Used by permission.
2. Strong, *Exhaustive Concordance*, H4159.
3. Strong, *Exhaustive Concordance*, H6383.
4. Dietrich Bonhoeffer, *The Cost of Discipleship* (New York: Touchstone, 1995), 152.

Chapter 29: Lord, You Are eXalted

1. Spiros Zodhiates, ed., *The Complete Word Study Old Testament* (Iowa Falls, Iowa: AMG Publishers, 1994), 2307.
2. Matthew 25:14–30; Luke 20:9–18.

Chapter 30: Lord, You Are Yahweh

1. Psalm 103:3–4, 10–12.
2. Strong, *Exhaustive Concordance*, H3068.
3. Herbert Lockyer, *All the Divine Names and Titles in the Bible* (Grand Rapids: Zondervan, 1975), 19.
4. James M. Freeman and Harold J. Chadwick, *The New Manners and Customs of the Bible,* rev. ed. (North Brunswick, N.J.: Bridge-Logos Publishers, 1998), 163.

Chapter 31: Lord, You Are Zealous

1. Luke 19:10.
2. Strong, *Exhaustive Concordance*, H7068.
3. Acts 1:8.
4. Revelation 19:11–21.
5. Strong, *Exhaustive Concordance*, G2205.
6. John 2:13–17.

Debbie Williams and Her Ministry

Hill Country Ministries, Inc., is located in the beautiful hill country of Kerrville, Texas, forty-five miles northwest of San Antonio. Founded in 1999 as a 501C(3), its mission is to spread the Word and love of God. It serves both individuals and the church by providing Bible study resources and inspirational gifts for all ages—for both Bible students and seekers. Its goal is to reach those who do not know Christ with the knowledge of Him and to disciple the Christian in the grace and knowledge of the Lord Jesus Christ.

Debbie Taylor Williams is founder and president of Hill Country Ministries. She has been teaching the Bible for more than thirty years and is the author of numerous Bible studies, including *Discovering His Passion*; *On Enemy Ground*; *A Glimpse of Jesus' Glory*; *Living by the Divine Nature*; *Knowing God in Psalms 1–20*; and *If God Is in Control, Why Do I Have a Headache?* and the author of *Prayers of my Heart*. Prior to leading a large community Bible study at her church, Debbie served as teaching leader for Bible Study Fellowship. She and her husband, Keith, have two children, Taylor and Lauren. Debbie speaks at conferences and events around the country and is known for her passion for Christ and ability to communicate and apply Scripture to everyday life.

Friends of Hill Country Ministries are those who support Hill Country Ministries by their prayers, volunteer support, and/or financial gifts. To find out how you can be a part of the ongoing work of Hill Country Ministries, please contact us at 830-257-5995, e-mail us at hcm@ktc.com, visit our Web site at http://www.hillcountryministries.org, or write to us at PO Box 2218, Kerrville, TX 78029-2218.

Bible Studies

- Pray with Purpose, Live with Passion
- A Glimpse of Jesus' Glory—Luke
- Consider It All Joy—James
- Contend Earnestly for the Faith—Jude

- Discovering His Passion
- Grace and Peace in Fullest Measure—1 Peter
- How to Live by the Divine Nature—2 Peter
- If God Is in Control, Why Do I Have a Headache?
- Knowing God in Psalms 1–20
- On Enemy Ground, On Holy Ground

For information on corresponding DVDs, contact Hill Country Ministries.

INSPIRATIONAL RESOURCES

- Cross Upon the Rock Paper Weight
- From My Heart Collection of Poetry
- Kid's Time Devotional Photo Journal
- Preparing Our Hearts for Christmas
- Rub-A-Dub-Dub Bible Poems for Tub
- Kid's Time 2, Praising God A to Z

CONFERENCES & RETREATS

To schedule Debbie for a speaking engagement, contact Hill Country Ministries, Inc., at 830-257-5995, or e-mail her at hcm@ktc.com.

PRAYERS OF MY HEART

WEEK AT A GLANCE (SAMPLE)

Prayers for My Family

	LORD, YOU ARE	HUSBAND	WIFE	CHILD	CHILD	EXTENDED FAMILY
SUN	Almighty	Strengthen to meet demands *PTL*	Empower me to live for You	Set eyes on You, through whom he can do all things	Strengthen and empower to live fully for You today	Mom— give phys & emot strength to recuperate
MON	Beloved Son	Be an extension of Your love to others	Help me love as You do	Exper Your love in a new, deeper way *PTL*	Fill with a knowledge of Your love	Jay – Come to faith in Your Beloved Son
TUE	The Comforter	Use to comfort Bob	Give me Your words to comfort Sue	Turn to You & exper comfort only You can give	Bless with the comfort of Your presence	Molly – Look to You for comfort
WED	The Door	Use us to point others to You, the door of sal *PTL*		Daily enter into Your presence in prayer		Carol – Enter salvation through You
THU	Eternal	Have Your eternal perspective as makes decisions	Use for Your eternal purposes and glory	Walk in Your eternal will with eyes set on You *PTL*		Dee – Set her eyes on eternity's hope
FRI	Faithful	Rejoice in Your faithfulness	I be a faithful servant to You	Faithfully live for You *PTL*	Rest in Your faithfulness	Al –Stay faithful to You
SAT	Guardian of My Soul	Guard our minds and hearts in You *PTL*		Guard his will to want You above all else	Guard her emotions; fill with Yours	Guard Pete and Mary's marriage as they look to You

"The staff and I are crazy about our Prayer Journals. Thank you, Sister!"
Beth Moore

prayers *of* my heart
a personal prayer journal
debbie williams

This beautiful journal includes twelve Month-at-a-Glance charts, fifty-two Week pages, along with complete instructions and examples for usage. *Prayers of My Heart* offers a quick and simple method of establishing and maintaining a deeper and more effective prayer life.

ISBN: 1-58229-443-7
Hardcover

Available where good books are sold.
www.howardpublshing.com

HOWARD
PUBLISHING CO.

Acts 5:29, 31

This story teach me about God that he is
forgiving because he made a way for us to
be saved from our sin through Jesus'
death on the cross.

Myself ... complaining sinner – experience discipline
from God.

Commands... look to God for my
Salvation. Repent.
↑ admit sinner – agree with God
about sin

Promises.... save us from sin, provide a
way out. He commands for my
good.

live on mission ... thankful for saved
from sin. Tell others about savior.